S0-BFD-466

PUGET SOUND

Pictorial Research by Henry Gordon
"Partners in Progress" by Karen Milburn
Produced in Cooperation with the Museum of History and Industry, Seattle
Historical Society of Seattle and King County
Windsor Publications, Inc. Northridge, California

Where Mountains Meet the Sea
An Illustrated History of
PUGET SOUND

James R. Warren

Windsor Publications, Inc.—History Book Division
Publisher: John M. Phillips
Editorial Director: Teri Davis Greenberg
Design Director: Alexander D'Anca

Staff for *Where Mountains Meet the Sea*
Senior Editor: Pamela Schroeder
Director, Corporate Biographies: Karen Story
Assistant Director, Corporate Biographies: Phyllis Gray
Editor, Corporate Biographies: Judith Hunter
Editorial Assistants: Kathy M. Brown, Laura Cordova, Marcie Goldstein,
   Marilyn Horn, Pat Pittman, Sharon L. Volz
Designer: Ellen Ifrah
Layout Artist: Christina McKibbin
Sales Representatives, Business Biographies: Al Amundson, Carter Reynolds

Library of Congress Cataloging-in-Publication Data
Warren, James R.
   Where mountains meet the sea, an illustrated
history of Puget Sound.

   "Produced in cooperation with the Historical Society
of Seattle and King County."
   Bibliography: p. 282
   Includes index.
   1. Puget Sound Region (Wash.)—History. 2. Puget
Sound Region (Wash.)—Description and travel 3. Puget
Sound Region (Wash.)—Industries. I. Gordon, Henry.
II. Milburn, Karen. Partners in progress. 1986.
III. Historical Society of Seattle and King County.
IV. Title
F897.P9W27   1986   979.7′7   86-11020

© 1986 by Windsor Publications
Published 1986
Printed in the United States of America
First Edition
ISBN: 0-89781-175-5

Endpapers: *This illustration, "Puget Sound & Mt. Rainier from
Whitby's Island," appeared in a report prepared by territorial governor Isaac I. Stevens, who surveyed the land as he headed west to
assume the governorship. Courtesy, The Bancroft Library, University of California, Berkeley*

Frontispiece: *This sunset photograph captures the haunting beauty
of the San Juan Islands in upper Puget Sound. The archipelago
includes over 170 named islands and hundreds of tide-washed
rocks, the summits of an undersea mountain chain. Photo by
Stephen Hilson/Aperture PhotoBank*

This drawing, the first known representation of Mt. Rainier, was done by John Sykes of Captain George Vancouver's expedition of 1792. Here the mountain is viewed from the south part of Admiralty Inlet. Courtesy, Museum of History and Industry, Seattle

This painting, probably done in the 1890s, depicts a quiet morning at the port of Dockton on Maury Island. The port was named in 1891 by the Puget Sound Dry Dock Company when it began building a large dry dock on the island. The artist is unknown.
Courtesy, Museum of History and Industry, Seattle

Contents

This book is dedicated to
Mrs. Victor W.S. Denny
Mr. and Mrs. H.W. McCurdy
and several other octogenarian friends
whose vivid memories bring the past to life

Acknowledgments

Many are owed thanks for assistance in preparation of this book. First thanks must go to the staff and the Board of Trustees of the Museum of History and Industry, for their assistance. I also must acknowledge the assistance of: My wife Gwen for her patience and proofreading; Colonel Carl Lind, the deputy director, for taking over more than his share of details in operating the Museum of History and Industry while I retreated to my word processor; Mrs. James F. Brinkley, Jr., president of the Historical Society of Seattle and King County, who helped all along the way; Dr. Norman C. Clark, an old friend, who read the text for historical accuracy; Howard Giske, the museum's photo technician, who reproduced scores of the pictures enjoyed in this book; Richard Caldwell, the museum librarian, who was helpful in many ways; Margaret Roberts, the museum public relations specialist; Barbro Ulbrickson, administrative assistant; Eunice Roselle, accountant; and all the many others who contributed time and effort.

And at Windsor Publications, a special thank you to editor Pam Schroeder, and vice-president Roland G. Behny, who put in a good word at the right time. This book would not have been produced without you.

Anders Wilse, the Norwegian photographer who practiced his art in Seattle between 1899 and 1905, distinguished himself with his scenes of the Northwest. He later returned to Norway where he was named the official photographer of the king. He is seen here to his ankles in Lake Washington preparing to preserve an image. Courtesy, Museum of History and Industry, Seattle

Introduction

Puget Sound, in the far northwest corner of the contiguous United States, is one of the world's great inland seas. For more than ninety north-south miles its tides rise and fall on the shores of twelve Washington State counties, bobbing ships at anchor before cities large and small, washing the foothills of mighty mountain ranges, undercutting the roots of giant evergreens, dousing beds of oysters and clams, and providing sustenance for one of the world's greatest varieties of water creatures, ranging from plankton to whales. It is sometimes called the "fertile fjord" and is one of the most picturesque bodies of water anywhere.

Originally Puget Sound, as it was named by Captain George Vancouver, encompassed only the area south of the Tacoma Narrows, but over time, common usage has resulted in the name being applied to all of the inland sea. For the purposes of this book, we have included under the term the region stretching from the Pacific Ocean to the southern reaches of the Sound.

The 2,000 square miles of its blue-green surface surround 300 islands ranging in size from tide-washed rocks to Whidbey, largest island in the lower forty-eight states. Its sinuous arms stretch into countless natural harbors, some of which have developed commercial port cities. These ports flourish, in part, because the route from Puget Sound to the Orient is much shorter than the route to these markets, say, from San Francisco.

Puget Sound developed over a span of 200 million years and more. Originally waters of the Pacific Ocean lay deep over this land, but as the eons passed, the shifting sea floor carried land masses eastward and jammed them against the continental shelf. At times the land masses crumpled upward and the northern Cascade Mountains were formed. Submerged lava flows accumulated one atop the other on the sea bottom and were shifted eastward and scraped atop the continental plate to form the Olympic mountains. Throughout the long period of volcanic action, among the Cascade crests, conduits issued forth lava, piling layer on layer, creating ever higher peaks. Between these newly formed Cascade and Olympic ranges, rivers flowed north and west to the ocean over the lowlands which later were submerged beneath the Strait of Juan de Fuca.

Finally came the ice. Over a period of two or three million years of intermittent cooling and warming temperatures, several monumental glaciers advanced and retreated, the last about 14,000 years ago. The shifting ice of these glaciers accumulated a mile in thickness at the northern end of the Sound, a half-mile thick where Seattle lies today, and heaped a terminal moraine south of present Olympia. As temperatures moderated, the glacier retreated and as ice dams were breached, the seawater rushed in to fill the glacier-gouged troughs we know as the Strait of Juan de Fuca and Puget Sound. Other glacial scars, protected by highlands, retained fresh water and became inland lakes such as Washington and Sammamish.

As the climate warmed, the forest spread down to the shores and fish and wildlife returned. And about 12,000 years ago, as the ice retreated, early man followed the other of God's creatures into this picturesque country where the mountains meet the sea.

The waters of the great inland sea that is Puget Sound surround some 300 picturesque islands. This photo of the San Juan chain was taken near Anacortes. Photo by Don Lowe/Aperture Photo

1
The Abundant Land

The origins of the first human inhabitants of the Puget Sound area are not certain, nor do we know with any precision when they arrived in the area, but it is believed that they came from eastern Asia some 12,000 years ago, across a frozen land bridge and down through the Columbia and Okanogan valleys. Very little is known about their development during a period of more than 10,000 years; virtually all we do know is that the ancestors of Washington's modern Indians were active in the area more than 1,000 years ago.

The Puget Sound natives encountered by the Europeans, including the Duwamish, Clallam, Nisqually, Swinomish, Puyallup, Lummi, and others, were part of the Coast Salish language group. This group was in turn part of the fascinating and highly devel-

Opposite: *Friendly Cove, named by Captain Cook, was the site of the Spanish village at Nootka Sound. Here Kendrick, Gray, and other early traders and explorers anchored. The 1792 sketch is by Harry Humphrys, who was with Captain George Vancouver. Courtesy, Museum of History and Industry, Seattle (MOHAI)*

This sketch with Mt. Baker in the background is of Admiralty In-let from Port Townsend. It was used to illustrate an article by A.T. Hawley titled "The Key City of the Sound," published in The West Shore, a very successful magazine printed in Portland, Oregon. The sketch was a large, foldout supplement in the maga-zine's April 1889 issue. The artist is unknown. Courtesy, Bancroft Library, University of California at Berkeley

Left: *Tetaku, wife of a Makah chief, is pictured wearing a cedar bark cape. The soft inner bark of the western red cedar (Thuja plicata) was haggled and woven into cloth. Note the dentalium shell earrings. The baby's head is bound to flatten it, as was the tradition. Courtesy, University of Washington Libraries*

Opposite: *Edward Curtis posed the Indians as authentically as possible to illustrate their culture. In this 1890s photo two Skokomish women sit by a canoe before a shelter of woven mats. The baskets, rain hats, and capes were woven from the inner bark of the red cedar tree. (MOHAI)*

Below: *This Anders Wilse photo displays the traditional baskets of Puget Sound Indians. Tools include mortar and pestle, horn spoon, knives, chisel, halibut hook with spruce handle, hammer stone, and net sinker. Courtesy, University of Washington Libraries*

oped Northwest Coast Indians, believed to represent one of the most sophisticated nonagricultural societies in the world.

In contrast to almost all other tribes living in what became the United States, the Northwest Coast Indians were affected little, if at all, by the culture of the Aztecs, Mayans, and other influential Mexican groups. Their folkways, social organization, beliefs, and means of survival were unique in many ways.

In contrast to virtually every other native group in North America, the Indians of the Northwest Coast enjoyed virtual freedom from want. The sheer abundance and variety of food made agriculture unnecessary; "hunting" was almost indistinguishable from "gathering." The mildness of the climate was of considerable importance, too. Men often went naked, and women traditionally wore skirts made of the twined fibers, haggled and softened, from the inner bark of the red cedar. In cold weather, animal skins,

furnished by otters and other fur-bearing animals easily caught, were worn. Capes and conical hats, which the Indians skillfully wove from reeds and bark fiber, were sometimes worn in the cold rains.

Their winter homes were longhouses of split-cedar board siding. Poles embedded in the earth around a sunken floor supported the roof. Several families occupied each longhouse, each family with its own quarters. The smoke from their fires escaped through holes in the roof. In summer, portable mat shelters were carried to fishing and food-gathering sites.

Salmon served as the staple of the local Indians, for good reason. Over the last million years or so, several species developed in the Northwest: the coho, sockeye, chinook, chum, and pink. The Indians learned to take advantage of the spawning runs of each species, and invented ingenious methods of catching and then drying this nutritious food supply. So important was the salmon to their culture that they incorporated it into much of their artwork and into their spiritual practices. They believed that the salmon migrated upstream to benefit mankind, died, and then were resurrected. For this reason, the Indians reverently returned salmon bones to the water.

Adding variety to the local diet were other fish—smelt, herring, candlefish, cod, halibut, and flounder—and shellfish, including clams, mussels, oysters, and crabs. Vegetables and fruit rounded out their diet and added variety. These included several kinds of berries, camas bulbs, wapato, and fern root, all naturally occurring in the productive climate.

The Indians were highly accomplished toolmakers, basket makers, and mat weavers. They also were fine woodworkers, utilizing the trees of the forest in many ways, especially the red cedar. This magnificent softwood splits easily into straight planks for building and for making storage boxes and paddles. Yellow cedar and alder were easily carved into utensils without cleavage planes; yew and maple were fashioned into bows and harpoon shafts, the latter used

by the Makahs on whale hunts. Canoes of cedar logs were crafted in a variety of shapes and sizes depending on the intended use—blunt-nosed and shallow for the rivers, higher-prowed and larger for the Sound and sea.

The abundant growth and kind climate, nature's gifts to the Northwest Coast Indians, allowed for a population density greater perhaps than in any other part of pre-Columbian North America north of Mexico. They also made possible leisure time, which gave rise to some remarkable artistic endeavors, and the development of the concepts of surplus wealth and status. A class system based on possessions and heredity evolved, whereby the free members of the tribe were divided into three groups: chiefs, nobles, and commoners. The oldest man of wealth and position in each village was usually chief, though that in itself did not automatically entitle him to make political decisions. Many chiefs were powerful, however, due to the force of their personalities and initiative.

Warfare and feuding, whether between villages,

Above: *This 1895 woodcut of Chief Seattle, for whom the city is named, was the work of Raphael Coombs, who probably used the only known photograph of the chief to create the likeness. (MOHAI)*

Opposite: *The Makahs harvested from the ocean in large canoes. This Anders Wilse photo taken in 1900 shows them returning from a traditional whale hunt. Courtesy, University of Washington Libraries*

families, or tribes, was a common feature of life, and provided another characteristic of their culture: slavery. Slaves, who could make up as much as 20 or 30 percent of the population, lived to serve their masters, and so did any children they might have. The only recognized escape from slavery was through ransom paid by the slave's family, village, or tribe, though some managed to escape.

A major social event of the Northwest Coast Indians was the potlatch ceremony, a ritual reaffirming group affiliations and also a business transaction conducted in a social setting.

In the potlatch ceremony (the word is Chinook for "giveaway"), held during the winter months, the wealth accumulated by a man could be appreciated by his friends and neighbors as he distributed it among them, in an atmosphere of conviviality and feasting. He expected peers to return the favor at some future date with gifts of even greater value. The potlatch was also used to distribute goods to the needy in times of scarcity. Yet, careful calculation by the giver ensured that poor recipients could never repay the giver, thereby the status quo was preserved. Potlatches were given for varying reasons, depending on the tribe, and they varied in scale but their preparation could take years of accumulating wealth.

One of the most fearsome experiences of the Puget Sound Indians, who were relatively peaceful, was to sight the great war canoes of other tribes, especially those of the fierce Vancouver Island people, sweeping down the Sound on a raiding expedition. For that reason, their settlements were usually built to face the Sound but with escape routes behind by which they could quickly vanish into the forest. At times, they would fight the raiding enemy. The estimable Chief Seattle, son of a chief, reputedly became the leader of several local tribes in about 1810 by organizing the defeat of invaders from a mountain tribe.

THE EARLY EXPLORERS

No one knows when the first Indian met the first European in what is now Washington State. Several old Indian tales describe the arrival of shipwrecked sailors and the presence of fair-skinned Indians (presumably the sons of such sailors and Indian women) prior to the 1700s, but none of these stories was confirmed. Although Sir Francis Drake said he reached the 48th parallel in 1577, which would make him the first known European in the area, his claim is dubious. Another claimant was the navigator of a Spanish ship, a Greek who assumed the Spanish name of

Juan de Fuca. He reputedly discovered a strait extending from the Pacific to the Atlantic in 1592, a strait that now bears his name (thanks to a British captain, Charles Barklay, who arrived in 1787).

The Russians were known to have explored the Pacific Coast from Alaska down to northern California beginning in the 1760s, and hunted sea otters and other animals—they even instituted large-scale native slavery in Alaska to aid their efforts. But the first substantiated voyages along the Washington coast were undertaken by the Spanish. Vessels under the command of Juan Perez, Bruno Heceta, and Juan Bodega y Quadra, arrived in Northwest waters between 1774 and 1776. Some of Heceta's men, as far as is known, were the first Europeans to set foot in what is now Washington. A few of them were also the first to die at the hands of the Indians, when Heceta sent a scouting party ashore on the mainland south of Cape Flattery, near the island known today as "Destruction."

Close behind the Spanish were the British, in the person of Captain James Cook, in 1778. As were the Spanish, the British were searching for the legendary Northwest Passage. What they found instead was a coastal network of inlets, straits, and islands teeming with fur-bearing animals. The value of these early discoveries may not have been immediately apparent, but it took little time for its discoverers to appreciate the region's attractiveness.

On Cook's ship was an American, John Ledyard, who was struck by the profits to be made in fur trading when he saw pelts bought for a few cents from the Indians later sell for $100 in China. After the Revolutionary War, Ledyard supposedly informed Thomas Jefferson of the opportunities to be made in this endeavor. Meantime, Massachusetts and New York financiers in 1787 dispatched two ships, under captains John Kendrick and Robert Gray, to investigate the trade possibilities. The young United States of America was now competing with three other countries for the riches of the Northwest Coast.

One of those countries—Spain—soon found that its claim to territory in the Northwest was impossible to maintain. After the Nootka Sound controversy of 1789-1790, between Great Britain and Spain, the latter country began to lose interest in the territory and left it for all practical purposes to Britain and America. Although Russia entered a claim, in 1810, to the territory from Alaska to the mouth of the Columbia River, that country, too, soon realized its ambitions were untenable. The remaining contenders for control of the area were the mighty British Empire and

Above: *The ship* Columbia *under Captain Robert Gray was the first American ship to circumnavigate the globe. This sketch by Hewitt Jackson shows the* Columbia *leaving the Strait of Juan de Fuca on her historic journey south in May 1792, during which Gray discovered both Grays Harbor and the Columbia River, which he named for his ship. (MOHAI)*

Opposite, top: *This contemporary sketch shows a shore boat of Captain George Vancouver's expedition of 1792 being sailed toward the mother ship* Discovery. *It is followed by canoes that appear to be of Haida construction. The Indians learned to use sails from the early explorers. (MOHAI)*

Opposite, bottom: *John Sykes, an artist who accompanied the 1792 expedition of Captain George Vancouver, sketched this scene of the expedition's boat encampment on the "Strait of Juan de Fuca." The exact location is not known. Courtesy, Bancroft Library, University of California, Berkeley*

John Jacob Astor, who founded the Pacific Fur Company in 1810, sent two parties—one overland, the other by sea—to establish a post near the mouth of the Columbia. Fort Astoria was built in 1811. The following year, with the War of 1812 threatening a British takeover, the fort was sold to the North West Fur Company. Courtesy, Washington State Historical Society

its former colony, the infant United States.

During the years 1790 to 1814 at least eighty-two American vessels are known to have engaged in the Northwest fur trade, compared to twenty-six British ships. The British traders were restricted by licensing requirements; the Americans were not.

Still, the British were a powerful presence in the area. In 1792 Captain George Vancouver, who had sailed under Captain Cook, arrived with orders to explore the inland seas and to negotiate details of an agreement to end the Nootka controversy. His great achievement was the charting of the northern Pacific Coast, of the territory he christened New Georgia. He also provided more than 200 place names, most of which—Mount Rainier, Mount Baker, Hood Canal, Bellingham Bay, Whidbey and Vashon islands, as examples—are still in use. Although the name he gave to part of the Sound north of present-day Seattle, Admiralty Inlet, is seldom used, his name for the lower waters remains. "Puget Sound," named for Vancouver's lieutenant, Peter Puget, over the years has extended to all of the inland sea.

In the same year, 1792, Robert Gray returned from Boston to undertake a second trading mission. While sailing along the coast, he brought his ship, the *Columbia,* close to shore searching for rivers and bays. In this manner he discovered and entered Grays Harbor. Then, on May 1, 1792, he safely negotiated the treacherous bar which had hidden the great river of the west from previous explorers. He named the river for his ship.

Gray's discovery of the Columbia, according to international law of the day, presented the United States with a claim to all lands drained by the river. Vancouver, nonetheless, upon hearing of Gray's discovery, sent his Lieutenant William Broughton on the *Chatham* to explore the stream. Broughton later maintained that Gray had not sailed far enough up the river to claim it (Broughton had been rowed nearly 100 miles upriver), though in his charts Vancouver retained Gray's name for the river. Despite Broughton's contention, Gray's discovery ultimately provided the United States with a strong argument for possession of the Oregon country, especially that land north of the river, which remained contested territory into the 1840s.

Other Europeans were busy exploring northern North America west to the Pacific, among them Britishers Alexander Mackenzie and Simon Fraser. But it was President Thomas Jefferson who had the greatest influence on the settlement of the Northwest by championing plans for an expedition through the western half of what is now the United States, both to provide geographical knowledge of the vast terrain and to prepare the way for the extension of the American fur trade. The Lewis and Clark Expedition, which reached the Pacific Ocean in the fall of 1805, not only added weight to the American claim for the region west of the Louisiana Territory, purchased in 1803, it also fueled American interest in the great, uncharted region. The Yankees proved characteristically energetic in pursuing opportunities in the Northwest.

In 1807, David Thompson of the British-controlled North West Company of Montreal established the first trading posts east of the Cascades. In 1811, he descended the Columbia River, only to find the Americans had established a trading post at Fort Astoria shortly before.

John Jacob Astor and his partners built posts at the mouths of several rivers in the territory, and the British were never far behind. Soon the entire area north of the Columbia and Snake rivers was dotted with commercial enterprises which relied on the efforts of trappers, fur brigades, guards, and trading ships. During the War of 1812, Astoria, at the mouth of the Columbia, was sold to the North West Fur Company. By 1824 the British, represented by the Hudson's Bay Company (which bought out its rival, the North West Company, in 1821), controlled the fur trade in the area, even though under the terms of the 1818 Joint Occupation Agreement, signed by Britain and the United States, the Oregon country was to be held jointly by both countries, with neither side assuming sovereignty. The company's chief factor, Dr. John McLoughlin, in the next few years would greet and aid many American explorers and trappers, and would in the end link his destiny with that of American settlers.

McLoughlin moved the company's headquarters upriver to Fort Vancouver and from there the first parties to explore the Puget Sound country were outfitted. This fort on the north bank of the Columbia, the British hoped, would be a means of retaining control of northern Oregon. But within a matter of only a few years, the British would concede even that area to the Americans.

2
Stars & Stripes on the Sound

The first four decades of the nineteenth century brought enormous changes in the territory of which Puget Sound was a part, and the man responsible for the first white settlement on Puget Sound, Dr. John McLoughlin, almost seems to have anticipated the future. One of the most intriguing characters to influence Puget Sound's early history, he realized that, at the rate sea otter, muskrat, beaver, and other animals were being trapped, the business would soon come to an end. He also convinced the Hudson's Bay Company directors to form the Puget Sound Agricultural Company in 1833 simultaneous with the establishment of Fort Nisqually, at the southeastern edge of the Sound. Puget Sound had heretofore attracted little attention, being relatively poor in beaver and sea otter pelts.

Opposite: *American Camp on San Juan Island was built when the British and Americans contended for the island beginning in 1855. The altercation became known as the Pig War, and although bloodless, for a time it threatened the peaceful relationship between the two countries. Courtesy, Washington State Historical Society*

SETTLING THE WILDERNESS

The farming settlement on the fertile Nisqually Plain raised crops, sheep, cattle, and pigs for the trappers and their families and even exported some to Russian colonies in Alaska. Although the settlement lost its importance in the 1840s when Americans began to arrive on Puget Sound, the success of the settlement, near present-day Tacoma, was an early adumbration of things to come.

The first non-trading settlers in the Oregon Country, apart from McLoughlin's traders-turned-farmers at Nisqually, arrived on a spiritual mission. They were American and Canadian missionaries whose charge it was to spread their religions (Protestantism and Roman Catholicism, respectively) to the Indians.

The first Americans to settle in Oregon were several Methodists, under Jason Lee, who founded their mission in the Willamette Valley in 1834. Two years later, Dr. and Mrs. Marcus Whitman and the Reverend and Mrs. Henry H. Spalding, Presbyterians, established Indian missions east of the mountains.

Neither the Protestants nor the Catholics had great success in converting the natives, though the Catholics, arriving in 1838, fared somewhat the better. Fathers Francois Blanchet and Modeste Demers established missions at the mouth of the Cowlitz River, at a site near Willamette Falls, and at Fort Nisqually. At the Fort Nisqually mission, several Indians, including some of the leaders of Puget Sound tribes—Chief Seattle included—received instruction.

Westward expansion captured the energy of Americans for several reasons. Some were philosophical, having to do with the desire to spread their enlightened free society from sea to sea. Others were practical. For one thing, a continent-wide America would help improve the security of the country. But most people moved west for their own enrichment.

Mountain men and missionaries had described Oregon as rich in timber, with fertile river valleys and a mild climate. Americans responded. Farmers, merchants, lawyers, craftsmen, millmen, doctors—they came primarily from small villages on the Great Plains and from the Eastern cities to this new promised land. The majority, however, came from the Midwest.

In 1841, an American naval expedition under Commander Charles Wilkes explored the Oregon Territory including Puget Sound. Wilkes, in his report, lauded Puget Sound's ideal harbors: "I venture nothing in saying, there is no country in the world that possesses waters equal to these."

While diplomatic negotiations between Britain and the United States progressed in the 1840s, the trickle of Americans into the territory was becoming more of a flood. In four years—between 1842 and 1846—nearly 10,000 Americans found new homes in the Oregon Territory, tipping the scales toward United States possession of the still-jointly-held territory. Most, though, settled in the valleys south of the Columbia River.

Clearly, all these people could not live together without some sort of government; so, pending formal diplomatic agreements between the United States and Britain, the settlers drew up a provisional government in 1843.

The first American settlers on Puget Sound arrived in 1845. These were the families of Michael T. Simmons, George Washington Bush, and four others. Bush, a successful mulatto stock raiser from Missouri, left the Willamette Valley because the Oregon provisional government had established a law preventing blacks from settling there. During the course of his remarkable career he became a wealthy and renowned farmer near Olympia as well as a community leader.

The other families, too—those of James McAllister, David Kindred, and George Jones—and two single men, Jesse Ferguson and Samuel Crockett, (in all thirty individuals), settled near Budd's Inlet on Puget Sound. Simmons chose a claim that included the falls of the Deschutes River which the Indians called Tumwater but which he named New Market.

A few more hearty souls soon joined these first arrivals. Charles H. Eaton, who had come to Oregon in 1843, his brother Nathan, Edmund Sylvester and his partner Levi L. Smith, Alonzo Marion Poe, Daniel D. Kinsey, and Antonio Rabbeson arrived on the Sound in 1846, settling near Simmons at New Market. Smith fixed his claim on the ground where Olympia stands today. His partner, Sylvester, chose a site near Chambers Prairie, but he and Smith had an agreement that each should own a half-interest in the land selected by the other. They planned to lay out a townsite on Smith's property which they would call Smithfield or Smithter. Smith, a bachelor, was an epileptic and died in 1848; Sylvester inherited his property.

The first settlements on Puget Sound almost coincided with the settling of the Oregon question. After long rounds of negotiations, in June 1846 the boundary between the United States and Canada was established at the 49th parallel as far as the Strait of Georgia, where it dipped down to give Britain all of Vancouver Island. The agreement also preserved free

The Puget Sound Indians used weirs to guide salmon into narrow spaces for spearing. This sketch was made by Captain Wilkes who led the U.S. expedition to the Puget Sound country in 1841 and illustrates a weir on the Chehalis River. Courtesy, University of Washington Libraries

navigation of the Columbia for the British and promised reparations for the property of the Hudson's Bay Company.

The year 1846 saw the building of a small gristmill at Tumwater Falls. A few months later Simmons and seven others formed a partnership called the Puget Sound Milling Company to erect a sawmill near the lower falls. That same month, a trail was blazed between New Market (Tumwater) and Smithfield (Olympia).

In 1847 several others increased the size of the settlement. The McAllister family, meanwhile, left their claim on Bush Prairie for a new site on the Nisqually flats where a small stream called Medicine Creek emptied into the Sound. (In 1855, when McAllister was killed by the Indians, the creek was renamed for him.)

While the number of settlers taking advantage of the rich new lands of the Pacific Northwest increased, another group, the natives, were declining in number. In the course of a few decades, the Northwest was transformed from an Indian realm to one in which Indians were having difficulty surviving. Once the undisputed rulers of their land, they were rapidly coming under the rule of whites. A primary cause was the Indians' susceptibility to the diseases introduced by the newcomers. The number of Indians in the Northwest in pre-contact days is unknown, but by the time the first missionaries arrived, in the 1830s, great deterioration was already evident. In the years 1836-1840 smallpox epidemics wiped out entire villages. Other diseases to which the Indians had no immunity, including measles, scarlet fever, and venereal diseases, contributed to the decimation and left the Indians even less able to determine their own destinies. The formidable influence of European traditions, values, religion, and language was noticeable even before the Indians were relegated to reservations in the 1850s. Nevertheless, compared to many other tribes in the United States, the Northwest Coast Indians have retained considerable land and managed to preserve some of their traditions.

After the settlement of the Oregon Question, political maneuvering and the great distances involved delayed the establishment of the Oregon Territory. General Joseph Lane, a hero of the Mexican War, was appointed governor and appeared in Oregon City on March 3, 1849.

As attractive as the Puget Sound area was, several hurdles faced potential settlers. The biggest hindrance was simply the difficulty of getting there, no matter how one chose to travel. (Most early arrivals

came from Portland, after having traveled down the Columbia River.) Despite the difficulties the settlers came. One catalyst for settlement was the Donation Land Claim Act, passed by Congress in 1850. It invited citizens to claim the land whether or not it had been surveyed and ignored both Indian title and the guarantees of remuneration promised the Hudson's Bay Company. Large claims—640 acres (one square mile) for a couple married before December 1, 1851—could be had free. Hurry-up marriages were arranged and, because women were in short supply on the frontier, more than one twelve-year-old girl became a bride. Immigrants arriving after December 1 were eligible for a claim half the size of the earlier pioneers'.

This promise of land succeeded in bringing many new residents to the territory, and a good deal of valuable property was acquired as a direct result of it. Because the area had not been surveyed, claims could take any shape, meandering to include the most valuable natural assets. Later the surveyor general would, only with difficulty, verify the boundaries of the oddly shaped holdings. Many of the cities and towns on Puget Sound were founded in 1850 and 1851 after word of the land-claim law reached the Pacific slopes. Port Townsend, Bellingham, and Seattle are examples. However, a succession of gold rushes (in eastern Washington, Idaho, Montana, and even British Columbia) lured more men than did the free land, though many later stayed on as settlers.

Whidbey Island, with its fertile plains, attracted families early in the process of settling Puget Sound. On October 15, 1850, Colonel Isaac N. Ebey staked a claim on Whidbey's west shore and was soon joined by Clement Sumner, Martin Tuftson, and Ulric Friend, all three of whom pioneered in the Oak Harbor vicinity. In March 1852, Dr. R.H. Lansdale recorded his claim nearby. In August, William Wallace and family moved there, bringing the first horses to the island. John Crockett and his father, Colonel Walter Crockett, took land on the island and in November 1852 Thomas Coupe appeared on Penn's Cove where he later laid out the town of Coupeville. As 1853 came to a conclusion, Whidbey was one of the most settled areas on Puget Sound.

Henry Wilson was the first American to make his home in the area of what became Port Townsend. His claim dates from August 1850, although he apparently remained at Steilacoom until the following year to run the store which Lafayette Balch had founded there.

Alfred A. Plummer and Charles Bachelder regis-

Indians living near Chimacum Creek in Jefferson County had adopted the clothes of their white neighbors by the 1880s. The seagoing canoe, hollowed from a single cedar log, has a high prow which was carved separately and attached with wooden dowels. Courtesy, Washington State Library

tered claims at the land office in April 1851, that date being regarded as the beginning of Port Townsend. In November Francis W. Pettygrove and L.B. Hastings looked the area over and decided to return to Portland to bring their families north. Pettygrove is considered a founder of Portland and provided its name, but when a fever epidemic struck the area, he moved his family north, where he also became one of the founders of Port Townsend. Benjamin Ross and family accompanied Pettygrove and Hastings to the area early in 1852. Later J.C. Clinger arrived with his wife and children. Pettygrove, Hastings, Plummer, and Bachelder agreed to lay out a townsite and develop a store.

In September 1851 Luther M. Collins, Henry Van Asselt, and Jacob and Samuel Maple came to the Sound country from California. Collins had earlier taken a claim on the Nisqually which he abandoned for his new choice in the Duwamish River Valley. He drove his twenty head of cattle along the beach at low tide and built a scow on which to transport household effects to his new site.

Some of the adults of the Denny Party which landed at Alki Point on November 13, 1851, are shown here with Arthur Denny, center. Pictured clockwise, from upper right: Louisa Boren Denny (Arthur's sister-in-law); Mary Boren Denny (Arthur's wife); Charles Terry; Carson Boren (Arthur's brother-in-law); William S. Bell; and David T. Denny (Arthur's brother). The following year, all but Terry moved across Elliott Bay to found the city of Seattle. (MOHAI)

The genesis of Seattle dates to November 13, 1851, when the Denny party arrived at Alki Point (now West Seattle), greeted by David Denny, who had been sent north along with John Low to scout the country. Low had returned to Portland with the message, "Come at once." Arrivals on the ship *Exact* included Arthur Denny, Carson Boren, John N. Low, and William N. Bell and their families, and Charles C. Terry, and Louisa Boren. With children included, they numbered twenty-six.

For a short time until Arthur Denny's log cabin was finished, they all sheltered in Low's cabin. The next two houses were built of cedar boards split off with wedges, a process they learned from friendly Indians.

No sooner had the newcomers settled in than the brig *Leonesa* appeared, looking for pilings for that booming gold-rush town, San Francisco. The pioneers accepted the contract from Captain Daniel S. Howard and finished loading on Christmas Day. The brig sailed away with orders for provisions to sustain the new settlement.

The following February, Arthur Denny, Boren, and Bell, seeking timbered claim sites near deep water, and dreaming of a port city they would establish, sounded Elliott Bay from a canoe using a length of Mary Denny's clothesline weighted with a horseshoe. Much to their delight, they discovered that the eastern shore of the bay provided just the potential they sought. Though Charles Terry and John Low remained on the point, the others moved across the bay. Later Low sold out to Terry and moved to the Olympia vicinity, and Terry himself finally joined Seattle's founders on the eastern shores of Elliott Bay.

In March, Dr. David T. Maynard appeared with a scheme to salt salmon in barrels for the California market. The others adjusted their claims to allow Maynard waterfront property necessary to his enterprise. Today, the Pioneer Square area of Seattle covers his claim.

In October 1852 Henry Yesler arrived seeking a site on which to erect the first steam sawmill in the area. Again the settlers adjusted their property lines to give him the "sag" where the shoreline cliffs had been eroded by a stream, providing the proper waterfront elevation for his mill. A long, narrow neck of property ascended the hill to the major portion of his claim. This became the original "skid road," later Mill Street and today Yesler Way.

Arthur Denny, a trained surveyor, Boren, and Maynard agreed to lay out a townsite for which Maynard suggested the name "Seattle" after the most influential chief in the area. All seemed to agree it was euphonious, unique, and an improvement over "Duwamps," the name given the voting precinct. Bell, in time, platted his own township, called Belltown, but within a few years it was absorbed by Seattle. David T. Denny, after his marriage to Louisa Boren, took his claim north of Bell's.

In 1852 Dr. Henry A. Smith settled north of the David Dennys on a cove later named for him. Early in 1853, Thomas Mercer and Dexter Horton came to Elliott Bay. Later John C. Holgate and his brother-in-law, Edward Hanford, took claims on Beacon Hill. Holgate, incidentally, is given credit for being the first American to choose a land-claim site on the Duwamish. He did so during an inspection trip in 1850, but returned to Oregon, fought in the Cayuse War, and when he finally returned, found the property already occupied by Luther Collins, so he selected a new site.

Sometime in 1852, on Bellingham Bay, Captain William Pattle, while searching near the shoreline for timber with which to fill a contract with the Hudson's Bay Company at Victoria, discovered a seam of coal on the beach. Two men who accompanied him, James Morris and John Thomas as well as Pattle, took donation claims nearby. Nearly 150 tons of coal were dug from their claims before a better-quality coal was found to the north by Henry Hewitt and William Brown, who had arrived on the bay with Henry Roeder, R.V. Peabody, and others on a schooner. This coal was shipped to California, for the most part. William Utter and H.C. Page were also in the party and agreed to form a milling company with a millwright named Brown from Olympia. They soon had the saws whining.

C.E. Roberts, J.W. Lyle, and others settled in the area soon after and a village called Whatcom developed. Later this village, with two nearby settlements, was incorporated into the city of Bellingham.

Out on the Strait of Juan de Fuca in March 1852, B.J. Madison, an Indian trader, chose a claim near New Dungeness and was soon joined by General Daniel F. Brownfield, Thomas Abernathy, J.J. Burrows, J.C. Brown, J.W. Donnell, C.M. Bradshaw, G.H. Gerish, Hoseah Lowrey, and others, forming the first American settlement on the Olympic Peninsula.

In the Puyallup Valley, several families who had hacked their way over the Naches Pass on what was supposed to be an open wagon road, found land on which to create new homes. Among them were Willis Boatman, John Carson, George Haywood, Isaac Lemon, A.S. Perham, Abiel Morrison, A.H. and Isaac Woolery, and William Kincaid. Not far away, Michael Connell and A.S. Porter settled on prairies which, to this day, carry their names.

FORMATION OF WASHINGTON TERRITORY
By the early 1850s, it had become clear to the settlers north of the Columbia River that the Oregon Territory was too vast and sparsely populated to be administered effectively by the Oregon territorial government. On July 4, 1851, the founder of Chehalis, J.B. Chapman, spoke in Olympia of the need for a new territory to be created north of the river; the name he suggested was "Columbia." A twenty-six member committee was appointed and met on August 29, 1851, at Cowlitz Landing to prepare a memorial to Congress requesting separation from Oregon.

They compared the long journey from the homes of northern Oregon citizens to Salem, the newly chosen seat of government, to that from St. Louis to

Boston, and explained it was even more costly and time consuming. Residents living south of the river unselfishly instructed delegate Lane, their former governor, to support the effort.

The first newspaper to publish north of the Columbia, founded in 1852 by T.F. McElroy and called the *Columbian,* became a champion of the separation struggle. Its editorials urged the scheduling of another convention at Monticello (now Longview) on November 25, 1852. From this a second memorial was sent to Congress asking that the new territory be established. Congress, while debating the bill on February 8, 1853, adopted the amendment of Representative Richard H. Stanton of Kentucky to strike the name "Columbia" and substitute in its place "Washington" to honor the Father of our Country. After Congress passed the amended bill, it was signed by President Millard Fillmore on March 2. The new territory extended from the Pacific Ocean to the summit of the Rocky Mountains and from the 49th parallel on the north to the Columbia River and 46th parallel on the south. Ten years later Idaho Territory was created, reducing Washington to its present boundaries.

Isaac Ingalls Stevens, a West Point graduate, an engineer by training—and a supporter of Franklin Pierce—was appointed to three posts by the new president: governor of the territory, superintendent of Indian affairs, and leader of the Northern Pacific Railroad survey. Arriving in Olympia late in September 1853, Stevens embarked on his eventful and controversial four years as governor of some 4,000 white residents and 21,000 Indians. The larger priorities of his administration would be road-building (for which the territorial residents had been agitating) the linking up of Washington Territory by rail to the rest of the nation, the purchase by the federal government of Hudson's Bay Company holdings, and the formal acquisition of the land from Indians, a plan that included the establishment of reservations to which Indians would be confined. Other goals included the improvement of the territory's mail service, the establishment of a school system and a university, and the arming and training of a militia. Stevens, who was forty-four when he took over as governor, had led an eventful life. As a lad from a poor Massachusetts farm family, he was appointed to West Point and graduated first in the class of 1839. Because of his high ranking, he was allowed to join the Engineer Corps of the U.S. Army and was assigned to a unit building fortifications along the Atlantic Coast. When the Mexican War erupted, he asked for active

duty, fought in seven battles, and was badly wounded in the taking of Mexico City. After the war, he was given charge of the U.S. coast survey.

After the Compromise of 1850, he believed the slavery issue was settled and that an army career would offer little challenge. He quickly accepted President Pierce's appointment as governor of the new territory.

January 30, 1854, was the date Governor Stevens set for the election of the territory's first legislators. Voters, numbering 1,682, elected nine councilmen (senators) and seventeen representatives. The first session began on February 27 and lasted into May. During that time the legislature organized the territorial government, established Olympia as the territorial capital, assigned a commission to write a code of laws, and created eight new counties: Chehalis (now Grays Harbor), Clallam, Cowlitz, Sawamish (now Mason), Skamania, Wahkiakum, Walla Walla, and Whatcom. Women's suffrage and prohibition bills were introduced but failed. Political parties were organized and Columbia Lancaster, a Democrat, was elected delegate to the U.S. Congress.

The Olympia they chose as the seat of government, with nearly 1,000 inhabitants, was the largest city on Puget Sound. Both the social and official life of the territory centered there. The houses were mostly log cabins facing muddy streets and expenses were astronomical for the time (potatoes were three dollars a bushel, flour was ten dollars a hundredweight, and eggs cost a dollar a dozen). Little competition, high labor costs because of manpower shortages, very high transportation costs, and a shortage of local production to meet the needs of a growing population all contributed to the high prices.

Treaty-making with the Indians of Washington Territory was a time-consuming process. The federal government did recognize Indian title to the land, but called for quick transfer to government control to prevent friction between white settlers and the native occupants.

The intentions may have been basically sound, but the process was flawed. In return for their land, the Indians were to receive a reservation which they alone would occupy, government-supported education, medical care and other services, and a cash payment along with goods and supplies. Some tribes also retained fishing rights at traditional sites and the right to farm and to pasture stock on unoccupied lands.

The appointment of Governor Stevens as superintendent of Indian Affairs was probably a mistake.

Above: *On the second floor of this frame structure, the twenty-seven members of the Washington Territorial Legislature met in session for the first time on February 27, 1854. The photo was taken about twenty years later. Courtesy, Washington State Historical Society*

Right: *By 1873, when this photo was taken, Olympia, then the largest city in the Territory, had lined its Main Street with maple trees. Courtesy, Washington State Historical Society*

The pressures of his many duties placed him under stress. He had neither the personality nor the understanding necessary to carry out the process without developing rancor. On the other hand, he was a military man who carried out orders. Between December 26, 1854, and January 31, 1855, he managed to convince Indian leaders of all Puget Sound tribes to sign treaties. Some later questioned whether the Indians fully understood what was happening and whether the true leaders were the signatories.

The Indians, especially those east of the Cascades, were loath to part with their land. Some historians say the Sound tribes had become more commercial minded and more willing to accept the consequences of the treaties. East of the mountains, where the land was less productive and trading less predominant, the Native Americans resented even more the process by which they were forced to hand over the land of their ancestors. Stevens ignored the signs and moved on to complete the treaty process.

Before the ink was dry on the signed documents and while the last treaties were yet to be negotiated, a gold rush developed in eastern Washington (which then included northern Idaho and western Montana). Prospectors moved across Indian lands and several lost their lives. An Indian agent, A.J. Bolon, on the way from The Dalles to eastern Washington to join Governor Stevens, was killed by the Yakima. Federal troops were dispatched and were repulsed with many casualties. This was but the first of many skirmishes between whites and the Native Americans.

Acting Governor Charles H. Mason, in charge while Stevens was away, warned that a state of hostility existed between the Yakima and the settlers and called for volunteers, two of the companies to be raised by Puget Sound residents. Hostile action spread to the Sound settlements. All across the territory, blockhouses were hurriedly raised. After two members of Charles Eaton's Rangers were killed (one was the popular James McAllister, the other a man named Cornell), the Olympia settlers rushed their families to the nearest stockades.

On October 28, 1855, the Indians struck at families on the White River just north of the present city of Auburn, killing nine people. Survivors rushed to the protection of Seattle's blockhouse.

Lieutenant William Slaughter, stationed at Fort Steilacoom, was ordered to lead his troops in pursuit of the hostile Indians. On December 4, he and his fifty regulars were encamped on White River not far from the massacre site. As darkness arrived, they built a large warming fire. Slaughter, sitting in a cabin with some of his men, was killed when Indians fired into their encampment; two other soldiers were also killed and several were wounded.

As January 26, 1856, dawned over Seattle, Indians massed in the forest on the hillside east of the Seattle settlement. After friendly natives alerted the settlers to imminent attack, the warship *Decatur,* which was anchored in Elliott Bay, fired a warning shot. Emily Inez Denny, a child at the time, described the scene in her book, *Blazing the Way.*

To a number of the settlers who were about breakfasting, it was a time of breathless terror; they must flee for their lives to the fort. The bullets from unseen foes whistled over their heads and the distance traversed to the fort was the longest journey of their lives. It was remembered afterward that some very amusing things took place in the midst of fright and flight. One man, rising late and not fully attired, donned his wife's red flannel petticoat instead of the bifurcated garment that usually graced his limbs. The "pants" were not handy and the petticoat was put on in a trice.

Louisa Boren Denny, my mother, was alone with her child about two years old, in the little frame house, a short distance from the fort. She was engaged in baking biscuits when hearing the shots and yells of the Indians she looked out to see the marines from the Decatur swarming up out of their boats onto Yesler's wharf and concluded it was best to retire in good order. With provident foresight she snatched the pan from the oven and turned the biscuits into her apron, picked up the child, Emily Inez Denny, with her free hand and hurried out, leaving the premises to their fate. Fortunately her husband, David T. Denny, who had been standing guard, met her in the midst of the flying bullets and assisted her, speedily, into the friendly fort.

The battle continued sporadically until dusk, at which time the Indians withdrew, burning the outlying houses and killing the cattle. The settlers suffered two casualties: Robert Wilson, an adult, and Milton Holgate, the fifteen-year-old son of a prominent pioneer family who, while standing in the doorway of the blockhouse, was struck in the head by an Indian bullet.

After the attack on Seattle, the Indians realized they could not match the firepower of the white settlers. The Hudson's Bay Company, to the surprise of the natives, sent not only supplies but armed vessels to protect the Americans.

Colonel William F. Prosser in his *History of Puget Sound,* published in 1903, quotes one long sentence from Admiral Phelps who served as a young lieutenant on the *Decatur* during the Indian attacks on Puget Sound settlements. That one sentence explains why, in Phelps' reasoning, the Indians went to war.

The early settlers, I believe, were always kind, just and considerate in dealing with the natives, and so far as I know retained to the last their friendship and good will; but as the country filled with new arrivals many rough characters, so called 'pioneers of civilization,' from the western frontier and other states, appeared, who, regardless of the rights appertaining to the natives, seized their reserved lands, drove them from the fisheries, deprived them of their just dues, surreptitiously shot some, hung others, and became ingenious in their methods of oppression, until their victims, roused from the lethargy enshrouding their faculties, began to exhibit signs of discontent, yet endured patiently, hoping for a beneficial change in their conditions, till the final blow to their anticipations came in 1854, with the delivery of some two hundred thousand dollars in presents, a preliminary measure on the part of the government to treaty stipulations with the tribes, which, being distributed by the agents in such fraudulent, unjust, and outrageous manner finally forced their eyes open to the certainties of the future, and from that moment they resolutely determined to be rid of the detestable pests fastening upon them.

Governor Stevens managed during his years as governor to antagonize several persons, even some of his supporters. He held strong opinions, was somewhat of a martinet, and to some of the settlers appeared to drink too much and to act erratically at times.

The territorial legislature, while praising Stevens' railroad survey, censured him for his treatment of the Seattle volunteers during the Indian unrest. Stevens had not only threatened to withhold their pay, he had backed a move to court-martial Arthur Denny for refusing to take his men away from Seattle. Denny believed the village needed their protection. Stevens even managed to irritate President Pierce, who went so far as to remove him from office in 1856, for declaring martial law in order to force transfer from territorial courts to military tribunals the cases of "squawmen" (whites married to Indian women) whom Stevens had accused of spying during the Indian wars. Pierce condemned the action and replaced

Emily Inez Denny (left) was the eldest child of David and Louisa Boren Denny (right) and the first white girl born in Seattle. She was a painter and writer of note, and her book Blazing the Way *is an excellent chronicle of pioneer life. She died in 1918 at the age of sixty-five. (MOHAI)*

Stevens with former Oregon governor Joseph Lane, but the Senate refused to ratify the shift and Stevens retained his office.

After it was certain the Indians had indeed been quieted, the volunteers were disbanded. A total of 1,896 men had served, all but 215 of them from the sparse population of the new territory. Nearly every able-bodied male had been involved.

Prosser reports:

The close of the war found most of the settlements in a wretched and pitiable condition. Houses, crops and improvements had been burned, destroyed or abandoned, stock killed by the Indians, and those settlers who had not been driven off or murdered were without the most ordinary means of subsistence. The future looked dark and discouraging in the highest degree. No one could tell whether the promised peace was to be permanent or not, or whether the professed friendship of the Indians could be relied on, after the bitter heartburnings created by death and bereavement on one side, or death and disappointment on the other, as the results of the war in which they had recently been engaged. . . . Under the circumstances, therefore, it was not surprising that the country recuperated slowly from the effects of a disastrous Indian war. Time was necessary to heal its wounds and to restore confidence to both races and to all settlers, whether in the country or in towns and villages, before an era of permanent prosperity could be ushered in. Many settlers did not return to their homes in the country until after the treaties made with the Indians were ratified by the United States senate in 1859.

THE PIG WAR

Though British assistance during the Indian unrest had been appreciated by the Americans, old frictions flared anew over San Juan Island.

The agreement of 1846 had established the border at the 49th parallel as far as the Strait of Georgia, then down "the main ship channel" to the Pacific. Two conflicting interpretations developed over which was the "main ship channel"—Canal de Haro northwest of San Juan Island or Rosario Channel, southwest of the island. The island of San Juan became disputed territory.

The Hudson's Bay Company pastured a herd of several thousand sheep on San Juan. The Washington Territorial legislature considered the island to be part of Whatcom County and all real and personal property there to be taxable. When the Hudson's

Bay Company refused to pay the taxes levied, the Whatcom County sheriff, in March 1855, seized and sold a number of the sheep to cover the bill. A sharp exchange ensued between the governor of Vancouver Island—the tall, fearless, half-Creole, illegitimate son of a Scottish merchant, James Douglas, who later would be knighted; and the short, fiery-tempered Isaac Stevens. The latter insisted the island was U.S. territory and warned: "Should he [the sheriff] be resisted it would be the duty of the Governor to sustain him to the full force of the authority vested in him."

The problem was communicated to the secretary of state in Washington, D.C., who urged patience and promised a quick diplomatic solution, but this was not forthcoming.

In 1859, an American settler on San Juan Island, Lyman Cutler, shot a Hudson's Bay Company pig which he found rooting in his garden. Governor Douglas sent his son-in-law and two members of the Colonial Council to collect $100 for the pig. Cutler balked at the price, and boldly defied arrest. The British threatened to summon Cutler before a British magistrate.

U.S. General Harney, after inspecting the security of the Sound, was troubled by the lack of defenses for settlers. After discussions with Governor Stevens, he transferred Captain George Pickett and his Ninth Infantry Company from Bellingham Bay to San Juan Island.

Governor Douglas dispatched three warships to the area to prevent further American troop landing. Pickett's men proceeded to erect fortifications. Thereupon, Douglas issued a proclamation protesting the "invasion of British territory" but later suggested the territory be jointly occupied. Pickett ignored the suggestion.

Just then, Admiral Baynes, commander of the British Pacific fleet, sailed into Victoria harbor with a strong naval force. Douglas ordered the admiral to drive the Americans off the island. But Admiral Baynes dallied. Why should two great nations, he asked, go to war over a pig? He did, however, reinforce the blockade of the island. When, under cover of a dense fog, the Americans managed to sneak three additional companies ashore, Admiral Baynes withdrew his ships.

A compromise now appeared attractive to both sides, and for good reason. Americans on Puget Sound numbered fewer than 3,000 and were spread thinly in small settlements at Bellingham Bay, Port Townsend, Seattle, Steilacoom, Nisqually, and Olym-

The Whatcom County settlement of Ferndale on the Nooksack River is pictured here in about 1880. Courtesy, Washington State Historical Society

pia, and around the sawmills at Ports Madison, Ludlow, Gamble, and other harbors on Admiralty Inlet and Hood Canal. Even so, they outnumbered the handful of British, who, for the most part, were concentrated on Vancouver Island. Furthermore, the British considered the Yankees to be aggressive and the volunteers that had fought in the Indian wars could be quickly reassembled. On the other hand, the Americans realized the British fleet clearly controlled the seas.

To make matters more confusing, the Fraser River gold rush had, beginning in 1855, attracted throngs of American miners. By the thousands, they "invaded" Victoria and the settlements on the Fraser and Thompson rivers. Some of the British feared the sheer weight of their numbers might jeopardize their country's hold on the territory north of the 49th parallel just as had been the case in Oregon.

When the U.S. Government sent General Scott to negotiate, the British again proposed joint occupation of San Juan Island and the Americans quickly agreed. All but one company of U.S. troops were withdrawn from the island. The British encamped a troop of marines near its western end. Thus did the matter rest for thirteen years until Emperor William of Germany mediated the dispute and awarded the island to the United States.

CIVIL WAR

Isaac Stevens, after serving as governor, was twice elected the territory's delegate to Congress and served in the nation's capital from 1857 until April 1861. He returned to Olympia careworn and worried over the threatening civil conflict. Word followed him west that Fort Sumter had fallen. As a Democrat at a time when the new Republican party was gaining ascendency, and as a soldier intent on performing his duty, he withdrew his re-election candidacy and hurried back to offer his services to the Union cause.

By May 10, 1861, Acting Governor Henry M. McGill (Governor Gholson had returned to his native state, Kentucky, to join the efforts of the Confederacy) had received President Lincoln's first call for volunteers. All able-bodied men were to enroll with the adjutant general. The order was largely ignored. Clinton A. Snowden in his *History of Washington*, explains:

The Democrats had always been in the majority in the territory. All the governors so far had been Democrats appointed by Democratic presidents, and all the delegates in Congress had been Democrats, and had been elected by considerable majorities. The majority had, therefore, long been opposed to any interference with slavery. . . . The majority accordingly were but little inclined to march across the continent to engage in the war on either side, and the minority probably did not, for some time, comprehend that the attack on Sumter had changed the issue from one about slavery, to one about union or disunion.

In October, Assistant Secretary of War Colonel Thomas A. Scott wrote Colonel Justin Steinberger that he was to raise a regiment of infantry in Washington Territory. After meeting with the legislature in January 1862 and visiting towns west of the Cascades, Steinberger concluded that at most three companies would result.

He received little help from the legislature, which refused until the next session even to pledge allegiance to the Union cause. However, the legislators agreed to raise $7,755, the territory's share of a direct tax levied by Congress, to help support soldiers in the field.

There were several reasons for the legislature's lack of immediate support for the Union cause. The settlers were suffering through one of the coldest winters on record. Government payments promised the Indian tribes by treaty had not been forthcoming and the natives were angry and suffering from the chill weather. Indians from north of the border made menacing moves just as the regulars in the military company at Bellingham Bay were withdrawn. With all the uncertainty, few men wished to enlist in units that might serve 3,000 miles away when they felt their homes and families needed protection.

Colonel Steinberger authorized a company to be filled by residents of Puget Sound and hoped two others might be recruited from east of the mountains. He traveled to California where he filled eight companies and transported them to Fort Vancouver to serve in the First Washington Infantry Regiment. Most of the men recruited on Puget Sound were stationed at Fort Steilacoom for the duration of their service.

Early in the war, Southern sympathizers were outspoken enough to cause some anxiety. Rumors of privateering off the coast were heard and, late in the conflict, the Confederate privateer *Shenandoah* did destroy several merchantmen and whalers in North Pacific waters. But the Unionists rallied support and women in the territory raised several thousand dollars for the Sanitary Commission to use in caring for wounded and ill soldiers.

The progress of the war was followed avidly through Eastern newspapers mailed to the Sound. Though they arrived months after the events, they were read with interest and passed from family to family. Not until 1864 would telegraph wires reach the area, permitting instant communication.

Of special interest were the careers of military men who had been stationed on Puget Sound. Colonel Silas Casey, for example, the former commander at Fort Steilacoom, led a division through the Peninsula battles and at Fair Oakes where he was brevetted a major-general. Lieutenant Augustus Kautz became a brigadier-general, commanded a division in the Army of the James, and later a division of "colored" troops, then in retirement returned to live on Puget Sound. Captain Rufus Ingalls, well known during the San Juan dispute, took over as chief quartermaster of the Army of the Potomac and fought in several major battles as a major-general. General John M. Wilson, the territory's 1855 appointee to West Point, served in the artillery, fought at Manassas, and ended the war in the engineer corps. Afterwards he was named superintendent of West Point.

Lieutenant Thomas S. Phelps of the U.S. Navy, who had served on the *Decatur* during the Indian attacks on Sound settlements, was assigned to the expedition sent to relieve Fort Sumter and served most of the war off the East Coast. He later achieved the rank of rear-admiral. Captain Guert Gansevoort, commander of the *Decatur* when it was in Puget Sound waters (Phelps was one of his lieutenants) served as chief of ordnance at Brooklyn Navy Yard and later as commander of the ironclad *Roanoke.*

Others fought for the Confederacy. Lieutenant E.P. Alexander, on duty at Fort Steilacoom when hostilities commenced, immediately returned to his home state of Georgia to enlist in the Southern cause. Captain George Pickett, famous on Puget Sound for his service during the San Juan dispute, led the Confederate charge at Gettysburg. When the conflict ended, General Grant, who had served a year at Fort Vancouver, sent a letter relieving Pickett of the onerous house arrest forced upon him as a Confederate officer following the war.

Major Granville Haller, who had fought the Indians east of the mountains and was later stationed at Port Townsend and on Bellingham Bay, served in several positions, including that of provost-marshal-general for the state of Maryland. Late in the war he was relieved of command "for disloyal conduct and the utterance of disloyal sentiments." Though he demanded trial and a confrontation with his accusers, this was denied until 1879 when his case was heard by order of Congress and he was vindicated. Meantime he had returned to Puget Sound. After his delayed trial, he was restored to his full rank of colonel, commanded the 23rd regiment, and retired from the army in 1882. He then moved to Seattle and became a wealthy and well-known citizen.

Perhaps the most memorable of all was former Governor Isaac Stevens, who was appointed a colonel with the 79th New York Highlanders, earned the rank of brigadier-general, distinguished himself at the Battle of Manassas, and was killed two days later on September 1, 1862, while leading his unit in a charge at Chantilly, Virginia.

By war's end, Puget Sounders were overwhelmingly pro-Union, and the Republican Party had taken control of territorial politics. Also in 1864 came news that would have pleased Isaac Stevens. Abraham Lincoln signed legislation designed to stimulate the building of a railroad linking Puget Sound with the Great Lakes. But a decade would pass before the dream came true.

Isaac Ingalls Stevens, first governor of Washington Territory, served from 1853 to 1857, then was elected by the settlers as their delegate to Congress. A West Point graduate, Stevens joined the Union Army when the Civil War began, and was killed at the battle of Chantilly in 1862. (MOHAI)

3
Cracking the Isolation Barrier

Isolation was the paramount problem facing the pioneers on Puget Sound. With the Cascade Range barring movement to the east and with an almost trackless wilderness on all sides, the first transportation systems to develop utilized the Sound, the sea, and the rivers.

SCHOONERS AND MOSQUITO FLEET STEAMERS

The first major settlements developed on inlets of Puget Sound where ships could serve them. The colorful age of the "mosquito fleet" dawned with these first settlements, and was so called after the small steam-propelled craft that flitted up and down the Sound, carrying passengers, freight, and mail to every inhabited bay and island. Each vessel developed a personality of its own and generated many a nautical tale, most of which are preserved

Opposite: *At the turn of the century Everett was a major lumber port where loaded schooners, such as the two pictured here, sailed for distant parts of the globe. (MOHAI)*

to this day as part of the rich folklore of the area. The mosquito fleet remained an integral part of the communication-transportation system until the automobile, a more convenient mode of travel, entered the picture.

We who live in an age of rapid communication and transportation find it difficult to imagine how completely Puget Sound settlers were isolated. Clarence Bagley, in his *History of King County,* described the pioneer mail transportation system:

A letter mailed in St. Louis or Chicago for the territory of Washington, went east to New York; there it was put on a steamship and taken to the Isthmus of Panama, then at first it went on muleback to Panama City, but after 1855, a railcar transported it. From Panama by steamer to San Francisco, and again from there by steamer, but not to Puget Sound. Portland then received and distributed all the eastern mails for the Pacific Northwest. From Portland, Seattle's mail came down by river steamboat to Monticello, near the mouth of the Cowlitz River; thence overland to Olympia. From there until 1858 it came by canoe, sloop or schooner. In those days, reply to a letter mailed to a friend in the East was not due for three months from the date of sending. Even when a steamboat carried the mails with somewhat of regularity between Olympia and way ports to Victoria it was only once a week. In most country regions, market day was Saturday, but in Seattle it was Monday, for that was steamer day.

As early as 1853, two tiny steamers, the *Water Lily* and the *Fairy,* busily plied the Sound. The following year, the *Major Thompkins* arrived to become the first mail and passenger steamer, but she sank near Victoria about a year later. The *Traveler* succeeded her, steaming from Olympia to Victoria for two years, then for a time was chartered by the Indian Bureau to carry officers and supplies to the various reservations. She was the first steamboat to work the Duwamish, White, Snohomish, and Nooksack rivers. In 1856 the screw-propellered craft *Constitution* left her wakes in the channels from Olympia to Victoria, but then her cranky engines were removed and she ended her career toting lumber under sail.

The *Eliza Anderson,* a small steamer of seagoing ability, made as much history and more profit than any of her pioneering sisters. In the months following the Fraser River Gold Rush, she was the only steamer of consequence scheduled on the Sound and her fares were high. Passengers from Olympia paid $6.50

to reach Seattle, $12.50 to Port Townsend, and $20 to Victoria. Horses and cattle were transported at $15 a head; sheep and hogs, $2.50; freight at $5 to $10 per ton depending on bulk. Later, when competition returned, fares plummeted, for the owners of the *Eliza* felt no compunction at lowering fares to freeze out competition. At such times a passenger could board the *Eliza* for 50 cents and travel to any destination on her route. By 1870, the *Eliza Anderson* was worn and run-down, so her owners debuted a beautiful new steamer, the *Olympia.*

As population increased, steamboating kept pace; Seattle yards in 1863 christened such sidewheelers as the *J.B. Libby* and the *Mary Woodruff.* The *Black Diamond, Ruby,* and *Chehalis,* and the first sternwheeler built in Seattle, the *Zephyr,* all slid down the ways in 1871. In 1876, William R. Ballard bought the *Zephyr* from J.R. Robbins and over the next ten years she earned him a small fortune. He invested in real estate, and the town called "Ballard," which later was annexed to Seattle, was named for him.

During the population surges of the late 1880s, the ships grew larger. Captain D.B. Jackson and associates brought the *City of Seattle* and *City of Kingston* into service, two crack steamers of latest design. John Leary had the *Bailey Gatzert,* which was 200 feet long, built in Ballard at a cost of $125,000. That same year the *Greyhound* began providing fast courier service between Seattle and Tacoma.

In 1883, the Northern Pacific Railroad spur line out of Portland was stretched to Commencement Bay. Thereafter, mail arrived at Tacoma via rail, but was distributed around the Sound by steamer. The ships of L.M. and E.A. Starr, among them the *Olympia, North Pacific, Alida, Isabel,* and *Otter,* successfully bid for the post office contracts.

In 1891, the Columbia River and Puget Sound Navigation Company purchased the *Gatzert, Fleetwood,* and *Telephone,* and built the *Flyer,* a speedy propeller craft that made four round trips per day between Seattle and Tacoma. This new company soon dominated the Seattle-Tacoma run, transporting more than a million passengers a year. At the time, the *Flyer* was logging more miles per annum than any other steamer in the world. This company also operated ferries between Alki and Manchester; Seattle, Bremerton and Port Orchard; Port Gamble and Shine; Mukilteo and Columbia Beach; Everett and Langley; Keystone Point and Port Townsend; Anacortes and Sidney, B.C.; Bellingham and Sidney; and from Port Angeles to Brinnon.

The Kitsap Transportation Company's complex

Above: *An unidentified tug tows two schooners (on left and right) and a barkentine on Puget Sound in 1900. The man standing second from the left is the well-known photographer H.W. Morrison. Courtesy, National Maritime Museum*

Right: *The stern-wheeler* Nellie *was built for use on the Snohomish River and could float on twenty inches of water. She is shown here in 1876 in front of the Exchange Hotel in Snohomish City. (MOHAI)*

schedule illustrates how completely water transportation served Sound residents. At one time they ran ferries from: Fauntleroy to Vashon and Harper; Ballard to Suquamish; Seattle to Port Blakely; and Fletcher Bay to Brownsville. On these runs, service was provided to tiny settlements such as Agate Point, Creosote, Eagledale, Ferncliff, Hall's Shipyard, Hawley Dock, Indianola, Keyport, Lemola, Manitou Beach, Manzanita, North Seabold, Pearson, Port Madison, Poulsbo, Rolling Bay, Scandia, Seabold, Suquamish, Virginia, Winslow, Wing Point, and Yeomalt. Each village had its ferry slip or log boom where passengers and freight were loaded and unloaded.

Lake Washington, too, had its fleet from pioneer days onward, the most noted being that of Captain J.L. Anderson who provided transportation between Madison Park and Kirkland and from Leschi Park to Mercer Island and Medina. A white flag, hung where it could be seen, signaled these small lake steamers to stand-to for passengers and/or goods often delivered by canoe or rowboat.

These waterway connections made it possible for retail, wholesale, and service activities to flourish in the cities. By the mid-1880s, Seattle, which was headquarters for most of the ship lines, had become the major port and would maintain this status even though it was years before a direct railroad link was established. Seattle's leaders had planned and worked toward this end, and with their centralized location and deepwater harbor, succeeded.

OVERLAND TRAVEL

From the outset, the pioneers on Puget Sound recognized that commerce and security required roads between the settlements. As early as 1852, Thurston County Commissioners discussed the need for a road from Fort Steilacoom to Seattle. In that summer before King County was split off from Thurston, Arthur Denny, who was then a county commissioner, saw to it that "viewers" were appointed to find the best route. They reported that the road should travel

... from Seattle to [Luther] Collins on the Duwampsh [Duwamish] river; thence on the dividing ridge most of the way, striking the Puyallup river one mile above Adam Benson's claim; thence to crossing of Steilacoom creek, thence to Steilacoom, the terminus.

With great exertion, the pioneers cleared several makeshift wagon tracks, following the ridges to miss the bogs and tideflats. In territorial days, when cash was scarce, a man could work off part of his taxes by laboring at road construction.

A new paper, *The Columbian,* in its first issue in

Above: *Small steamships of the Puget Sound "mosquito fleet" cross the bay below the cliff dominated by the Tacoma Hotel. The sketch was made in the 1890s after the railroad, with its tracks along the shore, had begun to compete for both passengers and freight. Courtesy, Bancroft Library, University of California, Berkeley*

Opposite: *The Puget Sound Tugboat Company's 151-foot steam tug* Goliah *is seen using her 1,000 horsepower triple-expansion engine to pull the four-masted steel bark* Acme *into port. Courtesy, National Maritime Museum*

Olympia in September, 1852, spoke of the importance of "opening new roads and improving old ones." At the time the only road of consequence, which meandered from Warbassport (Toledo) to Olympia, was scarcely passable in winter. On the trail between Olympia and Fort Nisqually, the river at "Packwood's Place" was crossed by an unreliable ferry that halted service during high water. The few flimsy bridges that were tediously built to span the rivers were invariably washed out by spring floods.

In December 1852, Thurston County commissioners authorized new roads from Yelm to McAllister's home on the Nisqually and from Steilacoom to Dewamps (Seattle) via the valleys of the Puyallup and White rivers. Several years would pass before these roads were cleared through the virgin forest.

Realizing that access was necessary if the region were to attract its share of settlers, the first Puget Sounders dreamed of building a road through the Cascades to Fort Walla Walla where it would intersect the Oregon Trail. *The Columbian,* in every issue, mentioned this need. In answer to the memorial of the Oregon Territorial Legislature, Congress in 1853 appropriated $20,000 for a military road from Fort Walla Walla to Fort Steilacoom and placed Captain George B. McClellan in charge of construction. He arrived on the coast in July but delayed building the road. The impatient settlers, urged on by the *Columbian,* raised $6,600 in pledges of funding and donated their labor for a cross-mountain passage. Roberta Frye Watt, a granddaughter of Seattle founder Arthur Denny, in her 1932 book *Four Wagons West* wrote of this episode:

With their own funds and voluntary labor, under the supervision of Edward J. Allen, they started out on the formidable task of building the road themselves through the Naches Pass. They hewed a rough road and built primitive bridges as far as the summit. Here they met Indians who told them that no parties were coming through the mountains that fall; so they turned back and did no more, since it was late in the season.

But a company known as "the Biles party," made up of twenty-nine wagons and one hundred and forty-eight people, had heard that the "Northern Oregon" settlers were building a road through to Puget Sound and came on through the mountains that way. The hardships and suffering of that first immigrant train through Naches Pass is an epic of pioneer history. Some of the oxen were killed in order to obtain raw-

hide for ropes for lowering the wagons over the precipices. To quote one of the party, it was "so fraught with hardships and peril and misery as to make all that had been suffered before scarcely worth mentioning."

The first session of the Washington Territorial Legislature in 1854-55 "located" roads on Puget Sound as follows: Steilacoom to Seattle, Steilacoom to Vancouver, Seattle to Bellingham Bay, Olympia to Shoalwater (Willapa) Bay, Seattle to the immigrant trail, and Olympia to Monticello (Longview). This was, however, a wish list they were long in realizing.

In spite of the difficulties, Stewart's Express Company was operating between Portland and Olympia as early as 1854. The 180-mile journey involved steamboat, canoe, and wagon and in good weather could be completed in thirty-six hours. Two years later Wells-Fargo took over the route and developed regular stops at Steilacoom, Seattle, Port Townsend, and Vancouver Island.

Pioneer writer Ezra Meeker described how this trail from the Columbia River to Olympia developed:

...The facts are, this road, like "Topsy," just "growed," and so gradually became a highway one could scarcely say when the trail ceased to be simply a trail and the road actually could be called a road. First, only saddle-trains could pass. On the back of a stiff jointed, hard trotting, slow walking, contrary mule, I was initiated into the secret depths of the mud holes of this trail. And such mud holes! It became a standing joke after the road was opened that a team would stall with an empty wagon going down hill ...

In 1858, the settlers on the Sound, especially those in Seattle, raised $1,050 to begin clearing the track over Snoqualmie Pass. Roberta Frye Watt described the effort:

That winter, through the good offices of Arthur Denny in the Council [Senate] and his colleagues in the House, Dr. Henry Smith and David Phillips, the legislature memorialized Congress on the need of connecting eastern Washington with the seaports of the Sound, and on the advisability of a military road to Walla Walla through the Snoqualmie Pass. The logical reasons in favor of this pass rather than Naches and other passes were set forth.

This memorial was favorably received in Congress. A

bill appropriating $75,000 was introduced, but was lost because of the dominating interest in the Civil War. For this reason this road remained but little more than a trail.

After the War, in the fall of 1865, the pioneers were determined to explore the Cascade passes to find " a more favorable line for a wagon road." The exploring party followed Indian guides through a lower Snoqualmie pass, the one we know today. After three days of surveying they returned full of enthusiasm. Solicitors quickly raised $2,500 and William Perkins contracted to clear a wagon road. Before the November rains came, his crews had completed twenty-five miles and the following spring built on to the summit. In October, 1866, a train of six wagons passed over the summit. Again we quote Roberta Frye Watt:

After the winter storms and spring freshets had done their worst, the people of Seattle realized what a tremendous undertaking the maintenace of the road was, for trees were blown across the road, bridges destroyed, and grades washed out. Not only was the condition of the road itself discouraging but it ended at Lake Keechelus, a beautiful lake with mountains towering near the water's edge on all sides. Here the travelers had to face the problem of loading wagons and horses on a log raft and poling across the lake. If the day was sunny, and the waters smooth, it did not seem such a formidable task; but reaching this lake on a stormy day was anything but cheerful and made even the stoutest heart fearful.

Seattle citizens, in 1867, lobbied the legislature and were awarded $2,000 on condition that King County raise a matching amount to complete the road to the Kittitas Valley. This road broke the barrier of the Cascades. Though it would remain a rough wagon trail until well after the turn of the century, it provided new potential for Puget Sound commerce and settlement.

Until 1907, all road construction revenue was derived from taxes collected at the county level, but as Cornelius Hanford stated in his book *Seattle and Environs:*

There was no general fund for continuous roads crossing county lines. For many years repeated efforts to change that condition were met by insistence upon Thomas Jefferson's theory of: Local government for local affairs. Taxpayers denied the power

of the state to compel them to pay for roads in distant parts, or even in neighboring counties...

...A few roads had been surfaced by spreading gravel, and being unprotected by legal restrictions against misuse, were cut into ruts and chuckholes by loaded vehicles running on narrow tires, and in some instances were plowed by dragging long sticks of timber thereon. Swampy places were bridged by corduroy— that is by laying flat pieces of timber upon the wet ground...

Not until 1905, when auto travel was increasing, did the state legislature enact laws creating the office of highway commissioner. It funded the act two years later. By 1910, most Puget Sound cities and towns were connected by graded roads, many of them gravel surfaced.

THE BUILDING OF THE RAILROADS

The age of the railroads had arrived in the East before Americans had settled on Puget Sound. In 1853, on his way to assume the governorship of the new Territory of Washington, Isaac Stevens led survey parties that scouted potential railroad routes to the Sound. But because the Willamette Valley of Oregon and parts of California developed more rapidly, railroad companies concentrated on providing service to these areas first. The rails of the Union Pacific reached California in 1869 and soon completed a spur line north to Portland. In 1864, the Northern Pacific received its charter and land grants alongside its proposed route from Lake Superior to the Sound.

Beginning in 1869, the Puget Sound region experienced a noticeable increase in population. The cause: Jay Cooke and Company, then the country's foremost bankers, had agreed to find financing for the Northern Pacific Railroad and in 1870 furnished $5 million to commence construction. Seattle became headquarters for surveyors working in Snoqualmie Pass and was assumed by many to be the leading contender for terminus status. In the ensuing building boom hotels changed their names to "The Western Terminus" and "The Railroad House." *Harpers Magazine,* in the September 1870 issue, described Seattle's vitality as coming from nearby coal mines, and from

...the popular belief that it is the place—the great terminus. The land for miles around has been bought by speculators, divided into lots, and auctioned off at Victoria, through the Willamette Valley and even in

Above: *The Columbia and Puget Sound Railroad train is seen pulling into Franklin, a small coal company town in King County twelve miles south of Maple Valley. In 1890, the year the photo was taken, Washington State produced 1.25 million tons of coal, most of it from mines in Puget Sound counties. (MOHAI)*

Opposite: *The Northern Pacific Railway chose Tacoma as its terminus and by 1888 was serving the city via a direct line over the Cascade mountains. Rail met sail on Puget Sound at this Northern Pacific wharf. Courtesy, Bancroft Library, University of California, Berkeley*

San Francisco. Nine months ago there were not more than 500 people in it, now there are 1000...

The Portland realty firm of Russell and Ferry coined the term "Queen City" in the 1870s to describe Seattle in a circular they broadcast nationwide.

The original settlers—Yesler, Bell, the Dennys, and others—began reaping a financial reward from their land claims as their hometown developed as a shipping and commercial center. Edmond Meany in his history of Washington wrote:

Industrial growth was present everywhere. The rivers and harbors were furnished with little steamers. Shipbuilding was begun and lumber exports pointed the way toward future wealth. Coal found a ready market. Fish and oysters were in demand. California to the south, Alaska to the north, the Islands and the

er to Portland were extended north to Tacoma. However, it was a difficult route involving a ferry across the Columbia to Kalama.

The Northern Pacific provided direct service over the Cascades to Tacoma in 1887 and the following year the Stampede Pass tunnel was completed, which moderated the grade at the summit. The Puget Sound region blossomed with the new economic and immigration possibilities. The direct line not only opened trade with populous areas to the east, it united the eastern and western regions of Washington Territory.

The railroads now began an advertising campaign to extol the advantages of moving westward. The number of immigrants to Washington jumped from 67,000 in 1880 to 239,000 in 1889. After the Panic of 1893 and the ensuing recession, still more families heeded the message, hoping to improve their lot on the western slopes of the Cascades.

Orient on the highway of the sea—everyone knew that Washington had a magnificent future. To hurry the dawning of that great day was the ambition alike of the patient pioneer and the impulsive newcomer. The one surest way to hasten that day was the construction of a railroad from the Mississippi River to tidewater on Puget Sound.

But in 1873 Seattleites received a severe jolt. The Northern Pacific chose Tacoma on Commencement Bay for its terminus. Soon thereafter, disaster struck financier Jay Cooke and Company, a worldwide depression ensued, and railroad building halted at Bismark, North Dakota. When activity resumed in 1883, the Northern Pacific tracks down the Columbia Riv-

Seattleites, after learning of their loss of the terminus, decided to develop their own railroad, the Seattle and Walla Walla. With local capital and labor they managed, in 1875, to extend the line as far as the Renton coal mines. It was a successful short, narrow-gauge line that eventually reached Newcastle and other coalfields. Later it was purchased by the Northern Pacific and became part of the spur line out of Tacoma. However, when the Northern Pacific refused to provide adequate service over this "Orphan" road, as it came to be called, Seattle's leaders decided rails should be built north to meet the newly completed Canadian Pacific. Meantime, they sent freight and some passengers north by ship to Vancouver rather than do business with the N.P.

1900 April the 29th 1900

HISTORY MADE!

THE PREMIER TRAIN OF THE
PIONEER NORTHWEST RAILWAY

The NORTH COAST LIMITED

NORTHERN PACIFIC
RAILWAY

NOW COMMENCING DAILY SERVICE
LINKING THE PROSPEROUS EAST WITH THE GOLDEN WEST

SEATTLE to ST. PAUL

And offering to the fastidious traveler

LUXURIOUS AND TASTEFUL ACCOMMODATIONS

THE NEW "ELECTRIC LIGHTS"

STEAM HEAT

Pullman's Palace Sleeping Cars

HIGHLY SCENIC ROUTE
FOLLOWING THE TRAIL OF LEWIS & CLARKE

Your Patronage Solicited!

Above: *By the turn of the century, both the Northern Pacific and the Great Northern railroads plus several smaller lines were serving Puget Sound. Then the principal means of passenger travel, rail service was constantly being improved. (MOHAI)*

Opposite: *The elegance of traveling first class by rail is depicted in this interior view of a Northern Pacific sleeper car taken in 1900. The walls unfolded to provide comfortable bunks. (MOHAI)*

By 1888, the Seattle, Lake Shore and Eastern Railroad was serving Snohomish and building northward, providing an important service to little towns, many of which were founded as the rails neared. In 1890, the Seattle and Northern tracks had reached Anacortes. The following year the Fairhaven and Southern extended from Sedro to the Canadian border. Soon these combined lines were feeding the Canadian Pacific, a fact that no doubt caused concern on the part of the Northern Pacific.

Now the Great Northern, under master builder James J. Hill, began grading its roadbed across the Midwest. In 1893, the first Great Northern train pulled into Seattle, providing the city with its own direct rail link with the Midwest and the East.

Since their rails followed the valleys, the railroads made many riverboats obsolete. Oceangoing vessels, too, lost some of their business to the rails, but the growing trade between Puget Sound and the Orient more than compensated. Direct steamship service to the Far East was inaugurated in 1887 by the Canadian Pacific. By 1904 Jim Hill's Great Northern was steaming two huge merchant vessels between Seattle and the Orient and a Japanese line began scheduled calls on Elliott Bay. In addition, the population growth in the Western states increased coastwise ship traffic.

Beginning in 1897, as a result of the Klondike gold rush, ships were suddenly in short supply and every vessel capable of floating was pressed into service. All Puget Sound ports were busier than they had ever been.

When the Panama Canal opened in 1915, waterborne transport would again compete for trade with the Eastern Seaboard. By then improvements were available, among them refrigeration units. Through the years, port facilities would be improved as the region worked to maintain its share of trade.

DEVELOPMENT OF INDUSTRY

The value of the natural resources on Puget Sound was recognized early. The British Hudson's Bay Company had, in 1833, sold 50,000 board feet of lumber to China. The Company also accumulated cedar shakes at Fort Nisqually for shipment to Hawaii and California. Most of the early settlers, at one time or another, spent days as "shingle shavers" to earn needed income.

In 1847, Michael Simmons and others, including George Bush, built the first sawmill on the Sound at the lower falls of the Deschutes in Tumwater. Several other water-powered mills were established be-

Right: *Port Hadlock, eight miles south of Port Townsend, was a sawmill town in 1890 when this sketch was made. New Hampshire-born Samuel Hadlock, who was a principal in the mill company, also laid out a settlement which took his name. (MOHAI)*

Below: *After the forests near the beaches had been harvested, transporting logs to the mills became a more laborious task. For a time oxen pulled the giant trunks over skid roads, then during the 1880s, logging railroads became common. The little engine "Minnetonka" is seen crossing a logging bridge in Thurston County. (MOHAI)*

Seabeck (1857), Utsalady on Camano Island (1858), Port Discovery (1859) and on the Snohomish River (1863). By 1870, forty-two mills were operating in Washington Territory, most of them on Puget Sound where the timber was heaviest and easiest to log and ship. That year, the mills of the territory employed 474 men who produced 128 million board feet of lumber.

Most of the first logs for the mills were furnished by settlers clearing their land for habitation, farming, and city building. Dr. David Maynard, Arthur A. Denny, the Hanfords, and other Seattle pioneers felled their tall firs and cedars with axes, and whip-sawed them into lengths for Yesler's Seattle mill. Clarence Bagley, in his *History of Seattle* speaks of the effort. "By sheer strength of their bodies the men laid low the stately trees that made the site of the future city a forest, rolled them to tidewater and towed them with small boats to the mill."

Not until the late 1870s did felling saws, first used in the redwood forests of California, appear on the Sound. After timber near the water was harvested, oxen dragged the logs, often over skid roads, to the water where it could be floated to the mills.

In those earlier mills, great circular saws, often six feet in diameter, cut a half-inch kerf, chewing much of the tree into sawdust. Thinner band saws were not introduced until the 1880s.

To clear land for cultivation, some settlers felled trees and burned them. In dry months the fires would sometimes spread to standing timber, filling the sky with smoke. Not until 1903 was the first state law passed to protect the forests, and not until 1917 was a State Forestry Department established.

During the two decades between 1870 and 1890, lumber developed into a huge industry. An infusion of out-of-state capital built bigger, more efficient mills. Steam donkey engines and logging railroads (the first apparently built near Marysville in 1883 by the pioneer logging firm owned by the Blackman brothers) were common in the woods. At the same time, improved machinery—powered band saws, carriages, trimmers and edgers—were being installed.

Elwood Evans, in a book about Washington State which he assembled for the World's Columbian Exposition of 1893, proudly listed fir, spruce, cedar, alder, maple, ash, yew, cottonwood, larch, and oak as trees growing in Puget Sound counties. He added: "Nearly one-third of the population is dependent upon the saw and shingle mills, sash, door, and other woodworking establishments." He placed an annual value of $19 million on these wood products, $9 mil-

tween 1850 and 1853, among them those of James McAllister on the Nisqually, Nicholas Delin on Commencement Bay, and A.T. Simmons on Henderson Bay. The first steam-powered sawmill on Puget Sound was operated by Henry Yesler at Seattle in 1853. J.J. Felt began operation of a steam mill at Apple Tree Cove a few weeks later. He sold it to George A. Meigs who moved it to Port Madison where a thriving town for a time rivaled Steilacoom and Olympia. Lumber from this mill was delivered all over the world by company vessels, though most of it went to California. That same year, 1853, William Renton and C.C. Terry put up a small mill at Alki Point, but the next year Renton moved it to more protected Port Orchard. James M. Colman bought this mill in 1862 and went on to become one of the Sound's most famous early mill owners.

The Puget Sound Mill Company established by W.C. Talbot and A.J. Pope of San Francisco, selected Port Gamble as a site for its mill. By 1854, the mill had thirteen saws operating and Pope and Talbot lumber was being sold in many foreign countries including Australia.

Other mills soon were established at Port Ludlow (1853), Whatcom Creek (1853), Black River (1854),

Cedar trees grow large in the Puget Sound country. Photos of these ancient giants were often used in promotional efforts to attract families to the region. (MOHAI)

lion of it exported to foreign lands. About 12,000 men in the state, he reported, were engaged in logging and production in 227 sawmills, 246 shingle mills and 73 sash, door, and other factories, and were paid salaries totaling more than $7 million annually.

Lumbermen, facing a growing public protest against cutting timber on the public domain, began purchasing huge acreages of timber. In some cases individuals called "dummies" would claim land under the Homestead Act, then as soon as legal, transfer the title to the company they served. Large tracts were also purchased from the land grants awarded the Northern Pacific.

Increasingly, lumbermen from the Midwest invested in forested lands on Puget Sound. Most, for a short time, were absentee landowners, but in the 1890s, many moved west. Minnesotans Chauncey Griggs and Henry Hewitt, Jr., representing several investors founded the St. Paul and Tacoma Lumber Company in Tacoma, then purchased 90,000 timbered Cascade Mountain acres from the Northern Pacific. Pope and Talbot, who had arrived earlier from California, were among the largest landowners in the Puget Sound region. In 1900, Frederick Weyerhaeuser, after nearly a decade of considering the move, purchased 900,000 timbered acres from the Northern Pacific at $6 an acre. It was his St. Paul neighbor, James J. Hill, builder of the Great Northern, who first interested Weyerhaeuser in the Puget Sound area and sold him the timber.

As a result of the speculative buying, land prices soared. In Snohomish County, a tract purchased in 1899 for $10,000 was sold ten years later for $110,000. Acreages of little commercial value a few years earlier were now eagerly purchased. Much of the forested land came under the control of a few companies. By 1913 three of the largest companies controlled 237 billion feet of standing timber, most of it in western Washington, compared to 205 billion feet owned by 17,000 small logging companies.

The national demand for Northwest lumber increased as the railroads developed to deliver it. The billion board feet Washington produced in 1888 was doubled by 1895 and trebeled by 1902. That year 150 new mills began adding to the production. In 1905, with new efficient equipment in common use, Washington produced 3.5 billion board feet, which was more than any other state in the Union.

Now overproduction became a problem. Mills cut back to five-day weeks, and closed for repairs during winter months. The uncertainties of the market and the efficiencies of the large mill companies began to

force out the small independent operations. By the turn of the century, though a few "gyppo" [independent] loggers still operated, the large companies, many of them headquartered in San Francisco, controlled most of the Puget Sound lumber production.

In 1900 the Pacific Coast Lumbermen's Association was born, and in 1911 joined with a similar Oregon group to become the West Coast Lumbermen's Association, with the aim of maintaining level prices even if this called for curtailment of production. The association also worked to establish uniform grading of lumber. But as the owners were organizing, so were the workers, leading to conflicts that later developed between the two groups.

FISHING

The first fishermen on Puget Sound were, of course, the Indians. From whales to herring and from salmon to clams they took advantage of nature's delicacies. The settlers bought fish from them or used Indian methods to supply themselves.

Until methods of preservation were improved, consumption was local although the Hudson's Bay Company did export salted fish to Hawaii, the Orient, and England. Some of the first American settlers, Dr. David Maynard among them, attempted to preserve salmon in barrels of brine for distant markets but the spoilage rate was high.

The first salmon cannery in the Territory was built on the Columbia River in 1866. Fifteen years later thirty-six canneries were operating on the river. Only two canneries were located on Puget Sound, both at Mukilteo. But by the 1890s, fish wheels, purse seins, and other means of capturing the salmon had depleted the river runs and Puget Sound became the favored location for canneries. In 1913, the peak year of the Puget Sound harvest, more than 2.5 million cases of salmon were canned.

By 1915, 600 licensed traps were in operation in Washington waters, mostly on Puget Sound, and the seiners were hauling in up to 1,000 fish at a time. More than 100 boats were operating off the southern end of Vancouver Island. Among the largest canneries were those operated by Pacific American Fisheries of Bellingham and the San Juan Fishing and Packing Company of Seattle. When the runs began to decrease on the Sound, canners moved north to Alaskan waters, though Seattle remained the principal port of the fishing fleet.

The improved methods of harvesting at a time when massive logging operations were stirring up rivers and effluents were beginning to spew into the

Above: *Captain William Renton built a sawmill at Port Blakely on Bainbridge Island in 1864. He gradually enlarged the facility until it burned in 1888. The rebuilt mill, larger than its predecessor, is shown in this 1890 image. Port Blakely became a thriving mill town by the turn of the century. Courtesy, National Maritime Museum*

Right and opposite, top: *In 1890, the Port Blakely mill was one of three sawmills on the Sound with the capacity to produce 100 million board feet a year. Ships delivered the lumber all over the world, including Hawaii, Australia, South America and, during the Gold Rush, to Alaska. Courtesy, National Maritime Museum*

Above: *In 1899, a variety of ships moored at the Port Blakely mill to take on loads of lumber. The raw materials can be seen floating in the log pond in the foreground. Courtesy, National Maritime Museum*

Above: *In this 1910 scene, Neah Bay natives work to butcher a thirty-six-foot whale brought in by Makah hunters. (MOHAI)*

Above: *In the 1880s, huge salmon catches such as these were common on Puget Sound. Here bargemen, using single tined pughs, unload at a Seattle cannery.* (MOHAI)

Left: *In the 1890s, seafood remained a major staple in the diet of the Native Americans. In fact, many made a living harvesting from the sea and selling to white neighbors. Here clam diggers work on a beach near Port Townsend. Courtesy, Washington State Library*

The German-built bark Artemis called at Puget Sound during the 1890s. Here she rests broadside a Seattle dock while two cutters, a sein boat, and a net scow float this side of her. Courtesy, National Maritime Museum

Sound, resulted in a dwindling of the fish harvest. As early as 1888, the United States and Canada met to develop international agreements to control the resources of northern Pacific waters. Conservation soon became a serious business.

AGRICULTURE

Wherever Europeans settled in western Washington, they tended to engage in sustenance agriculture. The Spanish at Neah Bay, in 1790, though there only a few months, landed cattle, sheep, hogs, goats, and poultry. The Hudson's Bay Company under Chief Factor McLoughlin, founded the Puget Sound Agricultural Company in the 1830s for purposes of farming, raising livestock, and dairying.

The Michael T. Simmons party that arrived at the south end of the Sound in 1844 planted fields and gardens on the prairies and river bottoms and soon had a gristmill grinding. Nurseries and orchards were established early in the histories of Tumwater, Olympia, Steilacoom, and the settlements on the White and Duwamish Rivers. Whatcom, Island, and Mason counties developed as early centers of agriculture.

Being perishable, most of the region's produce was grown for local consumption. As population increased, so did farm production. In the 1850s many orchards were planted in the Puget Sound country and the fruits that would survive the journey, apples for instance, were shipped to California. As the more fertile lands about the Sound were logged off, market gardening and dairy farming expanded.

By the 1880s, the mild, damp climate and fertile lowlands of the Sound country were providing a rich variety of vegetables and fruits. Among the common crops were cabbage, asparagus, beans, beets, Brussel sprouts, cauliflower, carrots, celery, cucumbers, kale, leeks, lettuce, onions, parsley, parsnips, peas, potatoes, radishes, rhubarb, spinach, squash, turnips, blackberries, currants, gooseberries, raspberries, strawberries, and some types of peaches.

The region also spawned a thriving seed business. A local farmer, A.G. Tillinghast, began growing seeds near LaConner in the mid-1880s. By 1904, cabbage seeds were being shipped east by the carload. In 1912, Charles Lilly began a national marketing effort and soon the Skagit Valley Seed Growers' Corporation was contracting with hundreds of farmers to supply Lilly with top quality seed. It has been said that many a fine Puget Sound mansion was "built of cabbage seeds."

Flower bulbs, too, were found to be financially rewarding for growers. Farmers near Bellingham,

This tender in 1902 carried a finny harvest between tally scows anchored at Puget Sound fishing grounds and nearby canneries. Neither the tender nor its location are identified. Courtesy, National Maritime Museum

Lynden, and Puyallup shipped tulip, daffodil, and other bulbs to Chicago, New York, and other cities.

Hop growing also proved to be profitable for many years on Puget Sound. The Meeker family had introduced the plant in the Puyallup Valley in 1865. Ezra Meeker in his book *Seventy Years of Progress in Washington* wrote:

My father, Jacob Redding Meeker, encouraged by a brewer of Olympia, Charles Wood, planted about a peck of hop roots on his farm near Sumner . . . He gave me a few sets or cuttings . . . The plants grew apace; bore a considerable crop the same year and we marketed at Olympia—180 pounds at 85 cents a pound . . . From this small beginning, in the following twenty-two years, more than twenty million dollars was paid out to hop growers of this territory and Oregon. My own exports to London reached the sum of over half a million dollars annual average for several years which caused me to follow or precede our shipments for four years where I remained "on the market" for six months of each year.

But the hop louse appeared and, as Meeker concluded:

After a five year struggle, the victory rested with the aphis that produced the live young faster than we could destroy them; our grand quality was destroyed; our market ruined; our occupation gone and there was no other alternative than to haul down the flag and destroy the hop yards.

Hop growing was shifted to the Yakima Valley and today Washington produces more hops than any other state.

Dairy farmers prospered in the valleys of Western Washington, especially in King, Snohomish, Skagit, and Whatcom counties. As the century turned, C.W. Orton of Sumner doubled the amount of milk from each cow through carefully controlled feeding and good management. Fred Stimson developed a record-producing herd of Holsteins at his Hollywood Ranch east of Lake Washington. E.A. Stuart bought a little plant at Kent, then expanded to Tolt (now Carnation) and soon was producing 40,000 pounds of canned condensed milk a day. He later expanded to an international market as the Carnation Company. By 1906, canned milk from the state had become a $500,000 a year business. Dairy cooperatives developed in Island and Mason counties and in several towns operated creameries. In 1910, Seattle Ice Cream Company was financed by Portland investors

and soon had branches in Everett, Tacoma, and elsewhere.

MINING
Though the financial return from minerals, with the exception of coal, was negligible during pioneer days, no natural resource influenced early Puget Sound history more than the gold rushes.

The dream of finding quick riches at a personal el dorado drove thousands from one reported gold strike to another, and while none of the strikes was directly on the Sound, the prospectors rushing through the area brought business to suppliers, and more importantly many stayed to enhance the permanant population.

In 1855, four French-Canadians, former employees of the Hudson's Bay Company, reported finding color on the upper Columbia near where it is met by the Pend Oreille River. Few facts were known about the find, but rumors spread rapidly.

At the same time, warnings were being received by Territorial officials that the Central Washington Indians were unsettled over the treaty-making recently concluded. Nonetheless, small parties of confident gold seekers set off over the mountains. The Indians feared this vanguard would contend for their lands, as had so often happened before.

Henry Mattice of Olympia apparently was the first casualty. He was killed by the Yakimas while crossing their reservation. O.M. Eaton and Joseph Fanjoy left their sawmill on the Black River and were followed a day later by L.O. Merilet, Charles Walker, J.C. Avery, Eugene Barrier, and a man named Jamieson. These men joined forces and started over Snoqualmie Pass when they chanced upon some Indians who offered to show them the lower route. Two of the party went with them to inspect the way. Those remaining in camp, hearing shots, correctly assumed their compatriots had been killed, and ran for the cover of the forest. Traveling at night, they worked their way back to Seattle. This was the start of the Indian War that ended with the attack on Seattle in January 1856. The number of prospectors who lost their lives to the Indians was never known but the estimates were probably exaggerated.

The Indian threat plus reports that the gold was not found in paying quantities halted the stampede toward Fort Colville. However, with miners flowing through the area, every valley came under scrutiny and in 1857, gold traces discovered on the Fraser River started a second rush. Governor James Douglas, in Victoria, required miners to purchase a license

Ezra Meeker and his father introduced hop growing to the Puget Sound country in 1867. His holdings near Puyallup included a warehouse (left) and towered, vented kilns for drying (in back). (MOHAI)

from the crown colony of Vancouver Island. The editor of the Olympia *Pioneer and Democrat* promptly informed his readers that miners on the Fraser were making from $25 to $50 per day, and that Indian women were panning out $10 to $12.

By May of 1857, ships were sailing north from California to Whatcom and Victoria carrying thousands of miners and their provisions. San Francisco merchants established tent stores on the shores of Bellingham Bay where the previously tiny settlement consisting of a sawmill, coal mine, and a few cabins was transformed in a few weeks to a city of 10,000. Late in the month, in a two-week period, forty vessels docked at Victoria and disembarked 6,133 passengers. By August, a 100-mile trail had been hacked through the wilderness from Bellingham Bay toward the Fraser River. The towns of Whatcom and Sehome (both later to become part of Bellingham) boomed.

Another result of the immigration was the establishment of a new crown colony called British Columbia. James Douglas then assumed the dual governorship of both colonies—Vancouver Island and British Columbia.

Other gold strikes would follow, but none would match the Fraser excitement until nearly forty years later when gold was discovered on the Klondike.

Non-metallic minerals—coal, sand, gravel, limestone, and clay—eventually were to be of more economic value to Puget Sounders than were the metal ores.

In the early days of settlement, "black gold" would bring needed infusions of cash. Hudson's Bay Company employees discovered coal on the Cowlitz as early as 1833. In 1849, Samuel Hancock, while trading with the Lummi, saw "black stones" at Bellingham Bay, but the Indians refused to let him search the area. In 1852, Captain William Pattle, while looking for stands of timber, stumbled upon a seam of coal on the beach of Bellingham Bay. Coal finds were reported in rapid order all up and down the Sound, and by 1890 coal was an important Washington export.

During the 1880s, when coal during some years was the second most important export from Puget Sound ports, Seattle benefited most. The largest amounts of coal were mined at Newcastle, Renton, and other mines east and south of Lake Washington and stored

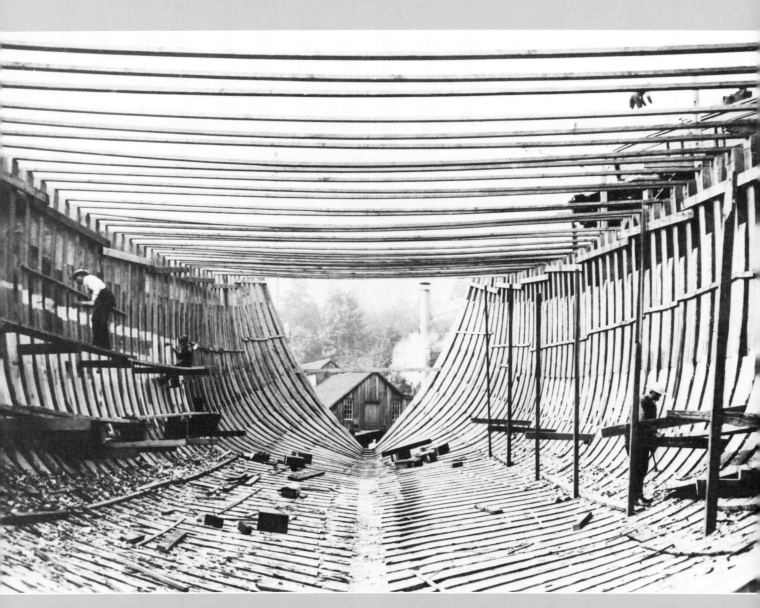

Opposite: *Before the ship canal was excavated between Lakes Washington and Union (it was dedicated in 1917) coal was barged to the south end of Lake Union. The city steam electric generating plant seen in the background was completed in 1914. (MOHAI)*

Above: *The Hall Brothers launched scores of ships, first at their yard at Port Ludlow (1874-1880), then at Port Blakely (1881-1903), and finally at Eagle Harbor (1903-1959). This 1904 photo was taken at the Eagle Harbor facility. (MOHAI)*

The tug Tacoma *is viewed floating on the waters of Eagle Harbor in 1910. The town of Winslow stands on the clearcut hillside above the Hall Brothers' shipyard. Courtesy, National Maritime Museum*

in bunkers on the Seattle waterfront.

This was the period when King County surpassed Walla Walla, Clark, and Thurston counties in population and Seattle became the largest city in the Territory. Coal played a part in this transformation, for it was an important commodity and many men were employed in its extraction and transportation.

In 1875, coal was discovered on Northern Pacific Railroad property near the Puyallup River less than thirty miles from Tacoma. This undoubtedly helped the railroad in its decision to extend its rails over Stampede Pass to Tacoma. The rail lines that extended to the Puyallup mines eventually met the Seattle and Walla Walla tracks that had been extended to the coal mines in south King County, providing Seattle with its first access to Northern Pacific service.

San Francisco interests soon gained control of most of the mines on the eastern shores of Puget Sound. One of the largest operators, the Black Diamond Company, took over many of the mines, including the one in the town named for it. The peak year in coal production was 1918 when more than four million tons were extracted. Then, as new fuels, principally oil, gained popularity, as hydroelectric power was developed, and as transportation improvements permitted inexpensive importation of better quality coal, production in Puget Sound mines slowly decreased until, in the 1950s, it ceased altogether.

MANUFACTURING AND COMMERCE

Early manufacturing concentrated on meeting the basic needs of local residents, the one exception being sawmills. Until after the Civil War, most of the sixty or so territorial industrial plants were mills located on Puget Sound and they exported vast quantities of lumber to the Sound.

In one of the more unusual pioneer enterprises, dogfish oil was marketed in Europe at seventy-five cents a gallon. The oil of this small shark, so plentiful in Puget Sound, was extracted at a rendering plant established on McNeil Island in 1872. As with many of the region's early business efforts, capitalization had originated in San Francisco.

Shipbuilding was an early and consistent business on the Sound. The Hall Brothers established the first shipyard at Utsalady in the 1860s and moved to Port Blakely a decade later. Soon nearly every town of any size was home to a small and elementary yard. Not until 1892, however, was there a dry dock large enough to accept sailing schooners. That affair was built at Port Hadlock and towed to Dockton on

Vashon Island. A few years later, the first huge Navy dry dock was completed at Bremerton.

From 1860 to 1870, the principal products of Puget Sound were lumber, flour, and leather, with lumber dominating. In the 1870s, the manufacture of butter and cheese, clothing, shoes, and boots developed, the latter principally for the loggers.

In the decade that followed, shipbuilding, blacksmithing, saddlery and harness-making burgeoned. Late in the decade, after the rails of the Northern Pacific surmounted the Cascade barrier, wheat from eastern Washington was transported to Tacoma where it was loaded on ships bound for England and elsewhere. Flour, too, became a major export. In 1901, an Everett flour mill, the largest in the state, was producing 600 barrels a day. Albers Brothers moved into Seattle and Tacoma in 1902 by purchasing existing mills. Sperry built a Tacoma plant in 1905 and Centennial developed mills in Seattle, Tacoma and east of the mountains. In 1910, O.D. and Will Fisher began building a huge flour mill on Seattle's Harbor Island.

The 1890 census, the first to report on manufacturing processes, indicated clay products, metal works, breweries, wood finishing shops, and printing establishments were among the major industries. During the decade, slaughterhouses and meat-packing plants grew in importance when Charles E. Frye established a large plant in Seattle and Thomas Carstens built meat-packing plants in both Seattle and Tacoma.

Stimulated by the Alaska gold rush and ballooning population, output of Puget Sound manufacturers trebled in the late 1890s. The value of dairy, clay, metal, bakery, and brewery products increased 600% or more during the decade. Lumber, though overall value of production increased, dropped to 40% of the total value of manufactured goods. The number of factories doubled as did the work force.

After the turn of the century, steel mills, paper and pulp mills, an airplane factory, and allied producers were established. Libby McNeill and Libby opened a Seattle office and developed a large cannery near Kent. Fruit growers built a cannery in Puyallup, the first of many, some of which were developed by cooperatives.

With the growth in manufacturing and production centering on the Sound, by 1900 the Puget Sound counties were in a more dominant position than ever in the state. The following is a 1900 listing of the top ten counties by value of industrial production. The number in parenthesis shows the ranking for that

county in 1890.

1. King	$29,843,408	(1)
2. Pierce	12,782,202	(2)
3. Spokane	6,424,337	(3)
4. Snohomish	5,650,314	(9)
5. Whatcom	5,264,661	(10)
6. Grays Harbor	4,749,278	(6)
7. Skagit	2,598,650	(16)
8. Lewis	1,678,870	(7)
9. Walla Walla	1,418,107	(11)
10. Thurston	1,315,213	(8)

In addition, a listing of the ten most populous counties of 1900 includes King, Pierce, Snohomish, Whatcom, and Skagit. Seattle, Tacoma, Everett, and Bellingham are listed among the state's ten largest cities by the census of 1910.

The isolation of Puget Sound had been overcome. The northwest corner of America with its rich natural resources had been tied to the rest of the country by rail and by sail, and soon roads and the airways would make the products of the Sound country even more available to world markets.

Left: *The bark* Loudon Hill *is pictured at a Mukilteo dock in 1899. British-owned, she carried salt, pig iron, liquors, and other general cargo to Puget Sound consumers. She sometimes carried lumber on her voyage home. Courtesy, National Maritime Museum*

Below: *In 1901, T. Takayoshi supplied his Port Blakely customers with Japanese merchandise, photographic services, and a laundry. Courtesy, National Maritime Museum*

4
Decades of Rapid Growth

In the late 1880s, the iron horse on its rails carried massive numbers of new settlers to Puget Sound. The last Territorial Governor, Miles C. Moore, reported that during 1887-1889, 95,000 newcomers arrived in Washington, an influx in three years that equaled the total territorial population of 1880. Seattle was welcoming as many as 1,000 new residents a month and Tacoma, Port Townsend, and other Sound cities were likewise booming.

The total assessed value of property and of manufactures was ten times higher in 1890 than in 1880. In fact, Washington was developing more rapidly than any other state and most of the growth was on Puget Sound. Seattle's population grew from 3,533 in 1880 to 42,837 in 1890, Tacoma's from 1,098 to 36,006.

This rapid increase in the number of residents put pressure on

Opposite: *The Pay Streak of the 1909 Alaska-Yukon Pacific Exposition attracted throngs with its carnival rides, exotic shows, eateries, and games. The fair, held on the University of Washington campus, served as grand finale to two decades of dynamic growth for the Puget Sound region. (MOHAI)*

BIRD'S EYE VIEW
CITY OF SEATTLE
AND VICINITY.
1904

Above: *Seattle's population exploded from 80,761 in 1900 to 237,194 in 1910. This 1904 map illustrated the city spreading over the hills. In those days Seattle claimed to be the largest city of its age in the world. Courtesy, University of Washington Libraries*

Opposite: *The Fremont fire department in 1886 answered alarms with this man-powered hose cart. Fremont, then a separate town, was annexed to Seattle in 1891. (MOHAI)*

developers, builders, government personnel, educators, and merchants. Streets were extended and extended again. Huge, high stumps incongruously reared their bulks into the sky beside downtown buildings. Wires, providing the new electric and telephone services, hung from hurriedly raised poles. Structures, erected by the dozens, rose as much as five stories above clanking new streetcar lines. Schools were frantically enlarged and new ones built. Church congregations, crowded into edifices grown too small, planned new houses of worship further from commercial centers.

Five of Washington's most rapidly growing counties—King, Pierce, Snohomish, Whatcom, and Skagit—were located on the eastern shore of Puget Sound. And in those counties, the urban population was quickly overtaking the rural. In 1880, only 9.5% of the territorial population lived in the towns. By 1900, this had increased to 41% and, by 1910, more than half the residents (53%) were urban dwellers.

ANTI-CHINESE RIOTS

For all the growth and development, the area seemed in a restless mood, a time of political and racial tension that spanned three decades. This unrest several times erupted into violence, most notably during the anti-Chinese riots of the mid-1880s.

The Chinese workers had first been brought into the country in numbers as railroad workers. As the Pacific railroads were completed, hundreds of the Chinese migrated to Puget Sound cities seeking employment. When a recession swept the area, white workers found jobs increasingly scarce. As the ranks of the unemployed increased, feelings against the Chinese also increased. Orators whipped the crowds with emotional speeches that condemned "cheap foreign labor."

On the night of September 7, 1885, near the present town of Issaquah, five white men and two Indians fired into tents where Chinese hop pickers were sleeping, killing three and wounding six. Four days later at Coal Creek east of Lake Washington, Chinese coal miners were beaten and their barracks burned.

Later that month, agitators called for an anti-Chinese Congress to meet in Seattle. Retired Colonel

Chin Gee Hee, a Seattle labor contractor, imported hundreds of his countrymen to build railroads and canals, harvest crops, and perform other manual labor. In 1906, he returned to China with about a million dollars where he built the Suning Railroad which he managed until his death. (MOHAI)

These twenty-seven men, including mayor Jacob Weisbach, front row center, were responsible for the removal of all Chinese residents from Tacoma in 1886. Although today this action is considered a blot on Puget Sound history, at the time these respectable business and professional men provided Tacoma's moderate voice on the Chinese question. Many others urged violence. Courtesy, Special Collections Division, University of Washington Libraries

Granville Haller reported: "Every socialist and anarchist who could walk or steal a ride to Seattle was a self-elected but none-the-less welcome delegate." The mayor of Tacoma, Jacob Weisbach, was elected chairman and the group resolved that all Chinese should leave Puget Sound by November 1.

The citizenry was split on the issue of whether the Chinese should be forced out or legally expelled. Only a few believed the Oriental aliens should have equal rights with citizens. When Governor Watson Squire, a strong law and order leader, asked whether federal troops were needed to protect the lives and property of the Chinese, both Sheriff Byrd of Pierce County and McGraw of King County responded they had sworn in enough deputies to control the situation. However, Byrd and his deputies proved to be on the side of the agitators, and on November 3 all Chinese were forcibly expelled from Tacoma, most of whom made their way to Portland or Vancouver, B.C.

In King County, Sheriff McGraw, intent on maintaining the peace and upholding the law, was backed by a number of leading citizens who were prepared to protect the Chinese. After the Tacoma turmoil, the governor issued a proclamation calling for support of law and order and wired President Cleveland asking for federal troops. On November 8, 350 soldiers arrived on Puget Sound from Fort Vancouver and were joined by members of the home guard. Meantime, many Chinese were dismissed by their employers and left the area. After a time of apparent calm, the troops were withdrawn.

The legislature in January 1886, was considering several bills that would forbid any alien ineligible for citizenship (as were the Chinese) from holding property. Other proposed bills called for cities to refuse to issue licenses to alien businessmen and to prevent employment of aliens. Several such bills passed the House but in the Council (Senate) opposition came from several members, including Orange Jacobs who called the proposed legislation probably unconstitutional and spoke of a free land that welcomed anyone wanting to settle here. Nonetheless, both houses did pass a law preventing aliens from owning land.

The Anti-Chinese agitators decided that if the legislature would not act to expel aliens, they would do it themselves. In February they forced Seattle's Chinese from their homes and marched them to the waterfront where a ship was preparing to sail for San Francisco. The captain, however, refused to let them aboard until passage was paid. A collection was taken and the Chinese began to file up the gangplank, until the captain realized their number was greater than the ship would hold. The Chinese were kept overnight in a nearby warehouse.

The next day, as the Chinese for whom there was no space on the ship were being escorted toward their homes by the home guard, a mob of agitators appeared and attempted to block the way. The guardsmen, reinforced by university cadets, formed a protective cordon around the Chinese. The mob was ordered to disperse. A few of the persistent agitators attacked the guardsmen and attempted to wrest their weapons from them. Shots were fired. One of the rioters was killed and others wounded. The Chinese, though frightened, escaped harm and were taken to their domiciles where guards were posted to protect them. Governor Squire reinstituted martial law and the President, having been contacted by the Chinese minister and reminded of important trade treaties with the Orient, again dispatched federal troops, this time ten companies, to maintain order. They would patrol the cities of Puget Sound for many months.

Although most of the Chinese left the region, in a few smaller towns such as Port Townsend, they were not forced away. However, even there some citizens made life difficult for them. For several years, few Chinese were seen on Puget Sound, but, a few at a time, they returned to make their homes on the inland sea they had found to their liking.

RISE OF POPULISM

The great age of discontent began in the 1880s when a series of recessions haunted workingmen and employers alike. Increasing numbers of disgruntled Seattle workers joined the new Knights of Labor. In 1886 this group and other organizations met and planned to make their discontent known to city officials whom they believed to be overly conservative and protective of the "old families." This newly formed political group nominated W.H. Shoudy for mayor. The conservative citizens promptly named Arthur A. Denny, one of the founders of Seattle, as their "Loyal League" standard bearer. Much to the dismay of the conservatives, Shoudy won by forty-one votes and Seattle's early Populists savored their first political victory.

In the 1890s, all across America, discontented citizens decried the "opression of big corporations and the wealthy." They believed the laboring man was being manipulated, a condition exacerbated by importation of cheap foreign labor. Neither the Republican nor the Democratic party seemed to them to be responsive to their pleas for relief.

This nationwide dissatisfaction resulted in the 1892 formation of the People's Party whose members were called Populists. Their leaders advocated government ownership of railroads and telegraph and telephone systems; the replacing of the spoils system with civil service; formation of national labor organizations; donation of public land to actual settlers only; and a graduated income tax. They berated the gold standard, which the United States had enforced since 1873, and urged government purchase of all silver mined in the country from which silver dollars would be minted. This would in turn increase the money in circulation which would, they believed, provide more jobs and higher wages.

In 1889, some of these populist concerns were reflected in the new Washington State Constitution. The provision prohibiting state officials from accepting free railroad passes is one example. Another is the provision which allows the legislature to regulate rates of common carriers. In 1892, eight Populist candidates were elected to the State House of Representatives.

The Populists' stock rose rapidly during the financial panic of 1893. With unemployment high and with no help in sight, Jacob S. Coxey of Ohio, in 1894, prepared to lead his "army" of unemployed workers to Washington, D.C., to demand relief for

CAPITALISM

WE RULE YOU

WE FOOL YOU

WE SHOOT AT YOU

WE EAT FOR YOU

WE WORK FOR ALL

WE FEED ALL

PYRAMID of CAPITALIST SYSTEM

This 1911 sketch by an artist disenchanted with the capitalistic system is typical of Progressive era efforts to rally support for the "class war" which, in the end, did result in improved working conditions and living standards for the laboring class. Courtesy, Special Collections Division, University of Washington Libraries

the jobless. He argued that Congress should issue large amounts of paper money to pay for public works. Coxey's Puget Sound organizer, Frank "Jumbo" Cantwell of Tacoma, gathered about 3,000 supporters in Puyallup where they demanded free transportation to the East Coast on the Northern Pacific Railroad. After Governor John H. McGraw threatened to call out Federal troops to maintain order, the unemployed left in small groups. However, Cantwell, his wife, and hundreds of others rode freight cars to the East Coast to join Coxey. In Washington, D.C., during a demonstration, several of the leaders of Coxey's Army were arrested for trespassing on the Capitol grounds. His supporters scattered back to their homes.

The Populists, realizing a third party had little chance of winning elections, declared their aim to be one of fusion with candidates of any party who would support their concepts. In positions where they could find no one to support, they would nominate their own candidates.

In the Presidential election of 1896, William Jennings Bryan, the free silver Democrat who had adopted many Populist causes, including the free coinage of silver, received the majority of votes in every Puget Sound county. However, nationally, Republican William McKinley was elected President by a majority of 600,000 votes.

Local Populists did, in 1896 however, succeed in electing able state legislator John R. Rogers of Puyallup to the governor's chair, as well as a majority in both the state houses.

On Puget Sound the recession ended rather abruptly under a shower of gold dust from the Yukon. The Alaska Gold Rush of 1897, which accelerated business and increased employment, resulted in a slackening of support for Populist causes.

In 1900, by fusing with Silver Republicans and Democrats, the Populists managed to re-elect Governor Rogers, but this time as a Democrat. In fact, the saying circulated that if you scratched a Western Democrat you would find a Populist. But Republicans, too, had adopted several Populist ideas.

In Washington State, Governor Rogers died of pneumonia shortly after being re-elected and the Populists, their power wasted by infighting and a lack of political experience, retreated to work through the Grange and workingmen's organizations. Nonetheless, many Populist concepts later became part of the state's constitution among them: the direct primary system for nomination of state and local officials (1907); women's suffrage (1910); and the adoption of

the initiative, referendum, and recall (1912).

But even prior to the passage of the statewide recall amendment, first class cities, under "home rule" concepts, were allowed to establish recall legislation. Seattle and Tacoma adopted such measures, and in 1911, with women now voting, both cities recalled their mayors. After being accused by the forceful Reverend Mark A. Matthews of the First Presbyterian Church of allowing city government to support vice operations, Hiram Gill was removed as Seattle's mayor. In Tacoma, Mayor Angelo V. Fawcett was recalled on a charge that his administration was lax in providing city services.

Reform activists were busy during the elections of 1912. Theodore Roosevelt and his new Progressive

The tide flats at the base of Beacon Hill hindered expansion of Seattle's city center. In 1894, a private corporation began to fill the area. Later the city and county channeled the Duwamish River and built the streets. This photo, circa 1900, was taken before the land was filled to street level. (MOHAI)

(Bull Moose) Party split the Republican votes between himself and Republican William Howard Taft, allowing Democrat Woodrow Wilson to be elected President. In Washington State, many former Populists supported Progressive Party candidates rather than the Taft Republicans; this resulted in Democrat Ernest Lister of Tacoma winning the governor's race in 1912. Progressive candidates were elected to the two congressmen-at-large, six state senate, and twenty-nine state representatives positions. In that 1912 election, Teddy Roosevelt received the overwhelming support of Washingtonians for the Presidency, 113,000 votes to Taft's 70,000 and Wilson's 86,000. In those years, Washington was noted as one of the most "progressive" states in the Union.

Above: *On dry days in the 1890s, when dust blew up from Seattle's earth-surfaced streets, the water tank brigade with its sprinklers was called into action. (MOHAI)*

Opposite: *A Seattle garbage collector is pictured here in 1915 when true horsepower was still in vogue. (MOHAI)*

THE NOT-SO-GAY NINETIES

In 1890, the Puget Sound country was on the threshold of the modern age. The rough, frontier way of life was fading from the scene just as were the pioneers whose obituaries were appearing ever more frequently in the newspapers.

Photographs of Puget Sound in the 1890s often show smokestacks belching black coal smoke, tide flats spiked with hundreds of rotting pilings, streets surfaced with mud and manure, and sanitation efforts at their most elemental. Puget Sound dwellers were indeed fortunate that tides and the vast flow of the rivers kept water pollution to a minimum.

Though transportation was much improved and rails now tied the state together, the horse remained the major means of locomotion. Each of the animals, now concentrated in the growing cities, produced up to twenty-five pounds of manure a day. Adding to the sanitation problems were barns where families kept cows, sheep, chickens, and other farm animals. Outdoor privies were still commonly found within the city limits.

Despite these difficulties, the cities of the Sound experienced unprecedented growth. These were years when new retail outlets were founded and flourished, many of which are still with us: Frederick and Nelson,

Right: *High-rise structures were still in Seattle's future in 1901 when the Chapin Building at Second and Pike was more or less typical of business buildings. (MOHAI)*

Below: *Max Levy (left, wearing a bowler) stands before his Chicago Clothing Store in the Port Townsend of 1890, then one of the larger cities in the new state of Washington. Courtesy, Jefferson County Historical Society*

Below: *The Chambers Block, seen here, was built in 1887 by Andsworth Chambers, son of a pioneer Olympia butcher. Chambers was later instrumental in building the Hotel Olympia. Courtesy, Special Collections Division, University of Washington Libraries*

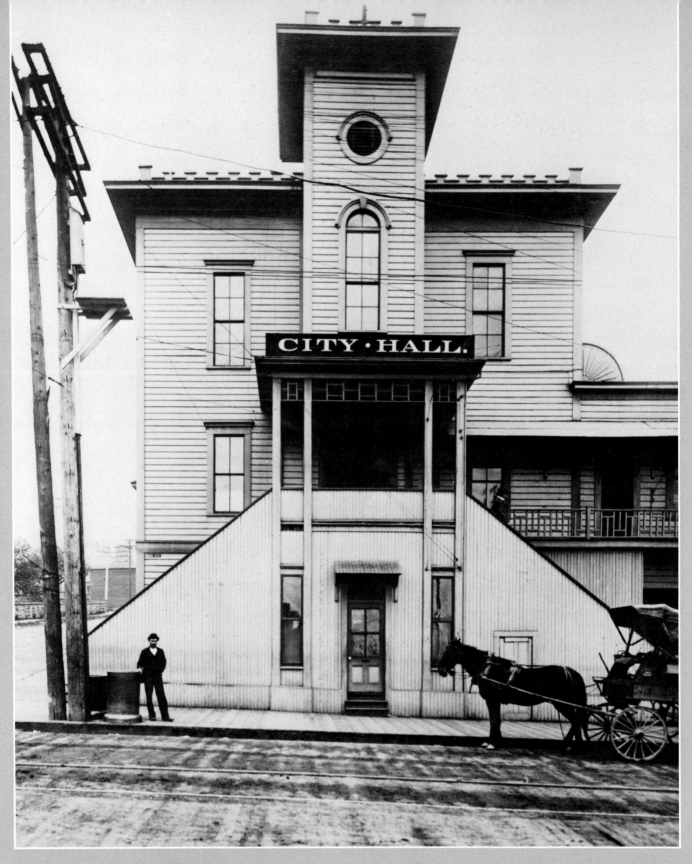

Fondly referred to as the Katzenjammer Castle, the first King County Courthouse, built in 1882, was sold to the city in 1891 for use as a city hall. Its nickname came from the haphazard construction of many additions to the right of and behind the original structure. (MOHAI)

Thurston County in 1894, the date of this photo, was home to about 13,000 residents. Nearly 5,000 of them lived in Olympia, the county seat and state capital. Here the eight-sided clock tower atop the grand new Chuckanut sandstone county courthouse dominates the modest skyline. In 1901, this building was purchased from the county and, with enlargements, served as the state capitol until 1927 when the present domed structure was completed. (MOHAI)

the Bon, Nordstroms, Bartells, G.O. Guy, and others serve as examples. Service industries multiplied with telephone, electricity, gas, banking, and transporation leading the way. The list of professionals grew longer by the month: doctors, dentists, lawyers, accountants, teachers, preachers, funeral directors, and publishers among them. The numbers of city and county personnel increased as fire departments were modernized, police departments took on additional territory, taxing districts developed, and elected and appointed governmental officials grew in number and increased their staffs. The counties built new courthouses and the cities new municipal structures. The state offices in Olympia were enlarged in the former Thurston County Courthouse and plans were developed for a capital complex that would soon be needed although it would not be built for another three decades.

HEALTH CARE
The two decades following 1890 witnessed considerable advancement in the field of medicine.

Disinfection and quarantine were then the common

Three representatives from religious organizations—Rabbi Koch, Dr. Gowen, and Dr. Mark A. Matthews—watch the laying of the cornerstone of the original Childrens' Orthopedic Hospital on Queen Anne Hill in Seattle in 1911. (MOHAI)

means of combatting communicable diseases. When scarlet fever or any of a dozen other childhood diseases swept the Sound region, schools would close and meetings would be cancelled. Tuberculosis, pneumonia, and other lung diseases were often fatal. Such old-time debilitations as ague were still common experiences, especially among the older immigrants who had come to Puget Sound from malaria country.

Treatment often involved habit-forming drugs. Cocaine and heroin were both regularly utilized in medicines, and opium, in the form of laudanum, was a common painkiller available in any local drugstore.

In 1874, the Medical Society of Washington Territory was organized to improve the practice of medicine. In 1890, the year after statehood, the Washington Medical Society replaced the territorial group and began exercising an expanded role.

During these years several hospitals were founded: Providence Hospital in Seattle, Tacoma General (1889); St. Peters in Olympia (1887); Seattle General (1889); The White Shield Home, Tacoma, founded by the Women's Christian Temperence Union as a maternity hospital for unwed mothers (1889); St. Joseph's in Port Townsend (1890); St. Johns in Tacoma (1891); St. Lukes, Bellingham (1892); and the U.S. Marine Hospital in Port Townsend (1896).

In 1889, the state constitution provided for a State Board of Health to collect vital statistics, obtain addresses of all state doctors and midwives, establish rules and regulations for the practice of medicine, cooperate with local health officials and to make recommendations for better protection of public health. Twenty years later, the legislature created the position of Commissioner of Health to enforce measures and sanitary regulations and to supress and restrict disease. After improvement of city water supplies, development of garbage and sewage disposal systems, and efforts to control communicable diseases, the number of deaths due to smallpox, diphtheria, scarlet fever, and typhoid markedly decreased.

EDUCATION
In the 1890s, most educational efforts concentrated on learning basic subjects by rote, and a high school education was considered more learning than most folks needed. Not until the mid-1880s did Puget Sound high schools offer annual baccalaureate exercises, and another decade passed before high school students were separated into buildings of their own.

In 1895, the "Barefoot Schoolboy Act" passed the legislature allowing school funds to be equalized, and

thereby raising the standards in poor counties to a level of those in the wealthier counties. By 1900, the twelve Puget Sound counties had developed eighty graded schools, half the number in the state. The average salary of teachers had risen to $60 a month for a six-month school year.

To improve teacher training, three state normal schools were established, at Ellensburg, Cheney, and Bellingham. The latter, though authorized in 1893, did not open until 1899.

Until 1895, the University of Washington was woefully under-funded. In the year of admission, 1889, the legislature provided only $10,000, although even that was an improvement over previous years. In 1900, seven years after the university had moved from its downtown Seattle location to its present campus, the state appropriation for operations had increased to $165,000. Enrollment that year climbed to 344 students of which 96 were taking college-level courses.

Over these years, several private colleges were founded: the Methodists opened the College of Puget Sound in Tacoma in 1888; a college founded in Tacoma by the Norwegian Evangelical Lutheran Synod of America and the Columbia Lutheran College, founded in 1905, combined in 1920 as Pacific Lutheran College (now University). Seattle College, started by Jesuit fathers in 1892, is now a major Catholic university. Seattle Seminary of the Free Methodist Church, which opened in 1891, is now Seattle Pacific University. Whitworth Academy, an institution of the Presbyterian Church, opened in Sumner in 1883, became a college in 1890, relocated in Tacoma in 1900, and in 1913 moved to Spokane. St. Martins College was founded by the Benedictine Order in Lacey in 1895.

These institutions, with diligent work and considerable sacrifice, survived depressions, wars, and other adversities to become part of the state's higher education system, which has trained many of the area's leaders, artists, business, and professional men and women through the years.

LIBRARIES
Local efforts to develop public libraries blossomed and wilted through the pioneer era until, during the 1880s and 1890s, libraries became permanant centers of cultural enrichment and learning.

The Andrew Carnegie Foundation grants to Puget Sound cities between 1901 and 1916 built twenty-one libraries, seven of them in Seattle, two in Bellingham, and others in Tacoma, Everett, Olympia, Bal-

Opposite, top: *These bird houses were the handiwork of the 1904 fourth grade class at Seattle's West Queen Anne Elementary School. The photo is believed to be the work of famed photographer Asahel Curtis. Courtesy, Seattle Public School Archives*

Opposite, bottom: *Education was avidly supported by most of Seattle's early residents. Denny School, built atop Denny Hill in Seattle in 1884, was a principal elementary school in the Seattle system until in 1929 the hill was regraded and the school razed. This is the faculty of the school in 1887. (MOHAI)*

Above: *Parrington Hall (left) and Denny Hall (center), the first two major classroom buildings on the present University of Washington campus, are shown here in 1915. Both, after several renovations, are still utilized. (MOHAI)*

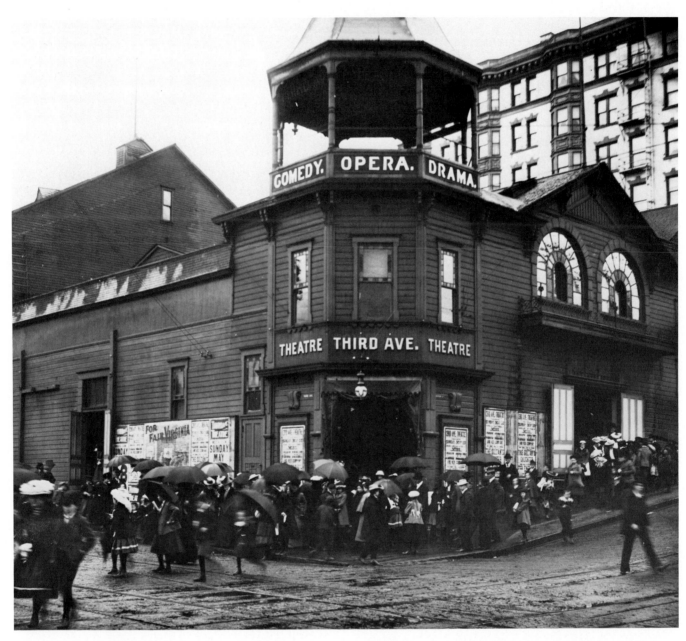

Above: *The Third Avenue Theater (also called Cordray's) was a popular Seattle vaudeville house at the turn of the century. It stood at Third and Madison. Behind it rises the Lincoln Hotel which was built in 1900 and burned in 1920. (MOHAI)*

Opposite: *A typical gay nineties Sunday crowd at the Leshi boat house on Lake Washington enjoyed band concerts, picnics, a small zoo, and convivial company. Courtesy, Washington State Library*

lard, Snohomish, Edmonds, Auburn, Port Townsend, Renton, Sedro-Wooley, Burlington, and Port Angeles. In most other towns, either small libraries were developed by the local population or traveling library services were available. Libraries were also established during these years in colleges, schools, and at state institutions such as the soldiers' homes, hospitals, and reformatories. The State Library, established in Olympia in 1853, took on added importance. For the first time all sorts of free reading material was available to the general public.

ARTS AND RECREATION

Many early settlers, when they had the time and the ability, delved into the arts and recreation. Early writers such as James Swan, Dr. Henry Smith, Arthur and Emily Inez Denny, and many other noted pioneers produced memoirs and historical writings that are enjoyed to this day. Authors such as James Stevens, Ella Higgenson, Sophus Keith Winther, Archie Binns, Nard Jones, and Betty McDonald are still in print. Historians Edmond Meany and Vernon Louis Parrington produced lasting works. Parrington won a Pulitzer Prize in 1929.

Music has been enjoyed here almost as long as there have been men and women to produce and hear it. The first piano was shipped around the horn

to the Reverend John Devore of Steilacoom in 1856. Brass bands were popular during Civil War years. The first pipe organ arrived in Seattle in 1882 to be installed in the Catholic church. Choral groups flourished during the 1890s.

Ladies Musical Clubs were organized in Tacoma and Seattle shortly after statehood. The Seattle Symphony first played in 1903 and several other symphonies developed over the years in cities up and down the Sound. Nellie Cornish founded her music and art school in Seattle in 1914 and the universities and colleges, public and private, developed music departments.

Art, too, was created by pioneer painters including Ella Shepard Bush who arrived in Seattle in 1888 and six years later founded an art school. Harriet Foster Beecher painted fine Northwest scenes and taught many young pioneers including Emily Inez Denny. In 1914, the first exhibit of Northwest artists was scheduled in Seattle and the following year the University of Washington established a School of Fine Arts. Today several Northwest artists are recognized worldwide, including Ambrose Patterson, Mark Tobey, Kenneth Callahan, Walter Isaacs, and several others.

From earliest days, Puget Sounders have enjoyed outdoor recreational activities. Town teams played

Built in 1892 as the Denny Hotel, the Victorian-Gothic edifice, designed by Stanford White, stood idle atop Denny Hill because of financial difficulties until it was formally opened in 1903 as the Washington Hotel. Four years later, as Denny Hill was being regraded around it, the partly demolished structure was consumed by fire. (MOHAI)

baseball in the 1880s. Yachting, too, blossomed in those years. Mountain climbing has been a challenge since the 1850s. The first golf club was established in Tacoma in 1893 and two years later Seattleites followed suit. In 1903, the state university's rowing crew challenged California. Soccer and rugby preceeded American football, but the latter, after 1889, out-shown the former in popularity. Tennis was planned in Tacoma as early as 1886 and soon after in Seattle. Archery, bicycling, and fishing were other early sports. Since 1915, skiing has attracted its thousands to Cascade and Olympic slopes.

UTOPIAN GROUPS
Near the end of the nineteenth century, Puget Sound became a magnet for utopian groups. In 1887, the Puget Sound Cooperative Colony of George Venable Smith was established at Port Angeles. There land was held in common, livable wages were guaranteed

from the sale of goods and produce, and no taxes or rents were charged. If a woman wished to work outside the home, a housekeeper was hired for her. For two years the colony made progress, but then dissolved when the leaders accused one another of fraud.

At Edison in Skagit County, a Socialist colony called Equality was developed during the 1890s. The nucleus of 100 members, many from Maine, built a sawmill and other industrial plants. Their long-range objective was to fit each person to the type of work he or she performed best, and to so obviously succeed that other communities would adopt their practices. Each person was to have complete freedom in thought and behavior. This emphasis on individuality soon resulted in failure of their industries and the colony became so disorganized that it collapsed.

In 1897, the Mutual Home Colony Association was established at an isolated location twenty miles from Tacoma. No roads led to the place for the members wanted no governmental control. Their plan soon attracted about 200 followers and might have survived longer had not some of the members advocated free love. After President William McKinley was assassinated by an anarchist in 1901, some Tacomans, hearing rumors that the colonists were anarchists, chartered a steamer to carry them to the colony so they could burn it out of existence. However, a minister and the steamboat owner, both of whom knew many of the colony members, convinced the mob that the colony was a nonviolent organization. The confrontation was avoided. Home Colony still existed in 1910, but that year several members were arrested for indecent exposure while swimming nude. Once the colonists began to practice a more acceptable life style they were left alone, but this also ended the utopian aspects of the enterprise.

ORGANIZING OF LABOR

Labor unions began forming in Seattle in the 1880s, largely as protection from the influx of migratory workers, especially the Chinese who, in times of recession, crowded into the area seeking work in mills, mines, canneries, and fields.

As business and industry developed and employed ever larger work forces, the employees were more easily reached by union organizers.

In the 1890s, it was reported that the average American family needed a minimum $13 a week to subsist, but a third of all factory and mine employees earned less than $10 a week. On Puget Sound, camps that housed logging, mine, and agricultural workers

were usually crude affairs, crowded and lousy, cold in winter and stifling in summer. The food was generally terrible. A common joke that went the rounds: "The meat is so tough you can't stick a fork in the gravy."

The American Federation of Labor, founded in 1886, increased its national membership to more than a million and a half during the depression years of the 1890s. By 1900, the infant union of Seattle waitresses and retail clerks had successfully bargained to limit the work week to six days with a 6:00 p.m. closing time.

Believing existing labor unions were too conservative, the Western Federation of Miners and the American Labor Union, at a Chicago meeting in 1905, helped form the revolutionary Industrial Workers of the World, known as the I.W.W. or the Wobblies. Out to organize unskilled and migratory workers of the West, those engaged in lumber, shipping, fruit growing and textiles, the I.W.W. opened offices in Seattle and Tacoma, Port Townsend and elsewhere to urge loggers and millworkers to join the "One Big Union."

The I.W.W. pitted the working class against the employing class, preaching that the two had nothing in common. The working class, the Wobbly leaders lectured, must "take possession of the earth and the machinery of production and abolish the wage system." A decade later, when the militancy of the I.W.W. leaders ran into the wall of intransigence erected by employers, blood would flow.

GREAT SEATTLE FIRE

On June 6, 1889, after an unusually dry three weeks, a fire started by an overheated gluepot in a woodworking shop burned 116 acres of downtown Seattle. Originally, firemen had hoped to contain the blaze but, as more hoses were hooked to hydrants, water pressure dropped. A brisk wind from the northwest spread the flames southward into the old part of town. The conflagration was so hot that even brick structures were gutted when their wooden sills and mansard roofs exploded into flame. All of the major hostelries and most of the boardinghouses were destroyed. The major retail outlets were gone, the wharves nothing but ashes. But in spite of the size of the disaster, there was no known loss of life. Cities up and down the Sound sent fire fighting equipment and later supplied food and shelter for citizens in need.

The fire earned headlines across the land and when the city fathers began rebuilding, taking the

Looking west toward Yesler's wharf and Elliott Bay, Seattle was in shambles after the great fire of 1889. The fire prompted then Mayor Robert Moran to construct a public water system. Business resumed in tents, and within two years the whole town was rebuilt. Courtesy, Special Collections Division, University of Washington Libraries

optimistic view that here was the opportunity to build anew, this, too, made headlines and earned praise for that doughty little city that would not let a catastrophe dim its dream. Within two years, most of the burned area was rebuilt with modern structures. many still standing in the Pioneer Square area of Seattle.

STATEHOOD

After several attempts at statehood, in January of 1889 various bills were introduced in Congress relating to admission to the Union of the Dakotas, Montana, and Washington. President Grover Cleveland signed the enabling act providing for the admission of Washington State on February 22, 1889.

In Olympia on July 4 a convention assembled to write a constitution for the new state, acceptance of which would be tested on the ballot of October 11, 1889. At the same time three associated issues were to be decided. Women's suffrage, which had been ap-

Fire was a common visitor to the wooden pioneer towns of Washington Territory. In 1889, after a major conflagration destroyed sixty-four acres of downtown Seattle, the city council passed an ordinance allowing merchants to serve customers in tents. (MOHAI)

proved by the territorial legislature in 1883 but later declared unconstitutional by the territorial Supreme Court, was now on the ballot for the voters to ponder. Prohibition, another issue of long standing, was also placed before the voters. The location of the state capital had also been a thorny problem. Several cities had been competing with Olympia for that political plum, and now, this matter was to be settled once and for all.

Voters approved the Constitution by a wide margin (40,152 to 11,879) but denied women the vote (16,527 voted for women's suffrage while 34,513 voted against it).

In 1910, an amendment to the state constitution would make Washington the fifth state in the Union to give the franchise to women. In 1920, the Federal suffrage amendment gave all U.S. women the right to vote. Prohibition was turned down in the 1889 election, but in 1916, prohibition became effective under Washington state law. Four years later a Federal amendment dried out the entire country. For capital location, the vote was as follows: Olympia 25,490; North Yakima 14,718; Ellensburg 12,833; Centralia 607; Yakima City 314; Pasco 120; Scattering 1,088. Olympia would not be seriously challenged again as the seat of state government.

Elisha P. Ferry of Seattle, a former territorial governor, was elected on that October 11 ballot to serve as the state's first governor. He was inaugurated on November 18 and all state and county officers assumed their duties on that day.

THE ALASKA GOLD RUSH
The Alaska Gold Rush capped the century and ended the six-year recession that had wiped out the hard-earned wealth of several pioneer families. Seattle grabbed headlines all around the world when the steamer *Portland* arrived from the Bering Sea with its "ton of gold." The results were unbelievable as tens of thousands of prospectors flooded through the area. The demand for transportation brought out of retirement every vessel that would float and some that wouldn't. Robert Moran in his Seattle shipyard built twelve shallow-draft river steamers simultaneously and sailed them as a fleet to serve on Alaskan rivers.

Cornelius Hanford, in his book *Seattle and Environs* wrote:

New industries thrived in preparation of foodstuffs in compact form, convenient and suitable for transportation and invulnerable to frost and decay; there were crystallized eggs and evaporated potatoes, onions and fruit. Portable houses were constructed, many new contraptions were invented and everything usable in camp life and in placer mining found ready purchasers. There was an extraordinary demand for dogs for sledge teams and horses to pack goods over Chilkoot Pass.

Before the Klondike excitement abated, gold was found in the sands of the ocean beach at Nome, extending the rush.

In July of 1898, a government assay office was established in Seattle and over the next ten years would purchase for the government more than $174 million worth of gold. Seattle established itself as the gateway to Alaska during these years and all of Puget Sound profited from the Alaskan connection.

SPANISH-AMERICAN WAR
While it wasn't much of a "conflict," the Spanish-American War did inflame the country with patriotic ferver. The First Washington Regiment of the National Guard, one of the best prepared in the country, was called to action early. They were sent to the Philippines to quell the insurrectionists led by Aquinaldo who had transferred his hatred of the Spanish to the Americans when they began to occupy the islands. Thirty-five battles and seven dead later, the regiment returned to a heroes' welcome at Schwabacher's Wharf in Seattle.

Shortly before the outbreak of hostilities, considerable attention was given to securing the inland waters of the Sound from any enemy naval force. The big battleships of those days were dreaded war machines, and with the vital Puget Sound Naval Shipyard being built at Bremerton, security became an important matter. Plans were drawn to fortify the Sound at key locations with coast artillery emplacements.

In 1898, Fort Worden was developed adjacent to Port Townsend. At the same time, Forts Casey on Whidbey Island and Flagler on Marrowstone Island were built. All had great concrete encasements housing the latest coastal artillery cannon. These three forts encompassed what was called the "Death Triangle," for any enemy ship attempting to enter the Sound would have to pass within range of these mammoth cannon. Any vessel that did survive that hail of artillery would next face the guns of Fort Ward built on Rich Passage, the entrance to Sinclair Inlet on which Bremerton is situated.

Fort Lawton in Seattle, also originally conceived as

AUSTRALIA.

In the effort to provide transportation for tens of thousands of argonauts headed for the goldfields of the Yukon, the Australia, a large steel steamer, was temporarily chartered by the Pacific Coast Steamship Company. Here the steamer is seen loading at a Seattle dock in 1898. Courtesy, University of Washington Libraries

a coast artillery base, developed as a regular army center. These military establishments provided not only security from foreign foes but were helpful feeders to the local economy. The initial construction costs of the three forts of the "Death Triangle" totaled nearly $10 million. In each case, as they were decommissioned a half century or more later, all or part of each became a state park, or, in the case of Fort Lawton, a huge Seattle park.

BOOSTING THE STATE

From the 1850s to 1910, promotion played a major role in attracting settlers to what originally was a largely unknown and misunderstood region. Numerous individuals and companies were involved in the efforts over the years.

James G. Swan must have been the earliest booster with his informative 1857 book *The Northwest Coast* which was widely read. Asa Mercer's attempts to attract marriageable women to the area received nationwide attention and, while in the East, he distributed a pamphlet he had written about the region. Elwood Evans prepared a historical sketch for the 1876 Centennial Exposition in Philadelphia and spoke in person there about the territory. Ezra Meeker all his long life promoted his state and on one of his journeys East met Horace Greeley who agreed to publish Meeker's promotional writings. These were picked up by papers as far away as London, and reached an estimated two million readers.

Local newspapers and immigration societies added their bit to the efforts, as did realtors such as Allen Chase Mason of Tacoma who purchased full-page advertisements in eastern papers, sometimes spending $5,000 a month. Colonel Coolican of Port Angeles established a Clallam County Immigration Society with recruiting headquarters in St. Paul. In Seattle, realtors Charles Conover and Samuel Crawford, in 1890, published booster pamphlets for distribution in the East.

The brokerage firm of Eshelman and Llewellyn advertised Seattle far and wide. As early as 1872, business directories were distributed. The 25,000 copies of Melody Choir's *Pioneer Directory of the City of Seattle and King County* were perused in every state in the union and in foreign countries, too. The reports of the governors, especially those of Watson Squire in 1884 and in 1885-1886, were given out by the Northern Pacific Railroad across the country and in Europe. D.B. Ward, state immigration agent between 1895 and 1901, distributed some five million pages of literature concerning the new state.

During the 1880s, after Chambers of Commerce were formed in most cities, information centers flourished and pamphlets were issued extolling towns and cities and their hinterlands. In 1897, the Puget Sound Bureau of Information, in cooperation with the Seattle Chamber of Commerce, responded to queries and disseminated information about the region.

The grand finale of this effort was the 1909 Alaska-Yukon-Pacific Exposition on the University of Washington campus. This world's fair resulted in millions of pages of informative material describing the Puget Sound region which was printed in newspapers and periodicals around the world. The railroads published folders describing the exposition and reduced their rates to attract visitors.

The 1907 legislature had appropriated $400,000 to fund an exhibition of products, resources, and advantages of Washington State. This plan was expanded to include exhibits from countries around the Pacific Rim and from many states. In a way, the exposition, which attracted 3,750,000, was the grand climax to an era.

Henceforth, the need for cautious development of the Puget Sound region would gradually replace the less sophisticated huckstering methods of enticing migration westward. The image of the region as the last frontier was fading into history.

Left: *In 1900, this detachment, Group C of the 9th Cavalry, was at Fort Lawton awaiting orders to be shipped to the Far East during the Boxer Rebellion. Courtesy, Special Collections Division, University of Washington Libraries*

Below: *Many famous politicians attended the Alaska-Yukon-Pacific Exposition to speak and be seen. Among them were former President Theodore Roosevelt, three-time Presidential candidate and famed orator William Jennings Bryan, and the incumbent President, seen here, William Howard Taft. (MOHAI)*

Left: *Live camels, ethnic music, and daring costumes marked the Streets of Cairo Oriental Village which was located in the Pay Streak carnival area of the 1909 Alaska-Yukon-Pacific Exposition. (MOHAI)*

Opposite: *The Alaska-Yukon-Pacific Exposition of 1909 was held on the new campus of the University of Washington. What had been a native forest was cleared to make room for formal land-scaping and elaborate though temporary fair buildings. (MOHAI)*

Below: *Luna Park on the southern shore of Elliott Bay in West Seattle was a popular summer resort, natatorium, and fairgrounds. During the winter of 1909, however, it stood forlorn and dusted with snow. (MOHAI)*

5
Entering the Modern Era

When, in 1900, the first auto rolled down a Seattle street at the astonishing speed of twenty miles per hour, few of the many curious onlookers could have foreseen how quickly the horseless carriage would replace equine power. By 1904, the noisy motor car had become such a nuisance that Seattle drivers were required to install a horn, whistle, or bell as a warning device, and a speed limit was established: four m.p.h. down the hills and eight m.p.h. up grade. In 1915, the state's more than 46,000 motor vehicles displayed license plates for the first time. Motor taxis and jitneys (private cars selling rides for a nickle), proliferated, as did trucks to deliver goods around the Sound.

This transportation evolution was indicative of the changes the citizens on Puget Sound would experience during the twenty

Opposite: *Members of Seattle's first motorcycle club pose near Volunteer Park circa 1914 with their kickstands down to hold them steady. (MOHAI)*

years between 1910 and the great depression of the
1930s. Innumerable inventions, such as the radio,
came into common usage during those years.

The opening of the Panama Canal in 1915 shortened the water route to Southern and Eastern states
by as much as 8,000 miles, and ships again began to
rival the rails in transporting bulky Northwest cargos
such as lumber and grain. Two years later the Lake
Washington Ship Canal formally opened, providing
large ships access to Lake Union and Lake Washington.

During these years ports were modernized in all
major Puget Sound cities, usually under the auspices
of newly formed countywide port districts such as
those approved by voters in King (1911), Pierce
(1918), and Thurston County (1922).

Another sign of the times was labor unrest. After
attending a heated 1908 Chicago convention, leaders
of the local Industrial Workers of the World (IWW)
returned more militant than ever and concentrated
on developing strikes and disrupting production. In
response, management stiffened its resolve. More
than 10,000 jobless men roamed Seattle's streets.
Seattle's Skid Road became the unofficial Wobbly
headquarters and the "Hotel de Gink," a huge old

Above: *Charles Hamilton flew his bi-plane at Seattle's race track,
the Meadows, in 1910. Hamilton hand-carved propellers for early
airplanes and established the Hamilton Aero Manufacturing Company, which became part of the Boeing Airplane Company in 1929.
(MOHAI)*

Opposite, top: *In 1886 the Seattle Electric Light Company supplied Seattleites with the first Edison three-wire system to be installed west of the Mississippi. In 1899, the Stone and Webster
Company was employed to consolidate the various independent
electric companies. Seattle Electric Company, forerunner of Puget
Power, was the result, and soon had line crews such as this one
busy. (MOHAI)*

Opposite, bottom: *This circa 1915 photo of an early repair shop in
Poulsbo depicts the beginnings of the automobile age on the
Sound. (MOHAI)*

A gala celebration took place on July 4, 1917 at the Hiram Chittenden Locks when Shilshole Bay and Lake Union were united by the Lake Washington Ship Canal. The grand opening drew vast crowds, but the locks were not the only attraction. The grounds also featured elegant gardens and lawns. (MOHAI)

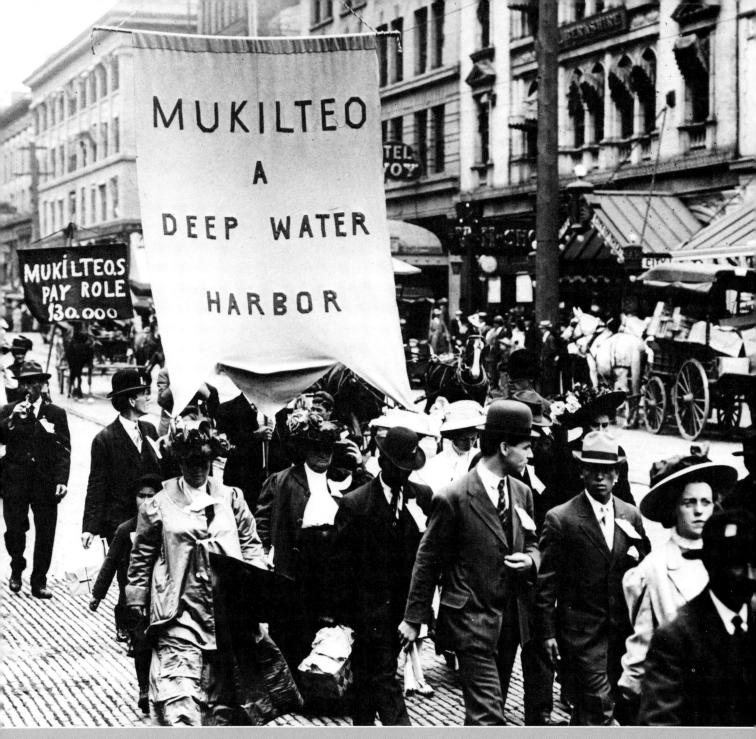

In 1924 some of Mukilteo's leading citizens paraded down a Seattle street to draw attention to their city's deepwater harbor. Though Seattle was already considered the queen city of the Northwest, others tried to lure some of the commerce away. Courtesy, Washington State Library

warehouse, was where many of them slept.

The mood grew ugly as fears of anarchy and rumors of pending violence raised emotions, but wartime employment reduced the number of unemployed before any serious confrontations developed.

By 1916, Europe had suffered through two years of war and the conflict was drawing the U.S. ever closer. Defense production employment soared. The time was ripe, the Shingle Weavers Union in Everett thought, to strike for increased wages. The mill owners promptly replaced the strikers with substitute workers.

The I.W.W. leaders, intent on following a plan that had resulted in gains elsewhere, decided to support Everett workers during the unrest. Meanwhile the mill owners, through the Commercial Club, gained the support and enhanced the powers of county sheriff Donald McRae. He promised to keep the I.W.W. out of Snohomish County. After weeks of often bloody confrontations, on Sunday, November 5, 1916, McRae and his heavily armed deputies prepared to meet a major challenge of the Wobblies. Three hundred supporters of the shingle weavers' union scheduled the steamer *Verona* to carry them from Seattle to Everett. As the ship nosed into the dock, the sheriff and his men warned them not to wharf. Someone fired a shot, then a full-fledged skirmish developed.

Five of the strike supporters were gunned down, two of them killed in the bay after they slid from the slanting *Verona* deck. Two of the sheriff's supporters also died. An additional fifty men were wounded, including the sheriff.

After they returned to Seattle, many of the Wobblies were arrested and several were held for trial, but in the end, all were exonerated of any crime.

After America entered World War I, some of the I.W.W. leaders preached non-involvement and urged their members to refuse to serve. This stand was too radical for the majority of Puget Sounders and the Wobblies lost most of their support.

WORLD WAR I

In 1917, after the Germans declared unrestricted submarine warfare on shipping, the United States on April 6 entered the war. Most of the recruits from Puget Sound, both volunteer and drafted, were assigned to the 91st Division at the new Camp Lewis near American Lake, the site where the State's National Guard had been training for years.

Pierce County taxpayers had voted $2 million in bonds to buy the land and give it to the government if a major military post were built there. The army accepted the 70,000 acres and promptly built a $7 million induction and training center which included

Opposite: *As part of the building of the Lake Washington Ship Canal, the waters of Lake Washington were lowered 8.8 feet to the level of Lake Union between July 12 and October 21, 1916. Here is the scene shortly after the dike was breached. (MOHAI)*

Above: *These men were on the little ship* Verona *when she tried to tie up at an Everett dock to unload IWW organizers and supporters during the Shingle Weavers' Union strike in 1916. They were met by the sheriff, deputies, vigilantes, and employer representatives, and in the ensuing gun battle seven men died and about fifty were wounded. Courtesy, Special Collections Division, University of Washington Libraries*

The Seattle Yacht Club first displayed its colors in 1892 and soon after located facilities off West Seattle (seen here). This boat house and moorages were sold to the government during World War I. After the war the present facility was built on Lake Union's Portage Bay, to which access was newly possible through the Lake Washington Ship Canal. (MOHAI)

more than 200 buildings to house and feed up to 50,000 men.

By September of 1918, after the 91st had left Camp Lewis and was fighting on European fronts, the 13th Divison moved in to train there.

The next month saw the start of the federal plan to establish student training corps on college campuses and a large naval program developed adjacent to Union Bay on the campus of the University of Washington.

With the services and industry absorbing much manpower, a shortage of agricultural workers developed. Women and youth took up the slack, drove tractors, and harvested crops. Professional and business men sweated away evenings and weekends in the fields. More land was in cultivation on Puget Sound than ever before, and liberty gardens were planted in vacant lots, many tended by Boy and Girl Scouts.

Puget Sound became a center of shipbuilding for the war effort. In 1914, only Moran Brothers yard was active in Seattle, but that year it was purchased by Todd Shipbuilding. Since the old Moran yard could not be enlarged, Todd added a new yard in Tacoma. By 1918, Seattle boasted seven busy shipyards employing 32,000 workers and was producing nearly 20% of the wartime tonnage.

Other shipyards were busy, too. Wooden ships were built at E.R. Ward's Olympia yard in 1917. Later Sloan Shipyards purchased and enlarged the yard to ten ways. Anacortes builders also constructed wooden ships. By 1918, nine Puget Sound yards were building steel ships, among the largest were Skinner and Eddie and Duthie and Ames in Seattle and the Todd yard in Tacoma. In all, during the year 1919, more than 50 ways launched 195 ships. In the war effort, Washington's shipyards built more ships than those of any other state.

Ship and housing construction required prodigious amounts of lumber. Logging camps and sawmills were busy places. The number of loggers jumped from 36,000 in 1914 to 53,000 in 1919. Some were engaged in specialized logging such as felling spruce trees to be used in the manufacture of airplanes.

When the war ended rather abruptly in 1918, many ships were still under construction. Some were never finished and for many years, rows of vessels floated side by side on Lake Union, many of the wooden hulls fast growing obsolete. This scene prompted some wag to call them "Wilson's Wood Row."

In August 1919, President Woodrow Wilson, deep-

Above: *During World War I, the Skinner and Eddy shipyard, one of Seattle's largest, employed hundreds of workers. This 1919 photo is by Asahel Curtis. Courtesy, Special Collections Division, University of Washington Libraries*

Opposite: *In 1919, after World War I had ended, Woodrow Wilson took to the hustings in a vain attempt to develop support for U.S. involvement in the League of Nations. Here he doffs his hat to Seattleites. (MOHAI)*

ly upset over the Senate's rejection of American membership in the League of Nations which he had worked so hard to establish, took to the hustings. On September 30 he appeared before a huge crowd at Tacoma's stadium, then moved on up to Seattle where he received a spectacular welcome. There, from the deck of the battleship *Oregon* he reviewed the Pacific fleet which steamed into Puget Sound for the occasion.

POSTWAR LABOR TROUBLES

The wages paid shipyard workers varied from yard to yard and in the West were higher than those generally paid elsewhere. During the war, the Emergency Fleet Corporation created a national board to establish uniform wage scales. The board decided $4.16 a day was proper, a wage lower than that being paid Puget Sound shipyard workers. The Metal Trades Council, which had held the labor power in the yards since most of the ships were being built of steel, expressed their outrage. On January 21, 1919, they called their members off the job until their demand for $6 a day was met. The Emergency Fleet Corpora-

tion director refused to make concessions.

Now A.F. of L. craft unions voted to strike. The Seattle Central Labor Council called for a sympathy walkout and the I.W.W. leadership, figuring this could be the climax battle in their class struggle, joined in. On February 6, 1919, a general strike—the first in the nation—closed down Seattle. No streetcars ran, restaurants closed their doors, the docks were deserted. As agreed, the strikers maintained vital services, such as telephone and electric service, medical services and prescriptions, hospital laundries, and milk supplies for infants and invalids.

Some newspapers predicted violence, but there was none. Mayor Ole Hanson demanded the strike be called off and threatened to bring in troops from Fort Lawton. By February 10, a few unions, on orders from their national headquarters, many of which had cautioned against the strike, ordered their men back to work and at noon the following day, the strike ended. Ole Hanson resigned as mayor, claiming he had saved the city from the Reds, and announced he was a candidate for the Presidency of the United States. He seemed to be the only one to take the

Above: *During the severe flu epidemic of 1918-1919, the Seattle Health Department ordered all citizens to wear masks in an effort to stop the spread of the deadly malady. Courtesy, Special Collections Division, University of Washington Libraries*

Opposite: *On February 6, 1919, Seattle became the first city in the nation to suffer through a general strike. Two days earlier The Seattle Star, had urged the strikers to reconsider. Courtesy, Special Collections Division, University of Washington Libraries*

U. S. OFFICERS TO DISCUSS STRIKE

The Seattle Star

FINAL EDITION
TWO CENTS IN SEATTLE

STOP BEFORE IT'S TOO LATE

This is plain talk to the common-sense union men of Seattle.

You are being rushed pell-mell into a general strike. You are being urged to use a dangerous weapon—the general strike, which you have never used before—which, in fact, has never been used anywhere in the United States.

It isn't too late to avert the tragic results that are sure to come from its use.

You men know better than any one else that public sentiment in Seattle—that is, the sentiment of the ninety per cent of the people who are not directly involved in the wage dispute of the shipworkers—*is against a general strike.* You know that the general public doesn't think the situation demands the use of that drastic, disaster-breeding move. *You know, too, that you cannot club public sentiment into line, and you know, too, that no strike has ever been won without the moral support of the public.*

The people know that there is a decent solution of the issue at stake. And the issue at stake is merely a better wage to the average unskilled worker in the shipyards. To a large extent public opinion is with these unskilled workers now, but public opinion will turn against them if their wage issue brings chaos and disaster upon the whole community unnecessarily. Seattle today is awake to the fact that she is on the brink of a disaster, *and Seattle is getting fighting mad.* The people are beginning to visualize the horrors that a general tie-up will bring. They see the suffering that is bound to come and *they don't propose to be silent sufferers.*

Today Seattle resents this whole miserable mess. Seattle resents the insolent attitude of the shipyard owners; Seattle resents the verbosity of Director General Piez, whose explanation does not explain, and just as emphatically resents the high-handed "rule or ruin" tactics of the labor leaders who propose to lay the whole city prostrate in a vain attempt to show their power. Let us not mince words. A general strike cannot win unless one of two things happens. Either the ship owners and Piez must yield or else the workers must be able to control the situation by *force.* The latter method no doubt would be welcomed by the agitators and the babblers of Bolshevikism. But the latter method is bound to be squelched without much ado, and you decent union men of Seattle will be the sufferers then. *A revolt--and some of your leaders are talking of a revolution--*to be successful must have a country-wide application. There isn't a chance to spread it east of the mountains. There isn't a chance to spread it south of Tacoma *and today fifty per cent of the unions of Tacoma have turned down the proposition for a general strike.*

Confined to Seattle or even confined to the whole Pacific coast, the use of force by Bolsheviks would be, and should be, quickly dealt with by the army of the United States. These false Bolshevik leaders haven't a chance on earth to win anything for you in this country, *because this country is America--not Russia.*

115

Below: *Washington citizens voted for prohibition in 1916, four years before the nation went dry under the Volstead Act. From then until 1934, federal and local officers were constantly hunting for stills which, once located, were quickly burned or trashed. Courtesy, Special Collections Division, University of Washington Libraries*

Above: *Employer-employee conflicts came to a head after World War I. To raise funds, some groups of workers scheduled "class war picnics" such as this one held in 1920. Courtesy, Special Collections Division, University of Washington Libraries*

suggestion seriously.

In the ensuing years, with business not trusting labor and with hard times dogging the area, the number of wage earners in the Puget Sound counties decreased substantially. Not until another wartime economy developed two decades later did the numbers of employed rise to exceed those of the World War I years. But the 1920s developed new leadership among the labor unions, the prime example being Seattle's Dave Beck.

In 1921, young Beck, a navy veteran, began driving a laundry truck as a member of the Teamsters' Union. By 1925 he was a major organizer. Roger Sale, in his book *Seattle, Past and Present,* wrote: "Organization was Beck's genius and passion ... He wore business suits and denounced communism and really believed in the American way." Though he was a tough, sometimes ruthless negotiator, business leaders learned he could be trusted to live up to a contract.

Beck's advancement in the Teamsters' Union was rapid and in the mid-1930s he and Harry Bridges of the Longshoremen's Union contested for control of Seattle waterfront warehouse crews. The Seattle Chamber of Commerce, fearful of Bridges' radicalism, sided with Beck.

Beck's success at building a bridge to the business leadership resulted in major gains for labor in Seattle and around the Sound. He went on to serve as president of the Teamsters' Union from 1952 to 1957. Accused of filing a fraudulent 1950 tax return for the Joint Council No. 28 Building Association and of allegedly pocketing $1,900 from the sale of a Cadillac belonging to the Teamsters, both charges he vehemently denied, he was sentenced to five years at McNeil Island. After two years and five months, he was paroled and in 1976 was granted a pardon signed by President Gerald Ford.

To again quote from the book by Roger Sale:

By the time Beck left the Teamsters, Seattle was one of the most unionized cities in the country and Washington one of the most highly unionized states. Most of the unionization was due to Beck. Labor became powerful by becoming bourgeoise and politically conservative if politically anything.

THE 1920s
The nation went dry on January 16, 1920, after Congress passed the National Prohibition Act over the veto of President Wilson. It made little difference on Puget Sound, for state law had closed the saloons

and forbade the manufacture and sale of alcoholic beverages after 1916. Even the beer breweries were dark and silent except those that were being used for cold storage, for fruit juice manufacture, and the like.

Prohibition was one law that many otherwise good citizens did not obey. Enforcement on Puget Sound was a hopeless task; its thousand bays and inlets and proximity to Canada, which was anything but dry, allowed good quality liquor to illicitly enter the area in quantity.

Ships loaded with liquor at Vancouver, B.C., cleared for Mexico and would return empty within twenty-four hours, which led prohibition enforcement officers to quip: "Seattle is now in Mexico?" Both commercial and personal size stills were available. Patent medicines containing up to 55% alcohol remained popular. Alcoholic beverages could be legally prescribed by physicians, and an amazing number of patients required such for their health. Essences were imported in many flavors to be added to grain alcohol, which sold for $4.60 a gallon. Denatured alcohol, at fifty cents a gallon, was more commonly used though it had to be distilled of denaturants first.

Below: The fertile river valleys, mild climate, and plentiful moisture result in bumper crops in Puget Sound counties. In this 1918 photo Japanese pickers are busy in a strawberry field near Carnation. Courtesy, Special Collections Division, University of Washington Libraries

Opposite: 1919 was a good year for strawberries as this scene of women sorting the produce at Seattle's Yesler Street Terminal attests. Soft fruits are a major crop in the Puget Sound country. (MOHAI)

"Nonintoxicating" grapefruit, rhubarb, elderberry, cherry, and pineapple juices would somehow, sometimes ferment in the bottle, but were consumed anyway.

The most famous of the rumrunners on the Sound was a former Seattle police lieutenant, Roy Olmstead, who retired from the force after being caught selling liquor. Though he later preferred wholesaling, he became somewhat of a folk hero and delivered his goods to some of the finest homes in the area. He eventually spent a few years at McNeil Island Federal Penitentiary where he took up Christian Science, and after his release, returned to the prison occasionally to work with his inmates.

Radio broadcasting came into its own during the twenties and many of the stations that developed are ancestors of radio-television broadcasters of today. In 1919, Vincent I. Kraft began operating 7XC which later became KJR in Seattle. In 1921, the *Post Intelligencer* aired news over KFC located atop its building. Many additional stations began broadcasting to Puget Sound listeners in 1922: KTW, which belonged

to and carried sermons of the First Presbyterian Church; KGY, which was started at St. Martin's College by Fr. Sebastian Ruth and later became Olympia's first commercial station; and KGB, which was started in the Tacoma Ledger Building.

In 1924, bootlegger Roy Olmstead and his wife began operating KFQX from their Seattle home. His wife, as Aunt Vivian, read children's stories, which were very popular. It was claimed her stories included signals telling the rumrunners where to land and unload their contraband. Regardless of the validity of the story, the station was raided and forced to stop broadcasting. Eventually it was leased by Birt F. Fisher who talked the Fisher brothers, O.W. and Dan, (no relation to Birt) into financing a new station which used the call letters KOMO.

By 1927, both NBC and CBS were feeding rudimentary network programming to Puget Sound. That same year KVOS in Bellingham began broadcasting.

Puget Sounders joined their brethren across the country during the faddish twenties by enjoying Mah Jong, crossword puzzles, and flagpole sitting. They

Opposite: *Richard Desimon, shown here with his produce, was at one time the president of the Pike Place Market. The Desimons were instrumental in creating the market, which opened in 1907, as an outlet for Puget Sound farmers. (MOHAI)*

Above: *In 1923 President and Mrs. Warren G. Harding journeyed to Alaska and Puget Sound. While touring Seattle they were photographed in front of the Seattle Press Club on July 27. (They can be seen in the rear seat of the auto.) Six days later the President, who was suffering from ill health, died in San Francisco. (MOHAI)*

idolized such heroes as Charles A. Lindbergh who visited the Puget Sound country in 1927 to promote the building of airfields.

A mini-depression slowed business on the Sound in 1921, but a disaster in Japan, the devastating earthquake of 1923 which leveled several cities, stimulated the export of building materials. With a dozen mills scattered about Commencement Bay, Tacoma was the leading producer of lumber during the decade.

During the twenties several federal acts were passed that affected life on Puget Sound.

On June 5, 1920, the Merchant Marine Act repealed emergency war legislation and permitted the sale of government-built ships to private owners. Several Puget Sound shipping companies were able to enhance their fleets at low cost. The "Jones Act," as it came to be called, required coastwise shipping to be carried on U.S. bottoms.

Four days later the Water Power Act was activated, creating the Federal Power Commission, which had the right to issue licenses, limited to fifty years, for construction and operation of powerhouses, dams, reservoirs, and transmission lines. Building of dams in the Northwest accelerated. As early as 1918, a Columbia River Basin Commission was advocating dams for reclamation purposes. That year Seattle was granted permission to plan the development of hydroelectric dams on the Skagit River. Gorge Dam was built in 1920-1922 and later Diablo and Ross Dams. In 1926, Tacoma City Light completed its Lake Cushman Dam on the north fork of the Skokomish River.

WASHINGTON IN THE TWENTIES
The population of the state increased nearly 19% between 1910 and 1920, by far the greatest part of the growth occurring in the Puget Sound region.

The Administrative Code of the State was reworked in 1921 allowing Governor Louis F. Hart to create several departments, —health, conservation and development, fisheries, highways, and licenses. This laid the foundation for the centralization of state government.

Banks began to consolidate during the decade. Between 1910 and 1930, forty-seven banks merged with twenty-three others, the largest amalgamation— that of Dexter Horton, Seattle National, and First National—became Seattle First National Bank.

President Henry Suzzallo of the University of Washington in 1926 felt the wrath of conservative Republican Governor Roland H. Hartley who had assumed the office in 1925. The quarrel probably stemmed, at least in part, from the stance Suzzallo had taken during the World War I years favoring the eight-hour day and other concessions for loggers and mill workers. Hartley, an Everett lumber baron, strongly disagreed with Suzzallo. In October 1926, the regents requested that Suzzallo resign, explaining that though they respected his success in educational matters, they differed with him in university finances. They apparently also favored educational changes that Governor Hartley requested but which Suzzallo opposed.

After Suzzallo left his post, labor groups and even the conservative *Seattle Times* accused the governor of prejudice and threatened recall action or impeachment. Hartley insisted he had nothing to do with the Suzzallo dismissal and said his supposed grudge against Suzzallo was mere fiction. In the 1928 election, Hartley won a second term by a sizable majority and the regents later named the new university library for their former president.

During the mid-1920s, folks in Pierce County noticed that activity at Camp Lewis had practically ceased. In fact, by 1925, the government had auctioned off nearly half the World War I buildings. Local citizens reminded the army that the agreement which had given the property to the government called for the return of the huge acreage to Pierce County should the government no longer need it for a military base. The army, realizing Camp Lewis was one of the largest and finest military sites in the country, promptly prepared a ten-year plan, raised the post to fort status, and began development of a permanant installation.

The largest military exercise in the nation would be staged there in 1937 when 7,500 soldiers maneuvered under General George C. Marshall and his aides, Major Mark Clark and Major Dwight D. Eisenhower. In 1939, after Hitler invaded Poland, the number of trainees at Fort Lewis jumped to 26,000 and after the bombing of Pearl Harbor to 50,000 at a time.

In 1937, from Fort Lewis acreage and adjacent land, developed a new airfield, named McChord. In 1943, it was the largest bomber training base in the country.

Shortly thereafter, a major hospital was built nearby and named for Colonel Patrick S. Madigan, father of army neuropsychiatry.

These military installations would be busy places during World War II, but that war came after Puget Sounders had suffered through one of the nation's severest depressions.

These men are checking the fit of the ammunition in the gun on the MB-3A, a single engine wooden frame pursuit plane built by Boeing in 1922. Courtesy, the Boeing Company Archives

W. E. BOEING
by
Roger Sult

Above: *This is the hull finishing room at Boeing Plant #1 in 1918. The men are working on an HS-2L, which Boeing built for the Navy during World War I. Courtesy, the Boeing Company Archives*

Left: *William Edward Boeing learned to fly in 1915. The scion of a wealthy Minnesota timber and mining family, he decided he could build a better airplane and in 1916 founded the Boeing Airplane Company. By 1928, the Boeing Company, with 800 employees, was one of the largest aircraft plants in the country. Courtesy, the Boeing Company Archives*

Opposite: *During the 1920s, Boeing Airplane Company draftsmen such as these worked on many different modes ranging from fighter planes to flying boats to the Model 80 passenger plane that transported twelve passengers plus crew. It first entered service in 1928. The age of air travel had arrived. Courtesy, the Boeing Company Archives*

6
Two Trying Decades: 1930 to 1950

Throughout the Great Depression that began with the stock market crash in 1929, the problems of unemployment, bank and business failures, home and farm foreclosures, hunger, homelessness, and hopelessness generated overwhelming difficulties for local governments. The municipalities of Puget Sound were no exception. But when cities and counties had used all available funds to care for those on relief, they had no recourse but to seek help from the state and federal governments.

During the first three years of the Depression, the Republican-dominated Congress and President Hoover, instead of providing direct relief, attempted to shore up failing businesses, including banks and railroads, so that they could pay their employees. Toward the end of President Hoover's term, the federal government

Opposite: *In July 1931, the Seattle City Council named Robert Harlan to fill the unexpired term of Frank Edwards as mayor. At the time, Depression shantytowns, dubbed "Hoovervilles," were springing up in the city. Harlan is shown here personally inspecting the one that was situated near where the Kingdome stands today. Courtesy, Special Collections Division, University of Washington Libraries*

Early in the Depression, as unemployment soared to about 25 percent of the work force, ever more desperate men gathered to demand jobs. Many had families needing food and shelter but the state and federal governments were not prepared to provide social services. Cities and counties quickly ran out of resources in attempting to meet the need. The rally of unemployed in the photograph occurred at the County-City Building in Seattle on February 10, 1931. (MOHAI)

did begin to provide loans to states and local governments for relief programs and for public works of a self-liquidating nature.

In Washington State, Roland Hartley was in his second term as governor when the Depression struck. A "capitalist" of the old stripe and political conservative, his last years in the Statehouse were trying ones. As the Depression persisted, he was ridiculed as a man with the mentality of the past. In 1932, for example, the Seattle City Council requested other Washington cities to join in their demand that the governor call a special session of the legislature to formulate a state plan to provide work for the unemployed. But Hartley, believing the state had no business in local relief efforts, remained resolute.

Representatives from Puget Sound, including Reno Odlin of Seattle, Harry Ramwell of Everett, Ralph Schaffer and E.W. Demarest of Tacoma, and other businessmen and community leaders journeyed east to meet with President Hoover on May 15, 1932, to urge immediate action to restore healthy foreign trade at a time when many countries were depreciating their currency, but they found a president beseiged with problems and facing an election race he would not win.

Though Seattle was still being served by more than eighty steamship lines, waterborne commerce through the port was falling precipitously—in dollar amounts, from $609 million in 1930 to $371 million in 1935. Tacoma's trade slipped from $145 million to $107 million during the same five years.

In the election of 1932, Franklin Delano Roosevelt won the presidency in a landslide, carrying Washington State two to one, and on his coattails rode an overwhelmingly Democratic Congress. In state political races, Governor Hartley's third term efforts fell before the overwhelming support given Clarence D. Martin, a moderate Democrat from Cheney. He carried every county. Swept in with him were Democrats in all elective state offices save that of the superintendent of public instruction where no Democrat had filed. All Democratic candidates for Congress won their seats, including the radical former University of Washington student body president Marion Zioncheck, who in 1936 committed suicide by leaping from an upper floor of the Alaska Building. Also elected to Congress was an Everett jeweler named Mon C. Walgren, who later would serve as governor.

When Governor Martin assumed office in 1933, unemployment plagued one of every four Puget Sound families. Martin assured his constituents that the state would assume the responsibility of providing relief for the unemployed, a responsibility previously shouldered by counties, municipalities, and charitable societies. He began to put men to work erecting state, institutional, and drainage facilities at a cost of $30 million. Over the next two years state and local governments would spend $46 million on relief.

From that time until the Second World War years, federal programs dominated activity on Puget Sound, as they did elsewhere across the land. President Roosevelt quickly called Congress into special session and, in 100 days, dozens of bills were passed including those to check the money panic (Emergency Banking Relief Bill).

On March 31, 1933, the Civilian Conservation Corps (CCC) was established and soon thousands of young men from ages eighteen to twenty-five were working on Puget Sound area reforestation, road construction, national park improvement, and other projects. Each received room and board in work camps plus thirty dollars a month, part of which was sent to their families. One of many CCC camps located on Puget Sound was developed on Orcas Island where youths were put to work creating the trails, campsites, roads, and other improvements at Moran State Park.

There followed literally scores of federal programs to assist those on relief, to help farmers survive, to keep homeowners from losing their shelter, to keep business and industry solvent.

The major bill of the session was the Public Works Administration (PWA) which provided $4 billion for public projects—roads, public buildings, bridges, and the like. Headlines in *The Seattle Times* read: "Big Public Works Program to Aid State's Comeback." Within a few months, Washington State's allotment was paying men to build a new Pacific highway between Olympia and Fort Lewis, to erect an addition to the Mukilteo school, beautify the grounds of Fort Lawton, install drainpipes at Sand Point, build emergency airfields, and to work on scores of other public projects.

One of the important appropriations of 1933 was the $60 million Congress approved to start construction of Grand Coulee Dam. Bonneville Dam was built about the same time and dedicated in 1938. The Bonneville Power Administration was created in 1937 to market the power from federal projects. The Northwest would profit from the low electric rates generated by these dams and by irrigation waters supplied by some of them, especially Grand Coulee.

In 1934, the Federal Crime Control Acts were

Above: *Members of the 935th Company of the Civilian Conservation Corps housed at Fort Lawton stride to their labors in 1935. Courtesy, The Seattle Times*

Opposite: *In the 1930s, WPA crews helped improve Tacoma Field, now the Tacoma-Pierce County airport. Courtesy, Special Collections Division, University of Washington Libraries*

passed in response to widespread racketeering and especially the 1932 kidnapping and murder of the son of Charles and Anne Morrow Lindbergh. These acts established the death penalty for kidnappers who carried victims across state lines. During the 1930s, Tacoma gained national notoriety as the scene of two kidnap cases. On May 24, 1935, nine-year-old George Weyerhaeuser of the prominent lumber-milling family, was abducted while walking home from school. He was released unharmed after a $200,000 ransom was paid. His kidnappers were apprehended and incarcerated. On December 27, 1936, Charles Mattson, the ten-year-old son of a Tacoma physician, was taken from the family home and later found murdered, his body mutilated. His kidnapper was never identified.

By 1934, white-collar professionals were being hired nationwide in sixty-four occupations under the Civil Works Administration (CWA). Included were 735 Puget Sound women being paid to work in recreational and educational undertakings. That same year, reforestation was started with federal funds in the logged-off portions of the Cedar River watershed. Among other Depression era projects funded by various government programs were: the landscaping of Seattle's Green Lake; installation of drainage systems in Puyallup; construction of a fish hatchery in Issaquah; installation of new steel grids on the Fremont Bridge; and clearing and cleaning of Colman, Frink, and other parks.

During the early 1930s, a Depression phenomenon was the sharp increase in the number of producing farms on Puget Sound. Unable to find employment, urban families returned to the rural areas where they could develop a certain amount of self-sufficiency. Land values fell drastically, many farms were repossessed, and then were leased at nominal sums. The rural counties showed the greatest increases in the numbers of working farms. In Clallam County, for example, the number of farms increased from 729 in 1930 to 1,010 in 1935; in Skagit County, from 2,721 to 3,155 in the same five-year period.

Nevertheless, low prices for dairy products, poultry, bulbs, hay, fruits, vegetables, and other agricultural products made life difficult for Puget Sound farmers.

In 1935, the newly created Works Progress Administration (WPA) funded 511 state projects including 178 improvements to schools, two new bridges at Port Angeles, improvements of airports at North Bend, Mt. Vernon, Tacoma, and Sand Point, completion of the Squalicum Creek breakwater at Bell-

In the 1930s, passengers rode this car to Phinney Ridge in north Seattle. Here it has stopped to load passengers in the Fremont neighborhood. Courtesy, Dennis Wilbert

During the Depression years, Joe Williamson delivered film for Bartell Drugstores. In 1940 he opened his own studios and became a noted maritime photographer. His collection of about 50,000 negatives now belongs to the Puget Sound Maritime Historical Society and is preserved at Seattle's Museum of History and Industry. (MOHAI)

A large Jewish community developed in central Seattle in the early years of the century. Al and Abe Hoffman (far right) had their photos taken in front of their grocery and delicatessen at 17th and Yesler in 1935. (MOHAI)

ingham, completion of the Blaine reservoir, and considerable work at the Bremerton Navy Yard.

Projects funded by the WPA and other programs in ensuing years include construction of the Showboat and Penthouse Theaters at the University of Washington, plus renovation of thirty campus buildings and construction of a wind tunnel for the engineering department; development of the Seattle Arboretum; construction of canneries in Kirkland and Kent for the preservation of surplus produce; the building of a warehouse at Salmon Bay for use by the fishing fleet; installation of the West Seattle Golf Links; and construction of the U.S. Courthouse in Seattle.

Other federal enactments that affected Puget Sound employment included: establishment of the Export-Import Bank to stimulate foreign trade; the Rural Electrification Act to build power lines to rural customers; the Merchant Marine Act to develop a well-balanced merchant marine; the Naval Construction Act authorizing a billion-dollar Navy expansion; and the National Housing Act which stimulated residential construction and improvements.

In 1935, the federal government began to withdraw from direct relief efforts in order to concentrate on large-scale national public works programs. The major agency was the Works Progress Administration (WPA) which by 1936, had put tens of thousands of Puget Sounders to work, most of them on manual labor jobs paying $40 to $55 a month. Also employed were authors, actors, artists, and musicians. With this help, several talented local men and women were able to continue developing their skills. Among the now nationally recognized painters who received federal contracts were Ambrose Patterson, Kenneth Callahan, Morris Graves, and Mark Tobey.

Though often belittled by detractors, the WPA was a saving grace for many families and many of the projects undertaken under the aegis of this federally funded program are, these fifty years later, still noticeable around the Sound.

Another federal program that had considerable impact on Puget Sound was the National Youth Administration (NYA) which employed youths aged sixteen to twenty-five. Under NYA many college and high school students continued their educations while working part time; others were employed full-time in public works. NYA camps, which existed until 1943, trained youths to work in national defense during the program's final years. These camps were found in various Puget Sound locations including the Georgetown neighborhood of Seattle.

A series of mid-Depression strikes caused bloodshed on Puget Sound. Under 1933 legislation allowing workers to organize and bargain, longshoremen struck Pacific Coast ports in 1934 and the employers brought in strikebreakers.

After several angry confrontations, a striker was killed at Point Wells and a special deputy died in a melee downtown. The police set up machine guns at strategic locations. In the end, an arbitration panel granted a coastwide agreement calling for no more than a fifty-hour week, a minimum ninety-five-cent hourly wage, and permitted hiring halls to operate.

The federal government in 1937 agreed to provide half the cost ($6 million) of a bridge across the Tacoma Narrows, and the Reconstruction Finance Agency loaned Pierce County the other half. As workmen completed the 2,800-foot suspension bridge, they remarked prophetically that it "acted funny" in a wind. Nonetheless, the bridge officially opened on July 1, 1940. Cautious residents waited for calm days to cross the bridge, however, as any wind sent ripples down its length. Before long the Tacoma Narrows Bridge—the third longest suspension roadway in the world—became known as "Galloping Gertie."

On November 7, four months after it opened, the roadway began twisting and writhing under the force of a 42-mile-per-hour gale. The final car crossing the bridge was abandoned on the span, its only occupant a cocker spaniel that bit its owner when he tried rescue efforts. Tacomans watched in awe as the bridge broke apart and most of it plummeted into the waters below. Motion picture footage and still photographs carried the dramatic images across the country. The bridge would be rebuilt in 1950.

Another Puget Sound bridge, built by the Washington Toll Bridge Authority in part with federal funds, would gain fame as the longest concrete pontoon bridge in the world. The First Lake Washington Floating Bridge, which cost $9 million, was opened in 1939 and linked Mercer Island and the East Side to Seattle.

Population growth stagnated in the Puget Sound country throughout the 1930s, and the ethnic make-up remained about the same. At mid-Depression, of the approximately 910,000 residents in the twelve Puget Sound counties, 97% were Caucasian. Of the nearly 16,000 Japanese, who made up the largest minority, 12,000 lived in King County, 2,700 in Pierce County, and 370 in Kitsap County.

In the twelve counties, Native American Indians numbered 5,119 and blacks 4,806. Only a scattering of other races lived on the Sound. These figures

would change in the 1940s as wartime jobs attracted immigration from other parts of the country.

By 1939, the belligerence of Nazi Germany had become apparent. The federal budget for that year included $1.3 billion for defense; a week later President Roosevelt requested and received an additional $525 million of which $300 million was earmarked for military aviation.

World War II began in Europe in September 1939 when Germany invaded Poland. Though the President declared the U.S. to be neutral, after the Senate repealed the arms embargo on November 4, 1939, American war materiel began to flow to allied countries, especially England. Defense contracts with Puget Sound industries had an immediate effect on the unemployment problem.

THE WAR YEARS
After the bombing of Pearl Harbor, with the Draft Act calling young men into the service, the President calling for massive production of the machines of war, and the War Production Board halting nonessential building in order to concentrate on war production, Puget Sound residents enlisted in the war effort with a will.

Opposite: *All Japanese families living in Puget Sound counties were evacuated inland during World War II. Two-thirds of the Japanese were American-born and therefore citizens. Not one was ever charged with espionage or a war crime and later many of the men joined the armed services. (MOHAI)*

Below: *Executive Order 9066 ordered Japanese-Americans out of designated military areas. In 1942 all of the West Coast was declared off limits and thousands of families were forced to quickly prepare for evacuation. Courtesy, Special Collections Division, University of Washington Libraries*

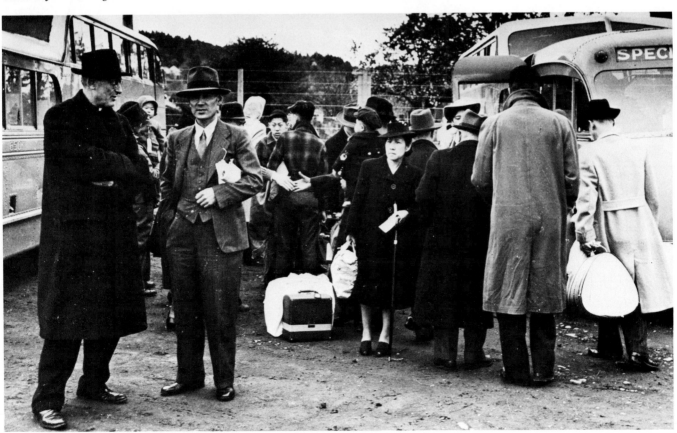

During World War II, with its acute manpower shortage, women were recruited to help in the war effort. The Boeing Airplane Company trained thousands of women to work in their plants. (MOHAI)

The productive capacity of industries on Puget Sound played a major role in gaining the final victory in World War II. Washington State, with approximately 1.5% of the nation's population, undertook 2.5% of its production. Nearly $5 billion in war contracts were assigned to Washington industries, most of them in the Puget Sound area. Nearly $2 billion worth of airplanes and a like amount in shipbuilding and repair contracts were let. Ordnance and other supply contracts totaled in the tens of millions of dollars.

This defense buildup began long before the Japanese attacked Pearl Harbor on December 7, 1941. The Boeing Airplane Company had developed the "Flying Fortress," the Bremerton Navy Yard had been enlarged and modernized, the shipbuilding industry was a hive of activity, and huge new dams were supplying needed power. Puget Sound's geographical importance as the major inland sea on the Pacific Coast, and its natural resources, when combined with the native aggressiveness of business and industry leaders of the region, attracted almost unbelievable wartime activity.

By 1944, the Boeing Company was turning out planes in three huge factories in Seattle and in Renton and operated six smaller plants in the state including facilities in Bellingham, Everett, and two in Tacoma. More than 41,000 were employed directly by Boeing, with additional thousands employed by companies subcontracted by Boeing.

The Bremerton Navy Yard was the only facility on the West Coast capable of handling large battleships and aircraft carriers. Here the front-line vessels damaged at Pearl Harbor were repaired and refitted. All through the war, battle-damaged ships were towed across the Pacific for repair at Bremerton.

Many private yards were contracted to convert passenger liners into transport vessels and to refit and arm cargo carriers. Vessels from the allied fleets, principally British and Russian, were maintained in a seaworthy condition by Puget Sound workers.

At the time Pearl Harbor was attacked, almost 80% of the Pacific Coast's shipbuilding industry was centered on Puget Sound. Baby flattops were built in Tacoma. Minesweepers, seaplane tenders, patrol, and picket boats slid down the ways in many different locations. Destroyers were built in Seattle and at Bremerton. Floating drydocks were in use at Tacoma and Everett. Victory and Liberty ships were under construction in various yards around the Sound.

Prodigious defense measures were undertaken to safeguard this production. The army assigned troops and artillery to protect the inlets and the plants. Fighter planes and bombers were concentrated on Puget Sound airfields. Barrage balloons, tethered to long cables, floated high over the Navy Yard and other installations as a deterrent to dive-bombers. Air patrols swept up and down the coast to intercept enemy submarines. Massive underwater nets were stretched across critical Puget Sound narrows to prohibit underwater incursions. Air-raid sirens were installed and tested each noon. Navy and Coast Guard patrols steamed through Puget Sound and coastal waters. The Boeing Company built an elaborate camouflage of streets and houses atop its Seattle plant to make it appear to be a residential area from the air.

As part of the security of the region, three months after the attack on Pearl Harbor, President Roosevelt signed Executive Order 9066 which instructed military commanders to evacuate persons of Japanese ancestry from designated military zones. On March 2, 1942, California, Oregon, and Washington were declared military areas and immediately Japanese families residing in these states were ordered to prepare to move. Those living on Bainbridge Island, near Bremerton, were the first to be evacuated.

The Puyallup Fair Grounds were used as temporary quarters for many of these families and eventually most were sent to Camp Minidoka in Idaho or Tule Lake in northern California where they were greeted by barracks encircled by barbed wire and guards. Within a few months, not a member of this most populous minority group could be found living on Puget Sound.

Though this action was carried out in the midst of wartime hysteria, when Japanese attacks on the West Coast were expected, the measure is considered in retrospect a miscarriage of justice. Not one of the Japanese-Americans—two-thirds of them native born—was ever found to have been an agent of the enemy. As the war progressed, many younger Japanese were permitted to migrate to the Midwest to work. Some of the young men enlisted and served as interpreters and decoders in the South Pacific. Many others fought in Italy with the all-Japanese 442nd Combat Team, the most highly decorated unit of the war.

After the hostilities ended, many of the Japanese returned to Puget Sound, though some made their homes elsewhere. The prejudices of the war years died slowly: in 1950, citizenship laws were altered to allow Japanese-born residents to apply for citizenship and in 1966 the state's alien land law was repealed making it possible for Japanese families to

own land.

The war stimulated the production of wood products and led to the development of new products using previously discarded materials. Production of plywood and finished lumber soared. Bark, now used to make tannic acid and cork, became an important lumber byproduct.

Dairy and poultry production, meat packing, truck farming, and fruit production also increased rapidly to meet wartime demands.

During the war years the population of Puget Sound cities surged as war workers arrived in increasing numbers. Seattle's population jumped by more than 100,000 and Tacoma's by 30,000. People of many classes, creeds, nationalities, and races moved to Puget Sound from all over the country, resulting in some social friction. Housing shortages developed and in towns and hamlets near factories and shipyards, temporary housing projects, most erected with federal money, blossomed almost overnight. Scarce commodities were distributed under a rationing plan. Women went to work in huge numbers, replacing the men who had gone to war.

On Puget Sound as elsewhere, physicians and dentists, many of them called into the services, were in short supply. Patient loads more than doubled. New automobiles were impossible to obtain and, as older models deteriorated beyond repair, public transportation in the cities took up the slack.

Recreational facilities were jammed. Some operated around the clock to serve workers on swing and night shifts. Movie theaters in small towns and large drew full houses. Taverns, especially those with restaurant facilities and/or dance floors, were packed on weekends.

With many military posts in the region—especially Fort Lewis, the nation's second largest training center—servicemen and women were much in evidence. Fort Lawton, Paine Field, McChord Field, Bangor, Keyport, Bremerton, Sand Point, Whidbey Naval Air Base, and dozens of other military establishments as well as Navy and Coast Guard ships added uniformed personnel to the population.

Seattle's Port of Embarkation was busy throughout the war, loading men and materiel on ships bound for Pacific battle zones and for allied nations, especially Russia. And arriving were shiploads of the wounded and ill to be treated in Northwest hospitals. And most tragic, hundreds of coffins crossed Puget Sound docks, the war dead being returned to hometown cemeteries.

V-J day was celebrated on August 15, 1945, following the dropping of the atomic bomb on Hiroshima and Nagasaki. The war was over and by mid-October, more than 35,000 servicemen from the state were on their way home and another 11,000 were about to be discharged. In the last five months of 1945, nearly half a million service personnel flooded through the Northwest ports of Seattle, Tacoma, and Portland on the way to processing centers and discharge.

As servicemen and women returned, the citizens of the Puget Sound country began to return to a peacetime mode of living. By 1946, war surplus stores were dispensing no longer needed government goods at bargain prices. Tiers of idle ships floated in Budd Inlet, some to remain there for two decades as mute reminders of a war that was fast becoming history.

Opposite: *Gas rationing during World War II was taken seriously. Officials frequently compared car license numbers with ration stickers posted in rear windows in an effort to prevent a black market in ration stickers. Here, on July 10, 1944, they perform their duties at Longacres race track in Seattle. (MOHAI)*

Above: *On August 14, 1945, World War II ended and Seattleites joined the world in celebrating V-J (Victory over Japan) Day, which brought the war to a close. (MOHAI)*

7
The Recent Past

The immediate postwar years were busy ones for the people of Puget Sound. Adjusting to a peacetime economy proved to be comparatively painless and positive in nature.

After eleven years of depression and four years of war, Puget Sound consumers went on a buying spree, purchasing new automobiles, appliances, furniture, and clothing as the goods became available. Television sets became a popular item after the first stations began broadcasting in 1947. Many servicemen and women returned to schedule long-delayed weddings and to set up housekeeping, which resulted in a demand for homes, furniture, and appliances. Many out-of-the-area veterans who had met local residents while stationed in the Puget Sound area returned and married and settled here. Spreading residential tracts began

Opposite: *In the 1930s and 1940s thousands of Puget Sound residents enjoyed the Seattle Rainiers, a Triple A baseball team that played at Sicks Stadium. Courtesy, the Seattle Times*

to change the landscape around the cities as suburban developers scurried to meet demands for new homes. A baby boom followed. Enrollments at colleges and universities increased rapidly as veterans took advantage of the GI Bill.

Census figures indicate that those who found jobs on Puget Sound during the war years tended to remain.

County	1940 Population	1950 Population
King	504,980	732,992
Pierce	182,081	275,876
Snohomish	88,754	111,580
Whatcom	60,355	66,733
Kitsap	44,387	75,724
Skagit	37,650	43,273
Thurston	37,285	44,884
Clallam	21,848	26,392
Mason	11,285	15,022
Jefferson	8,918	11,618
Island	6,098	11,079
San Juan	3,157	3,245

In spite of fears that unemployment would result from the increased population and peacetime economy, jobs were available for most including returning veterans, who had first rights to previous employment. New industries such as leisurewear, sports gear, electronic and medical supply manufacturing developed and the lumber mills were busy supplying building materials for residential and commercial construction.

As they had often done before, the state's voters in 1946 shifted their political allegiance to the right and elected Republicans to five of the six congressional seats, choosing conservative Republican Harry P. Cain over one-term Democratic Senator Hugh B. Mitchell.

The Republican dominated state legislature, during those years, formed a council to operate between sessions. This council, in turn, developed a Joint Fact-finding Committee on Un-American Activities chaired by Spokane Representative Albert Canwell. The ultra-conservative majority of the committee decided to "expose" Communist sympathizers they believed were active in such institutions as the Washington Pension Union, the Seattle Repertory Theater, and the University of Washington.

Liberal or socialist thinkers were considered "pink" by the committee and past membership in any "pinkish" organization was considered an evil brand. Committee investigators did not seem to delve very deeply into any of the charges nor to consider whether an individual had been "un-American" in his activities. In some cases, accusation was enough to mark the person.

Their 1948 hearings in the old Seattle armory were stormy. Liberal groups frequently picketed the hearings with signs declaring the committee itself was "un-American." During cross-examination before the committee, five witnesses from the University of Washington were slapped with contempt of legislature citations. Names of professors suspected by the committee of being tainted by communism were given to the university's board of regents who, in turn, referred the list to a committee of professors chosen by the faculty senate. This committee sent recommendations (not unanimous) to university president Raymond Allen who added his own interpretations of the importance of the hearing, but acquiesced to the recommendations of the majority of faculty committee members and kicked the report back to the regents. The hotly debated conclusion saw three faculty members terminated and three placed on probation. A reporter at the *Seattle Times,* Edwin O. Guthman, won a Pulitzer Prize for a series of articles, which proved that philosophy professor Melvin Rader had told the truth when he refuted the Canwell witness' charge that he had attended a Communist school. The Canwell committee played out its scenario under the bright lights of the mass media and their actions often turned self-defeating. In 1948, Canwell was defeated in a re-election bid. Four year later, when he ran against Don Magnuson of Mercer Island for a congressman-at-large position, he lost by a wide margin.

Three years later, when the legislature voted to bring out the Canwell committee records (reportedly some 40,000 pieces of material stored in a sealed room in Olympia), only a few scraps of paper and a couple of books were found. Former Representative Canwell, when subpoenaed, explained that he had burned most of the records which, he explained, were to be used only by the committee. After this episode, repeated efforts of right-wing legislators to reconstitute the committee suddenly were dropped.

In 1952, Democratic Congressman Henry M. Jackson of Everett, nationally recognized as one of the ten most effective House members, decided to challenge Senator Harry Cain for his seat. Late in the campaign, Cain invited his friend and fellow "Commie hater," Senator Joseph R. McCarthy of Wisconsin, to come west and take a few licks at

The Canwell hearings of 1948 heard charges that many Washington citizens were or had been members of the Communist party. Considered a witch hunt by many, the hearings were controversial and often picketed. Courtesy, The Seattle Times

The 1949 earthquake rocked the Puget Sound area, shaking down cornices and trim from old buildings. This Oldsmobile was crushed at the corner of Second and Yesler in Seattle. Courtesy, The Seattle Times

*Dedication day at Seattle-Tacoma International Airport in 1947
drew enthusiastic crowds. (MOHAI)*

Above: *Mrs. A Scott (Dorothy) Bullitt on May 1, 1947, purchased radio station KEVR, then the least listened-to station on Puget Sound. She changed the call letters to KING and the station soon had a sizable audience. She later purchased KING-TV, for a time the only operating station on Puget Sound. Mrs. Bullitt was the first woman to be named a "First Citizen of Seattle." Courtesy, The Seattle Times*

Opposite: *In 1958 when President Harry S. Truman visited Seattle, he was greeted by his long-time friend, Governor Mon Walgren. Between them are Senators Warren G. Magnuson and Henry Jackson. Courtesy, The Seattle Times*

Jackson, who had earlier called McCarthy a "tarpot politician." McCarthy, recovering from abdominal surgery, was in a foul mood at a Seattle Press Club banquet and became angered at the usual humorous baiting. Later he stalked out of the KING-TV studios when executives there deleted a portion of his speech as potentially libelous. "Scoop" Jackson won the election easily and joined Warren G. Magnuson in the upper chamber. Thus began three decades known as the Magnuson-Jackson era during which the two Washington senators became the most powerful duo in Congress.

THE 1950s

The decade of the 1950s brought major postwar development on Puget Sound. The age of suburbia spawned a rim of growing cities around the major metropolitan cores. Bellevue, east of Lake Washington from Seattle, experienced a population surge that would soon earn it the status of fourth largest city in the state. Small crossroad settlements such as Lynnwood and Mountlake Terrace, which were not even incorporated until the fifties, became instant cities.

Housing was being built at a tremendous rate to satisfy the needs of returning veterans and other young marrieds now beginning their families. A baby boom resulted in school districts scurrying to provide educational facilities for increasing numbers of school-age children.

Community college districts were separated from their parent school districts and each was given its own governor-appointed local board. Two-year colleges were rapidly developed around the Sound as large numbers of students, including thousands of former servicemen and women utilizing the G.I. Bill, flocked to their campuses.

New freeways were built including Interstate 5 which connected all major cities east of Puget Sound. These new access routes sped the growth of many smaller towns they served.

New shopping malls, the first being Northgate north of Seattle, were built near freeway exits to serve regional populations. Soon these commercial centers were serving all major suburbs. Department stores that before the war had attracted customers to a single downtown emporium, now erected branch stores in dozens of these new shopping malls.

The state's capital city was mentioned in the headlines frequently during the decade beginning with the celebration of its centennial in 1951 when carnivals, parades, and a "Street of Yesterday" all reminded citizens and visitors of its age.

The legislature that year expressed concern over the cost of computers used by the state. The IBM company was collecting about $100,000 a year in rentals, but this amount would be miniscule compared to costs in later years as the state utilized the new technology to keep up with its increasingly complex services.

As the new freeway was constructed around Olympia and travelers began bypassing the heart of the town, merchants lost potential customers. About the same time, the legislature funded a $2.5 million state office building to be located in Seattle. Some of the downtown Olympia merchants, fearing fewer state workers would be stationed in the capital city, sued to stop decentralization of state services. Thurston County Judge Charles T. Wright heard the case and eventually concluded that all state agencies must operate from Olympia.

It was in 1952 that John M. Fluke, Sr., who had been raised in Tacoma, moved his fledgling engineering company from Connecticut to Snohomish County. The company became the third largest manufacturer of test and measuring equipment in the United States. Other high-tech companies soon developed on Puget Sound and, two decades later, were so influential the region was called "Silicon Valley North."

In 1956, Democratic State Senator Albert Rosellini of Seattle, who in the glare of media publicity had chaired the legislative interim committee on crime, was elected governor. A new lieutenant governor also appeared on the scene, a former University of Washington football coach named Johnny Cherberg who had suffered through a player revolt the year before. A Democrat, he not only was elected to the post but became so adept in the position that these thirty years later he is still sitting in the lieutenant governor's chair.

Governor Rosellini inherited a crisis in the state's correctional institutions. In 1953, the State Reformatory at Monroe exploded with riots during which inmates burned the machine shop, garage, and powerhouse. The new governor hired 66-year-old Dr. Garrett Heyns from Michigan as Director of Institutions and under his able direction the situation rapidly improved.

In 1957 Dave Beck, the one-time Seattle laundry truck driver who possessed considerable skill as a union organizer and negotiator, and who had been elevated to the national presidency of the Teamsters' Union, was called before a Senate committee investigating corruption in labor unions. He was grilled by committee counsel, young Robert Kennedy. Beck, who maintained his home in Seattle, decided, under pressure from other union leaders, not to run for re-

election to the post. A grand jury charged him with "assisting with the filing of a fraudulent 1950 tax return" for the Joint Council No. 28 Building Association, and alleged he had sold a 1952 union-owned automobile and pocketed the $1,900. The federal government's charges that Beck owed $240,000 in back income taxes were dismissed as were all charges but the two brought forward by the grand jury. Of these Beck was found guilty and served two and a half years in McNeil Island Federal Penitentiary, but later received pardons from the state (1965) and from President Gerald Ford (1975). Now in his nineties, comfortable from real estate investments, Beck was named Seattle's Maritime Man of the Year in 1984.

After the Korean Conflict ended in 1953, consumers went on a short buying spree but it soon ended and late in the year Puget Sound's economy began to falter. For the first time in eleven years, the production of aluminum in Washington State dropped, in part due to a power shortage but also because of reduced demand. As housing construction caught up with need and as defense contracts were cut back, economic woes struck many families. However, highway and dam building continued at a vigorous pace, and prodigious amounts of sand, gravel, stone, and cement were used in their construction.

Lumber, shingles, pulp, paper, plywood, and hardboard remained major industries. Smelting of ores, production of non-metals such as clay, cement, and limestone, and processing of aluminum, steel, and iron remained important to the Puget Sound economy.

The increasing number of dams in the Northwest generated increasing amounts of inexpensive electricity, and Washingtonians, more than half of them cooking and heating with electricity, were using more power per capita than residents of any other state.

The Boeing Company developed a prototype jet transport, the 707, and rolled it from the hangar in 1954. The plane would revolutionize world transportation, and several variations, the 720, 727, 737, and 747 would follow. To build the 747, Boeing built a huge new plant near Paine Field in Everett. The company was also involved in several space projects and built the integrated components for the Saturn V rocket that lifted payloads to the moon. The lunar orbiter and lunar rover, which transported astronauts about the surface of the moon, were Boeing developments.

The Metropolitan Municipal Corporation Act (METRO) was lobbied through the legislature in 1957 by Seattle lawyer James Ellis and others. Now various municipalities, counties, and other political jurisdictions could cooperatively remedy environmental and civic problems. In 1958, the voters of King County and Seattle approved funding for a Metro sewer project costing $80 million. With the sharply reduced flow of effluents entering their waters, Lake Washington and other lakes and streams immediately began to cleanse themselves.

Seven years later Ellis would promote Foreward Thrust, a plan to develop rapid transit, a domed stadium, new parks, street improvements, and so on. Thirteen separate Forward Thrust items were on the February 1968 ballot and the voters of King County approved most of them with a bonding package of $333.9 million, the nation's largest per-capita public improvement plan ever approved.

THE 1960s
For Puget Sound, the 1960s began with a swagger but ended with a limp. The University of Washington Huskies won the Rose Bowl on New Year's Day, 1960 and repeated the feat in 1961.

Five years after the Russian sputnik first beeped from space and three years after the first American satellite soared aloft, the 1962 Seattle World's Fair, known officially as the Century 21 Exhibition, opened. The exhibition concentrated on the future and man in space, attracted ten million visitors, and ended with a surplus of revenue which was distributed to charity. It also left a legacy which Puget Sounders enjoy to this day—an opera house, coliseum, science center, space needle, center house, playhouse, monorail, and other structures at the Seattle Center.

So much for the swagger.

As if to portend the events of the coming decade, on Columbus Day of 1962, the tail end of a Pacific hurricane, carrying gusts of up to 100 miles per hour, lashed the Northwest, felling thousands of trees in the forests, wrecking old structures, breaking windows, downing power lines, closing bridges, and causing damage estimated at $70 million. Nine people died as a result of the gale.

A second natural disaster shook Puget Sound in 1965, a major earthquake that rumbled through the region causing eight deaths and millions of dollars in damage.

The turbulent 1960s brought major social changes to the Sound as well. An omnibus civil rights bill which passed Congress in 1964 banned discrimination in jobs, voting, and public accommodations, but did little to alleviate widespread discontent. There were many marches and speeches and several con-

frontations on Puget Sound. For a time the Black Students' Union interrupted normal operations at Seattle Central Community College and at the University of Washington. Minor violence erupted when activists attempted to force contractors to hire more blacks on federally-funded construction jobs. The struggle for equality seemed omnipresent.

As the decade wore on, broader support developed for ending the U.S. involvement in the Vietnam War. After the Communist's Tet Offensive in 1968 had taken many American lives and after American servicemen were sent into Cambodia, antiwar efforts grew increasingly urgent as more Americans became disenchanted with the war. Some of the local extremists adopted the violent tactics of protestors elsewhere, using bombs, arson, and physical threats as weapons. Several members of the Seattle Liberation Front, one of the more radical organizations, were charged with the 1969 burning of the Air Force Reserve Officers' Corps building at the University of Washington.

Still another movement, that of preservation of the environment, developed strong support during the 1960s. When, in 1964, the Italco Company built an aluminum plant near Ferndale, there was opposition, but nothing compared to that generated by the plans of the Northwest Aluminum Company to build on Guemes Island. "Save the San Juans" became a cry echoed around the Sound, and the supporting voices spoke so loudly that the company decided to drop its option on 750 acres on Guemes and seek a site in some other state.

In 1968, the Washington Environmental Council was formed and lobbied successfully for laws to protect the state's shoreline and waters. Stringent environmental controls were placed on all polluting processes of manufacture. Weyerhaeuser closed its old sulfite mill in Everett, stating that the cost of the necessary pollution controls made the decision for them. Simpson-Lee also closed pulp and paper mills in Everett, though a surplus of pulp in the region may have been a partial reason for doing so.

One of the more startling results of environmentalist action occurred in 1977 when the state legislature and Governor Dixie Lee Ray were wrestling with the question of whether the huge new oil tankers should be allowed in Puget Sound. Senator Warren G. Magnuson—as usual reading his constituency well— forced through both the Senate and House a federal bill prohibiting such tankers from sailing east of Port Angeles. That ended the debate.

Progress was made on several other fronts during

Left: *John F. Kennedy campaigned in Seattle in 1960. Accompanying him in the automobile are Senator Warren G. Magnuson and Governor Albert Rosellini. (MOHAI)*

Below: *Then Vice-President Lyndon B. Johnson came west to take part in the opening ceremonies for Seattle's Century 21 Exhibition in 1962. With him are Governor Albert Rosellini (left) and Senator Warren G. Magnuson (center). (MOHAI)*

Left: *Governor Daniel J. Evans is seen standing beside Presidential candidate Richard M. Nixon at a pre-election rally in 1968. (MOHAI)*

Below: *In 1962 students from the University of Washington protested President John F. Kennedy's blockade of Cuba by marching in front of the Federal Office Building in Seattle. Courtesy, The Seattle Times*

Above: *In protest against a decision by U.S. District Court Judge George Boldt which upheld the fishing rights of Native Americans, non-Indian fishing vessels blocked a Washington State ferry in 1978. Courtesy, The Seattle Times*

Opposite: *In 1966 members of the Muckleshoot Indian tribe walked past the Muckleshoot Community Hall east of Auburn at the beginning of their Auburn-Federal Way trek to call attention to their dispute with the state over fishing rights. Courtesy, The Seattle Times*

the 1960s. The Evergreen Point Bridge across Lake Washington was opened on August 18, 1963, then and now the longest floating bridge in the world. Its $30 million building bond issue was paid off and tolls removed in June 1979, less than sixteen years after it opened. In January of 1967, the last section of Interstate Five through Seattle was completed. The huge North Cascades Park was also established by the federal government in 1967.

In regional politics, a major legislative redistricting, the first in sixty-four years, brought the state closer to the one-person, one-vote ideal and gave Puget Sounders, with their large proportion of the population, even greater political clout.

The region entered the pro-sports world in 1967 when the National Basketball Association Supersonics played their first game. Twelve years later they would win the NBA championship for Seattle. In 1969, the Seattle Pilots, the Northwest's first major league baseball team, played for one year at the old Sick's Stadium, then moved to Milwaukee. Eight years later the Seattle Mariners reinstituted major league baseball in the region, and were joined shortly thereafter by the Seahawks football team. Meantime the University of Washington Huskies, under Coach Don James, developed a tremendous following and were invited to a bowl game nearly every year.

To provide an adequate arena for professional sports, King County voters in 1968 approved a $48 million bond issue for a domed stadium and the structure was promptly dubbed the Kingdome.

As the decade of the sixties came to a close, the aerospace business sank into the doldrums. Defense orders were down; the supersonic transport development had been cancelled; and the high cost of oil had increased the price of air travel, forcing some airlines to delay orders for new planes. Over several months in 1969 and 1970, Boeing was forced to cut its work force by more than half.

The lumber industry began suffering when increasing interest rates, fueled by inflation, depressed the home market. All around the Sound, mills closed or reduced their output. Unemployment in the state in 1970 reached 12.3%, more than twice the national average, and was even higher in certain Puget Sound counties.

As unemployment increased, hundreds of families were forced to leave the region to find work. Seattle's sardonic billboard—"Will the last person leaving Seattle please turn out the lights"—received national attention.

THE 1970s
While the decade of the 1960s was tormented by unrest over civil rights, the Vietnam war, ecological matters, and unemployment, the following decade would offer oil shortages and struggles concerning Indian fishing rights.

155

The summer of 1970 marked the high tide of Indian efforts to regain fishing rights provided them by the treaties of the 1850s. They faced opposition from commercial and sports fishermen. That summer, state game wardens and others were sent to end out-of-season Indian fishing on the Puyallup River. Physical skirmishes developed and supporters of the Indians (actor Marlon Brando was one) joined in the struggle. In 1974 Judge George C. Boldt, in a decision that still reverberates around the Sound, declared that the Indians had rights to half the salmon and steelhead harvest.

To show their unhappiness with Judge Boldt's decision, commercial fishermen began illegally gill-netting salmon, with fisheries' patrol officers in hot pursuit. In 1976 a young Seattle fisherman, caught in one of the confrontations, was shot and paralyzed. Later, commercial fishermen forced the issue to the U.S. Supreme Court, where the Boldt decision was upheld.

In 1973, the old Bangor Naval Base on Hood Canal was chosen as the site for a Trident submarine base. Over the next six years, the population of Kitsap County would increase by 32,000 (30 percent). A third of this growth was attributed to the new base.

With the end of the Vietnam war in 1975, Puget Sounders greeted a new wave of immigrants—refugees from Southeast Asia. Hundreds of these families (a larger percentage than was taken by most other parts of the country) were sponsored and assisted by local organizations and individuals.

On February 13, 1979, part of the Hood Canal floating bridge sank in a severe windstorm. Ferries were sent to carry passengers and vehicles across the waterway until the bridge could be repaired.

As the seventies waned, the debate over nuclear power plants reached a crescendo. Opponents were concerned about ecological matters, safety, and escalating costs. In Skagit County, potential site of some of the plants, the citizens produced a heavy "no nukes" advisory vote. At Satsop, Hanford, and other sites, construction was halted or slowed. The Washington Public Power Supply System (WPPSS) was overwhelmed three years later and defaulted on hundreds of millions of dollars owed to bond holders.

THE 1980s

Though the local economy appeared on the upswing and Boeing received a billion-dollar order from Delta Airlines and developed a backlog of orders from other lines, economic woes continued to dog the timber industry as high interest rates persisted. Perhaps

as much as did any factor this resulted in the state awarding its nine electoral votes for the Presidency to Ronald Reagan, who promised to lower taxes and control inflation.

Several Puget Sound medical facilities gained national attention during the eighties—the Childrens' Orthopedic Hospital, the Fred Hutchinson Cancer Research Center, Group Health Cooperative, and the University of Washington Medical School among them. A retired Burien dentist, Dr. Barney Clark, on December 2, 1982, became the first human recipient of an artificial heart in an operation at Salt Lake City. He lived with it for 112 days.

Senator Henry Jackson, the government's leading voice concerning military affairs, a thirty-year member of the Senate, former Democratic Party chairman, and presidential candidate died suddenly on September 1, 1983, at the age of seventy-one. Governor John Spellman appointed former Republican governor Daniel J. Evans to fill the vacancy.

Two years previously, Slade Gorton had defeated the state's senior senator, Warren G. Magnuson. For the first time in the memory of most Puget Sounders, Washington State sent two first-term senators to the nation's capital.

The long recession that began in the seventies showed signs of ending in 1983 as increasing defense funding began to feed into the Puget Sound economy.

To the satisfaction of the huge numbers of environmentalists in the region, Governor Booth Gardener, elected in 1984, gave high priority to the removal of pollution from the harbors of the major cities and from bays and inlets receiving effluents from manufacturing plants.

The 1984 Olympics brought fame and gold medals to several young people from the Puget Sound country, among them Phil Mahre, men's slalom; Debbie Armstrong, women's giant slalom; Candy Costie and Tracie Ruiz, synchronized swimming; Mary Wayte, freestyle swimming; Carl Buchan, Jonathan McKee, Bill Buchan, and Steve Erickson, sailing; and Shyril O'Steen, Betsy Beard, Kristi Norelius, and Paul Enquist, rowing.

City skylines continued to change during the eighties. In Seattle Martin Selig's Columbia Center, its seventy-six stories reaching 954 feet into the sky, captured highest building status. In Tacoma, the Tacoma Dome and new container cargo facilities altered the landscape. Bellevue, which twenty years ago was a small town, sprouted high-rises and skyscrapers.

A new optimism seemed to have replaced the feelings of the schizophrenic sixties and the dour seventies. Increased trade with Pacific Rim countries, new non-polluting industries, especially those high-tech in character, an increase in activities based on healthy defense budgets, and other factors tended to provide momentum to the economy.

Puget Sound in the 1980s remains the hub of the state's industry, finance, and government, as well as the gateway to international commerce with Pacific Rim countries.

Because of the country's increased trade flow with Pacific nations, total tonnage through Puget Sound ports has expanded dramatically since 1970. Japan, Canada, Taiwan, South Korea, Singapore, Hong Kong, and the Philippines are all major trading partners and the door to the Peoples' Republic of China is opening. Seattle and Tacoma remain the primary supply links to Alaska.

Though the harvesting of the region's natural resources remains an important facet of the economy, diversification has broadened the base of employment. In the decade following the "Boeing Bust" of 1968-1970, employment in manufacturing increased 28%. The percentage of workers in aerospace, forest products, and food processing has steadily decreased as diversification took hold. Machinery, fabricated metals, shipbuilding, and advanced technologies such as electronic equipment and computer software have increased in importance.

The Boeing Company, which commands more than half the world's commercial jet market, delivered 204 of the 335 new jetliners sold in 1983. It has added the 757-200, the 767 advanced twinjet, and the 767-300 to its family of jets. It was the top recipient of Defense Department research and development outlays in 1983 and ranked fifth overall among defense industries with more than $3 billion in contracts as a prime contractor for the Airborne Warning and Control System (AWACS) and the Air Launched Cruise Missile, and with major assignments in production of the B1 bomber and MX missile system.

Over the past decade, the population of the Puget Sound area has increased by more than 25 percent. Census figures for 1983 show the Seattle, Everett, and Tacoma metropolitan areas are home to 2,184,000, slightly more than half the state's residents. Puget Sound employees earn nearly three-fifths of the state's total personal income. Of the state's 4,285,100 residents in 1983, 2,815,300 (66%) live in the twelve Puget Sound counties.

Tourism has developed steadily and is now the fourth most important industry on the Sound. In the past few years, Seattle has more than doubled its first-class hotel space and a $100-million state convention center is under construction. The Seattle-Tacoma International Airport served 10.1 million passengers in 1983 and ranked ninth nationally by volume of cargo handled.

An indication of how a century of development has affected life on Puget Sound is vividly revealed by comparing the often exaggerated pleas of developers to attract new settlers during the 1880s with the cautious, sophisticated, analytical processes of our day.

The Puget Sound Council of Governments (PSCOG), which was formed in 1957 by local elected officials who sought cooperative solutions to common problems, is but one example of several such organizations attempting to analyze options and preserve the quality of life. More than fifty governmental jurisdictions in King, Pierce, Snohomish, and Kitsap counties, the four most populous counties on the Sound in which three-fourths of Puget Sound cities and towns are located, work with and support PSCOG. The council has recently studied potential consolidation of fire services in South Snohomish County; it has developed an atlas of 9,000 acres in Pierce County showing existing and potential industrial sites; it has analyzed the disposal of hazardous wastes and of solid wastes; and it has updated regional airport system planning.

The majority of residents now living on Puget Sound will be here to welcome the new century, which is little more than a decade away. If Puget Sounders have their way, the life-style will remain much as it is today, the environment will be preserved, and the economy will continue to diversify.

And because of goals like those of the Puget Sound Council of Governments and other organizations which represent the citizens of the region, Washington State will most likely continue to be listed among the ten states with the most rapid population growth. The PSCOG is estimating that in the last two decades of the century the population of King, Pierce, Snohomish, and Kitsap counties alone will increase by almost 800,000.

Such figures would undoubtedly astonish the settlers of a century ago who were doing everything within their power to find ways to increase the region's sparse population. They succeeded and the movement to the Northwest has continued ever since. And it appears that it will continue without end, for the shores of this great inland sea we call Puget Sound do indeed offer a life-style unmatched anywhere in the world.

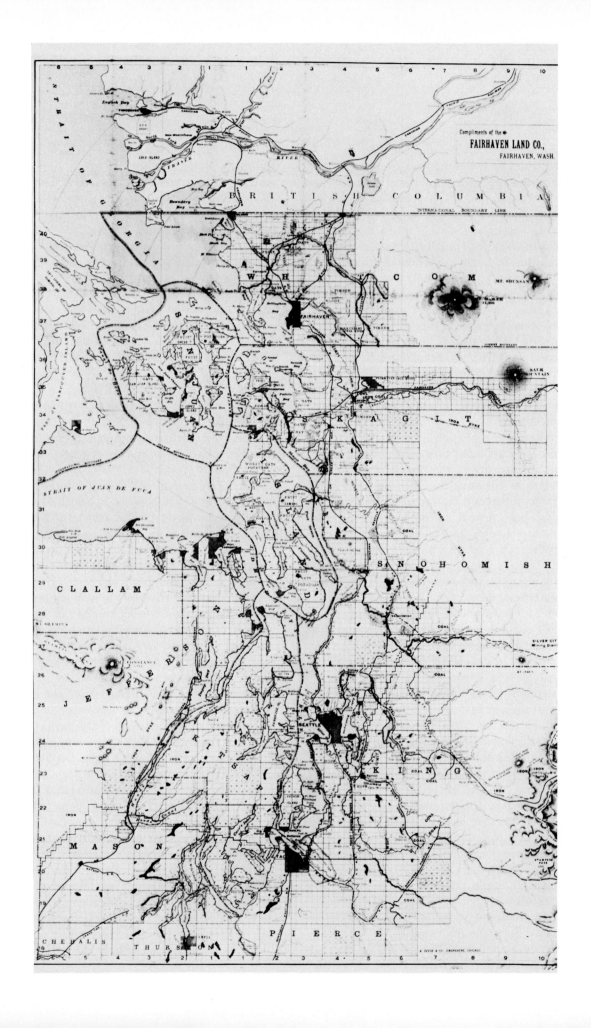

Compliments of the
FAIRHAVEN LAND CO.,
FAIRHAVEN, WASH.

8
The Counties of Puget Sound

Of Washington State's thirty-nine counties, twelve have beaches washed by the tides of the Strait of Juan de Fuca and Puget Sound. The three most populous counties in the state—King, Pierce, and Snohomish—are located here. The King County executive ranks second only to the governor of the state in the number of his constituents, and his counterparts in Pierce and Snohomish counties serve more citizens than do the mayors of any city but Seattle.

The history of the Puget Sound country could be told through the history of these counties. However, the restrictions of space in this book do not allow such an expansive undertaking. Because county government has played an important role in our history, we dedicate this chapter to brief histories of each of the Puget Sound counties and their incorporated cities and towns.

While each of these counties has a unique history, there are, of course, similarities too. Climate is one. As Robert Walkinshaw wrote in his 1929 poetic tribute titled *On Puget Sound:*

Although Puget Sound is in the latitude of Newfoundland and has a northern landscape and semiarctic twilights, it is blest the whole year through with kindly weather. In summer, the moisture of the ocean winds is cooled by the snows and suffused over the sky, often in an almost imperceptible haze. Even July and August noons are gentle as flowers. And when October is past and the flame of the vinemaple has smouldered down among the underwoods, this moisture of the winds is turned into greyish cloud. The sunshine is casual. Many of the nights are filled with softly falling rain. But when day breaks, the valleys are always green and at the spring. From beyond the eastern and western mountains, tales of winter storm are like voices spoken in the far distance . . . . Here is the beauty and stark grandeur of a North that has no harshness. In this, more than in all else, lies the appeal of Puget Sound.

This Pacific climate bathes all the counties of the Sound, though precipitation may be influenced by the rain shadows of the mountains.

Each county has its heritage society, most have historic museums, and, at one time or another, detailed histories have been published about each county. For those who seek further information, these local historical societies stand ready and willing to provide it.

Opposite: *This 1891 map showing the twelve counties of Puget Sound was published by the Fairhaven Land Company, a development company, as a "Complete Railway and Navigation Guide for Travelers and Settlers." Courtesy, Special Collections Division, University of Washington Libraries*

CLALLAM COUNTY

Population (1983): 52,500 (eighth most populous county among the twelve on Puget Sound)
Area: 1,753 square miles (fifth largest county on Puget Sound

Employment: Federal, state, and local governments employ 4,167 (25.98 percent) in part because Olympic National Park headquarters are in the county. Manufacturing (especially wood products), services, and retail trade (much of it for tourists) provide most of the remaining jobs.

Clallam County, with borders on the Strait of Juan De Fuca and the Pacific Ocean, was organized in 1854. The name comes from the local Indian inhabitants and means "strong people." A museum at Neah Bay displays the heritage of the sturdy Makah tribe, noted seafarers of old who hunted whales in the open sea from large canoes.

John Everett and John Sutherland crossed the strait from Victoria in 1849 to establish trap lines at Lakes Everett (now Crescent) and Sutherland.

In 1857, Angus Johnson became the first white settler in the area at False Dungeness, the former name for Port Angeles. After the settlement was founded, Victor Smith, who arrived in 1861, an appointee of Secretary of the Treasury Salmon P. Chase, managed to have Ediz Hook and surrounding area, 3,520 acres in all, set aside as the second national city (Washington, D.C., was the first). This preserved the land for government purposes until the reserve was opened in 1891 and auctioned off at a minimum of five dollars a lot. By then squatters had occupied most of it.

The Puget Sound Co-operative Colony, conceived by George Venable Smith, brought new people to Port Angeles in 1887. Shares in the venture were purchased with cash, labor, services, or property. All workers shared alike and scores of families joined the colony. On Ennis Creek they built the first mill, docks, stores, hotel, offices, and machine shops in the area. After 1889, the colony slowly dissolved as its holdings were sold at auctions. However, many of the families remained.

There are three incorporated towns in Clallam County.

In 1890, **Port Angeles** incorporated, taking its name from the harbor called Puerto de Nuestra Senora de los Angeles (Port of Our Lady of the Angels) which was named by the Spanish explorer Eliza in 1791. Port Angeles promptly wrested the county seat away from New Dungeness.

By 1892, it was a town dependent largely on wood products and over the years some of the nation's largest milling companies built at Port Angeles including Crown-Zellerbach, Rayonier, and Fibreboard Products, Inc.

Today Port Angeles is a town of 17,100. From here the Washington State ferries run to Victoria.

Sequim *(1983 population: 3,180; incorporated in 1913)* The name derives from an Indian word, "such-e-kwai-ing" meaning "quiet water." One of the driest and sunniest towns in Western Washington (it sits in the shadow of the Olympics which dry out the rain clouds), it has attracted large numbers of retirees. The town was settled in 1854 by John Bell and platted in 1907.

Forks *(1983 population: 3,180; incorporated in 1913)* The town received its name because of the nearby confluence of the Calawah, Bogachiel, and Soleduck rivers. The first settlers in the area—Ole P. Nelson, Peter Fisher, and Ely Peterson—arrived before 1878 and were joined that year by the Luther Ford family.

Port Angeles, the most northwesterly city in the continental United States, rests between the picturesque Strait of Juan de Fuca and the magnificent Olympic Mountains in this circa 1929 photo. (MOHAI)

ISLAND COUNTY

Population (1983): 47,000 (ninth most populous of the twelve Puget Sound counties)
Area: 212 square miles (second smallest county in the state)
Employment: two-thirds of the earned income is from federal, state, and local government jobs, the Whidbey Island Naval Air Station (Ault Field) providing a good share of this. Retail trade and services provide another 20 percent of the employment.

Island County was organized on January 6, 1853, by the Oregon legislature to provide government for the islands of Whidbey and Camano. The islands attracted settlers early because they were heavily timbered in places, and also provided large prairie and wet lands on which farming could develop. By the 1890s, the islands were in daily communication with the rest of the Sound through a fleet of small steamers and they provided considerable quantities of grains, hay, beef, and mutton for urban dwellers. Two sawmills were turning out 2.25 million board feet a year, the largest being that of the Puget Mill Company at Utsalady on Camano.

Whidbey, which lays claim to being the largest island within the continental United States, was named in 1792 by Captain George Vancouver for Master Joseph Whidbey of his expedition. Whidbey was in charge of the small boat expedition that first circumnavigated the island, thereby proving it was not part of the mainland.

The name **Camano** was given to the other island by Charles Kellett when he clarified the British charts in 1847, replacing the name McDonough, which Wilkes had given the island six years previously in honor of the American naval hero on Lake Champlain in the War of 1812. The name, which Eliza had given a smaller island in 1790, honors Spanish nobleman Don Jacinto Caamano. Thomas Cranny is said to have been the first American to settle on the island in 1855 and to have built the first sawmill there.

Four small islands are also included in the county, including eleven-acre **Ben Ure Island** which was purchased in 1908 from the federal government by Benjamin Ure. He subdivided this into estate-sized tracts. **Smith Island** was named for a Hudson's Bay Company employee. Its smaller compatriot, to which it is joined at low tide, is appropriately called **Minor Island.** Beginning in 1858, a lighthouse operated on Smith, westernmost of the islands in the county, but was abandoned in 1957 after wave erosion undermined the site.

The seat of county government is at **Coupeville** (population 1,005 in 1983). This settlement was originally called "Port of Sea Captains" for the number of mariners who retired there, but later was officially named for Captain Thomas Coupe who took a land claim there in 1852. Isaac N. Ebey settled nearby that same year and in 1857 was killed by Tlingit Indians from Alaska who were seeking revenge for the death of a chief in an earlier fracas with white settlers.

Oak Harbor is the county's largest city with a population of 12,150. The second oldest settlement in Island County, it is named for the native oaks found nearby. The first settler, a Norwegian named Zakarias Toftezen, claimed land on this site in 1849.

Langlie, with a population of 710, is the only other incorporated town in the county. It was platted in 1890 by Jacob Anthes who had earlier logged the area. He named the town for Judge J.W. Langlie, a partner in a land development company.

Island County attracts many tourists to its parks, among them Deception Pass State Park (2,292 acres), Fort Ebey State Park (227 acres), Fort Casey State Park (227 acres), and Camano Island State Park (134 acres). Keystone Underwater Park provides an area for scuba diving. The Oak Harbor State Game Range occupies 589 acres.

Island County's first courthouse, in Coupeville, was originally built as a store in 1855 and was remodeled in the 1890s. Courtesy, Special Collections Division, University of Washington Libraries

JEFFERSON COUNTY

Population (1983): 16,000 (eleventh largest among the twelve Puget Sound counties)
Area: 1,805 square miles (fourth largest among Puget Sound counties)

Employment is in government (28 percent), retail trade (24 percent), manufacturing (18 percent), and services (15 percent).
Agriculture, forestry, fishing, wholesale trade, and financial institutions supply the remainder of positions. It is the site of much recreational activity because a large part of Olympic National Park falls within its boundaries.

Jefferson County, named for the second President, was established on December 22, 1852, by the Oregon territorial legislature. At the outset, Port Townsend, the county's only incorporated town, was named its seat of government. The name derives from the adjacent bay which Captain Vancouver named for the Marquis of Townshend, but Commander Wilkes, in his charts, dropped the "h."

Port Townsend's first settler, Henry Wilson, arrived in 1850. Charles Bachelder and A.A. Plummer came in 1851, and later that year Loren B. Hastings and Frances W. Pettygrove traveled up from Portland. Pettygrove had been a founder of Portland and had named that village after his home town in Maine but a fever scare had convinced him to take his family north. Plummer, Pettygrove, and Hastings laid out the town of Port Townsend.

By 1890, the population of the county exceeded 6,000, a U.S. Army military post had been established at Fort Worden, and several sawmills in the county were producing nearly forty million board feet of lumber per year.

Port Townsend in those days was site of the U.S. Marine hospital and of a large mill, a sash and door factory, blind and molding manufacturers, machine shops, and a brewery. Furniture, carriages, harnesses, cigars, mattresses, and other goods were made there.

The value of foreign goods imported through Port Townsend, then Puget Sound's port of entry, between January 1 and August 31, 1892, totaled just over $1.5 million. Consuls representing Britain, France, Chile, Germany, and Hawaii had offices at Port Townsend.

After the recession of the 1890s, Port Townsend stagnated. Many citizens moved to cities east of the Sound where railroad service was becoming available.

Today, the population of Port Townsend is slightly over 6,000, about what it was in 1890. It has developed as a tourist mecca and many of the historical

structures built during its heyday are preserved.

Several unincorporated settlements exist in Jefferson County. Among them:

Quilcene, the name of a river, a bay, a mountain, and the settlement, all of which derive from a Twana Indian word meaning "saltwater people."

Port Ludlow was named by Commander Wilkes in 1841 to honor U.S. Navy Lieutenant Augustus C. Ludlow who was killed in the War of 1812.

Brinnen was named for early settler Ewell P. Brinnen.

[Port] Hadlock was named for Samuel Hadlock who in 1870 erected the sawmill of the Washington Mill Company.

Irondale was the site on Port Townsend Bay of the iron works erected by Western Steel Corporation, ostensibly to use the iron ores found nearby. However, Chinese ore, imported for a short time, was all that was ever put through the furnaces.

Kala Point was named by the Wilkes Expedition in 1841, probably from an Indian word. It is the site of considerable residential development.

Chimacum, a creek and a town, were named for a warlike band of Indians that once lived in the vicinity.

Opposite: *These five women, members of James G. McCurdy's Sunday School class, had their images preserved by their teacher. McCurdy, a Port Townsend banker and amateur photographer, took the picture in the early 1920s at Chetzemoka Park, probably during a church picnic. Only the two women on the left—Annie Jarvis and Madeline Butler—are identified. Courtesy, Jefferson County Historical Society*

Above: *The Snow Creek Logging Company used this huge donkey engine and its long steel cables to drag logs down the slopes to the waters of Discovery Bay. From there the logs were floated to nearby sawmills. Courtesy, Jefferson County Historical Society*

KING COUNTY

Population (1983): 1,315,800 (most populous county in the state)

Area: 2,128 square miles (largest county on Puget Sound, eleventh in size in the state)

Employment: In 1980 manufacturing accounted for 26 percent; services, 18 percent; government, 13 percent; retail trade, 10 percent; transportation and public utilities, 9 percent; wholesale trade, 9 percent; financial, insurance, and real estate, 8 percent; and construction, 6 percent.

King County was established by the Oregon territorial legislature in 1852. The first settlers were Luther Collins, Henry Van Asselt, and Jacob and Samuel Maple, who took land on the Duwamish River in 1851. The Denny party arrived a few weeks later at Alki Point. The following year members of the Denny party sounded Elliott Bay and platted Seattle.

Henry Yesler established the first steam sawmill on Puget Sound in Seattle in 1853. Lumber was the first major export, though coal, from mines east of Lake Washington, soon became a valuable commodity. Agricultural products harvested by the pioneers included hops, hay, oats, fruit, root crops, celery, and asparagus.

After the railroads arrived on the Sound, King County's population grew rapidly. The incorporated cities in King County are:

Seattle *(1983 population: 489,700; incorporated 1865)* Platted in 1852 by Arthur Denny, David Denny, Carson Boren, and Dr. David Maynard, it was named, at the suggestion of Maynard, for the elderly but friendly Indian chief.

Elwood Evans explained in his 1890 report, *State of Washington:*

Owing to advantageous harbor location, the proximity of coal and timber, it being the center and point of distribution for milling points and logging camps, the larger portion of steamboats engaged in the Sound trade made it their starting point, and to such fact may be attributed its commercial supremacy. Over thirty steamboats of every size run from here to every point on the Sound and upon the navigable waters tributary to it.

After the arrival of direct transcontinental rail service in the early 1890s, Seattle rapidly developed as a major metropolis. The pioneer leaders had worked diligently to attract settlers who would provide industry, retail and wholesale outlets, and legal, medical, and other services needed by settlers around the

Sound. Today, the Seattle-Everett-Tacoma metropolitan districts are home to a population in excess of two million.

Bellevue *(1983 population: 73,900; incorporated 1953)* Bellevue was platted in 1904 around a post office which was opened in 1887 by Isaac Bechtel. Not until the First Lake Washington Floating Bridge was completed in 1940 did the area become readily accessible from Seattle. The population in this suburb grew from 12,809 in 1960 to its present size twenty-three years later. It is now the state's fourth largest city and third largest on the Sound. It was named in the 1880s with the French term meaning "beautiful view."

Renton *(1983 population: 32,700; incorporated 1901)* Renton was originally called "Black River Bridge." The present city developed after coal was found nearby in 1853 by Dr. R.H. Bigelow. The town was named for Captain William Renton of the Port Blakely Mill Company. Renton was also one of the founders of the Renton Coal Company.

Auburn *(1983 population: 29,000; incorporated 1891)* The town was platted in 1886 by Dr. Levi Ballard and named "Slaughter" for Army Lieutenant Slaughter who was killed by Indians not far from the site in 1856. The name offended some residents (the hotel was called the "Slaughter House"), and in 1893 they petitioned the state legislature to change the name to that of Auburn, New York, which had taken its name from the line in an Oliver Goldsmith poem: "Sweet Auburn! Loveliest village of the plain."

Redmond *(1983 population: 26,300; incorporated 1912)* Settled in 1871 by William Perrigo and Luke McRedmond, it was first called "Salmonberg" because of the large numbers of fish spawning in the nearby Sammamish River, then was renamed "Melrose" for Perrigo's former home in Massachusetts, and finally "Redmond" for Luke McRedmond who platted the site in 1891 and served as the first postmaster.

Kent *(1983 population: 25,500; incorporated 1890)* The first settler in the area was S.W. Russell. Originally the community was called "Titusville" after James H. Titus on whose land claim it developed. In 1884, a new plat was named "Yesler" after Henry Yesler, builder of Seattle's first sawmill. In 1888, John Alexander and Ida L. Guiberson developed another plat for which Ezra Meeker, author and hop-grower, suggested the name "Kent" after the English hop-growing center. Here the first Carnation condensed milk plant was founded in 1889.

Mercer Island *(1983 population: 21,150; incorpo-*

rated 1960) The island was named for Thomas Mercer, early Seattle pioneer who arrived in 1853 and named Lake Washington. One of the first developments on the island was promoted as "East Seattle" by C.C. Calkins. Two governmental units, a town and a city, existed on Mercer Island but were combined in 1970.

Kirkland *(1983 population: 18,850; incorporated 1905)* The city was founded in 1886 and named to honor Peter Kirk, an English millionaire whose plan for smelting Cascade Mountain iron ore in what he hoped would be the "Pittsburgh of the West" turned sour when the ore was found to be too expensive to mine and of questionable quality. The Second Lake Washington Floating Bridge (Evergreen Point) made Kirkland-Seattle commuting quick and easy. Population nearly doubled to 15,000 in the eight years following the 1962 bridge opening.

Des Moines *(1983 population: 10,250; incorporated 1959)* This city is one of the state's fastest growing municipalities (500 percent in two decades). The original settler in 1872 was John Moore. In 1889, F.A. Blasher, a principal in the Des Moines Improvement Company, named the new plat after his hometown in Iowa. Originally a site for summer homes on a crescent-shaped beach, it is now a residential city with marinas and retirement homes.

Bothell *(1983 population: 7,600; incorporated 1909)* Bothell is named for Mr. and Mrs. David C. Bothell, whose son George founded the town after he and his brother John built saw and shingle mills and logged the area.

Normandy Park *(1983 population: 6,000; incorporated 1953)* The town was developed by the Seattle-Tacoma Land Company in the 1920s and was named to reflect the original plan to restrict construction to French Normandy architecture.

Enumclaw *(1983 population: 5,775; incorporated 1913).* Allen Porter homesteaded near here in 1853. In 1884 the town was platted by Frank Stevenson and his wife, and was named for the nearby promontory which Indian myths indicated was the home of thunder and evil spirits. Soon lumber mills and dairies were established in the town.

Issaquah *(1983 population: 5,550; incorporated 1892)* Coal was discovered near here in 1859. Settlers took claims in the valley in the 1860s and a village developed. It was referred to—as was the river, the lake, and the valley—as "Squak" after the Indian residents. In 1892, the town was incorporated as Gilman after Daniel Hunt Gilman, a railroad officer. Post office officials changed the name to "Olney" to prevent name duplication with another town. In 1899, the present name, a more euphonious, Anglicised version of the Indian name, was adopted. The floating bridge across Lake Washington brought suburban status to Issaquah in 1940.

Tukwila *(1983 population: 3,600; incorporated 1908)* Tukwila was first settled by the Joseph Foster family in 1853. The Seattle-Tacoma Interurban brought growth beginning in 1902. The first town plat was called "Garden City," but the name "Tukwila" soon supplanted it. It is an Indian word meaning "land where the hazlenuts grow."

Clyde Hill *(1983 population: 3,120; incorporated 1953)* The town was first settled in 1884 by Hans Nicholson. Before World War II many Japanese settled on truck farms in the area. After the war, the suburban boom resulted in residential development which has intensified since. The town took its name from the old Clyde Road (now 92nd Northeast), a major thoroughfare named by an early settler whose home had been near the Firth of Clyde in Scotland.

Medina *(1983 population: 3,100; incorporated 1955)* Thomas L. Dabney (Dabney Point) purchased property here in 1876. Other settlers followed him including Floyd Croft who, in 1894, operated a shingle mill, raised tobacco on his farm, and built a dock. The name, that of the sacred Moslem city where Mohammed was born, was suggested by Adelaide Belote. After 1900, the lake shore section, including Evergreen Point, became known as the "gold coast" for the wealthy landowners. Medina was platted in 1914; in 1919 the Overlake Golf Course was developed. Medina is now a suburb of fine homes near the east end of the Evergreen Point Bridge.

Lake Forest Park *(1983 population: 2,430; incorporated 1961)* The town was named in 1919 by Ole Hanson, one-time Seattle mayor and real estate developer, after a city near Chicago, and has become a site for fine homes at the north end of Lake Washington. Platted development began in 1907 after loggers had harvested the forest in the area.

Pacific *(1983 population: 2,330; incorporated 1909)* This city on the King-Pierce County line was platted in 1906 by real estate developer C.D. Hillman. Its name reflects the peaceful environs.

North Bend *(1983 population: 1,705; incorporated 1909)* A Dane, Matts Peterson, first claimed land here in 1865. Hop-growing was popular hereabout in the 1880s and the town developed as a waystop on the trail to Snoqualmie Pass. Mary and Will Taylor platted the town in 1889 as "Snoqualmie," but with Snoqualmie Falls down the way, the railroad renamed it North Bend for the nearby northerly turn of the Snoqualmie River.

Algona *(1983 population: 1,506; incorporated 1955)* This south King County town was first called "Valley City," a name rejected by the post office. The citizens then selected "Algoma," an Indian word meaning "valley of the flowers," but the post office inadvertantly changed the "m" to "n."

Snoqualmie *(1983 population; 1,475; incorporated 1903)* Jeremiah Borst was the first permanent settler in the valley in 1858. The town developed around a hop ranch that had its own hotel, which attracted many pioneer families. The town was platted by the Snoqualmie Land and Improvement Company in 1889.

Black Diamond *(1983 population: 1,095; incorpo-*

Unincorporated Juanita on the northeast shore of Lake Washington originated as a sawmill town called Hubbard. In 1905 it began developing as a summer resort area. In the 1930s it was a popular recreation center with a fine swimming beach, canoeing, and a dance pavilion. It is now a residential area and the site of a popular public park. (MOHAI)

rated 1961) This was the site of a major coal mine of the Black Diamond Coal Company of California. The miners worked in shafts more than 6,000 feet long. Though little or no coal is mined today, the town continues as a regional shopping center.

Yarrow Point *(1983 population: 1,041; incorporated 1959)* William Easter first patented a claim here. In the 1880s, Seattle businessmen Bailey Gatzert and Jacob Furth built summer homes on the Point. Leigh S.J. Hunt developed an estate there, which he named "Yarrow" from a Wordsworth poem. The town was platted in 1901.

Duvall *(1983 population: 953; incorporated 1913)* This town on the Snoqualmie River first developed in the 1870s as "Cherry Valley" but later was named for James Duvall, the man who first claimed land there in 1875. The town was platted in 1911.

Carnation *(1983 population: 950; incorporated 1912)* Located on the site of a former large Snoqualmie Indian longhouse, the town's original settler was James Entwistle who claimed his land in 1858. The oldest part of town was platted in 1894. The original name was "Tolt," anglicized and shortened from an Indian word meaning "swift running waters." In 1909, E.A. Stuart established his Carnation Milk Farm there. In 1917, the town elected to change its name to "Carnation."

Hunts Point *(1983 population: 525; incorporated 1955)* The town is named for Leigh S.J. Hunt, Seattle publisher and east side promoter who bought property there. In 1871, Marshall Blinn, Kitsap County lumberman, secured the property. In 1892, Francis Boddy built a sawmill and home on the Point. Today some of Puget Sound's wealthiest families live on Hunts Point.

Beaux Arts *(1983 population: 307; incorporated 1954)* This town is near where George Miller established a farm in 1883, and is the site of an artistic community founded in 1908 by Sidney Laurence and members of Seattle's Western Academy of Fine Arts.

Skykomish *(1983 population: 220; incorporated 1909)* This town is located on the Stevens Pass Highway in the northeast corner of King County. It developed when the Great Northern railroad built through the pass in 1890-1891, and was named for the river which below the town joins the Snoqualmie to become the Snohomish. Skykomish was platted in 1899 by John Maloney and his wife.

In King County, 539,000 residents live in unincorporated areas which, in effect, makes the county the largest local governmental unit in the state. Some of these population centers are considering incorporation.

Federal Way, where in the 1800s several sawmills operated and where the Weyerhaeuser Company has built an attractive corporate headquarters, is one such center. The name of the area derives from the school district which took its name from the Pacific Highway built through the area with federal funds in 1930.

Burien takes its name from German immigrant Gottlieb von Boorian who, in 1880, settled on the lake that also bears his name. The town grew rapidly during World War II because of its proximity to the Boeing airplane plant.

Woodinville was named for the Ira Woodin family that settled there in 1872. In 1877, a railroad began serving the area. Here is located the Chateau Sainte Michelle Winery on the old Hollywood Farm. The area is developing as a suburb.

Juanita, originally "Hubbard," developed around Dorr Forbes sawmill in the 1880s. Since 1905 it has offered a popular resort and swimming beach.

Kenmore was named by John McMasters after his former home near Ottawa, Canada. In 1903 he took over the sawmill there and leased acreage from Watson Squire, former governor and senator. The town is now a major shopping and residential area.

Richmond Beach was platted in 1889 and named by George C. Fisher, who homesteaded the forested area in 1872. He named it for his home in England.

Maple Valley welcomed its first settlers in 1873— John McCoy and family and James Maxwell. In 1882, the first sawmill began operations under the George Ames, C.O. Russell, and Henry Sidebotham families. They named the community "Vine Maple Valley."

Vashon-Maury Islands are in King County and ferries carry hundreds of commuters from the islands to Seattle each day. Vashon Island was named by Captain Vancouver in 1792 to honor his friend Admiral James Vashon. Maury Island was named by Wilkes in 1841 for William L. Maury, an expedition surveyor. Though the two islands are joined by landfill today, they were once separated by a narrow channel. The first permanent settlement occurred here in 1877 when the S.D. Sherman family arrived. In 1865, a Chautauqua camp was established there and a shipyard and drydock once operated at Dockton.

White Center was named by George White, a right he won after the toss of a coin in 1918. It was the site of pioneer farms in the 1870s. A sawmill operated there starting in 1888. Today it is a residential area adjacent to Seattle's southern boundary.

KITSAP COUNTY

Population (1983): 161,600 (third in population among the twelve Puget Sound counties)
Area: 393 square miles (tenth among the twelve Puget Sound counties)

Employment: Governmental services (federal, state, and local) employ more than 57 percent of the workers, many of whom work at the three Naval installations (Bremerton Naval Yard, Bangor Trident Submarine Base, and Keyport Torpedo Station) and several state agencies including the veterans' home at Retsil. Service industries employ nearly 17 percent, retail trade about 13 percent, and manufacturing about 3.1 percent of the work force. Many workers commute to and from Seattle and Kitsap County on Washington State ferries.

Kitsap County was established in 1857 and named "Slaughter" by the legislature for Lt. William A. Slaughter of the U.S. Army who was killed by Indians two years earlier. However, the legislature agreed that the residents could select a different name if they wished. They promptly, if ironically, chose the name of the most able of the local war chiefs, a man called Kitsap, who may have been indirectly responsible for the death of Slaughter.

In early days, the largest sawmills on Puget Sound were built on the heavily wooded peninsula with its several deepwater harbors including Ports Gamble and Blakely. By 1890, six large mills and many shingle mills were producing immense quantities of forest products.

Incorporated towns include:

Bremerton *(1983 population: 35,475; incorporated 1901)* Bremerton is the only large city in the county. The first settler in the area, Andrew Williams, arrived in 1872. William Bremer, a Seattle realtor, in 1890 became interested in properties fringing Sinclair and Dyes Inlets. Largely through his efforts, the U.S. Government purchased a site here for a U.S. Navy drydock, which became the major naval base in the Pacific Northwest. The town that grew about the base was called Bremerton for the farsighted realtor. Eventually nearby settlements of Charleston and Manette were absorbed by the city.

Port Orchard *(1983 population: 4,850; incorporated 1890)* This city is the county seat. In 1854 William Renton and Daniel Howard built a sawmill here. Originally called Sidney after Sidney Stevens who platted it, the town later was renamed after the inlet that stretches between Bainbridge Island and the Kitsap Peninsula. This inlet, Port Orchard Bay, was named by Captain Vancouver in 1792 for the

clerk of his ship *Discovery,* H.M. Orchard.

Poulsbo *(1983 population: 3,600; incorporated 1907)* The town was settled in 1883 by Jorgen Eliason. Many Norwegian immigrant families congregated here because the mountains and water reminded them of their home country. Located on Liberty (originally Dogfish) Bay, it is the trade center for the northern section of the county and a growing city because of developments at the nearby Bangor Trident base. The name was provided by I.E. Moe in memory of a small settlement, Paulsbo, near his home in Norway. The post office misread the handwriting and ever since the spelling has been Poulsbo.

Winslow *(1983 population: 2,440; incorporated 1947)* Winslow is located on Bainbridge Island's Eagle Harbor where the Seattle ferry docks. It was named for Winslow Hall, one of the brothers who operated a large shipyard there. Bainbridge Island was named by the 1841 Wilkes Expedition for Captain William Bainbridge, a U.S. naval hero of the War of 1812.

Several unincorporated but growing centers of population exist in Kitsap County.

Historic **Suquamish** is the site of Chief Seattle's grave. It is adjacent to the Port Madison Reservation of the Suquamish and allied tribes. Like Suquamish, **Silverdale** in the central part of the county is increasing in size. Originally Silverdale's name was to be Goldendale, but because there was already such a town in Klickitat County, it was decided to drop down a notch on the precious-metal scale. **Seabeck** was the site of Marshall Blinn's great sawmill. He named the settlement after his home in Maine. The mill burned in 1886 and again in 1914, after which it was not rebuilt. The 700-acre townsite was purchased by the Colman family of Seattle and an interdenominational church conference grounds was established there. **Chico** was one of the early locations for summer homes and was named for an Indian leader who, at his death in 1909, was said to be 105 years old. **Colby** was originally "Coal Bay," named in 1884 for lumps of coal found along a nearby creek. **Kingston,** unlike most of the other small towns, is still served by a ferry out of Edmonds. It is situated on Apple Tree Cove which was misnamed by the Wilkes Expedition when, from their ships, they mistook the native blooming dogwood for apple trees. **Southworth,** where the ferry from Vashon docks, is named for the point on which it is located, which Wilkes named for a quartermaster of his expedition. **Manchester,** an old lumber town, established in 1883 as Brooklyn, was renamed by the settlers in hopes it would become a busy seaport like its namesake in England. **Indianola** was named in 1916 by a development company because the land was part of an allotment grant to a Port Madison Indian. **Bangor** was named for the town in Maine, which was named for a town in Wales. **Hansville** was named for early settler Hans Zachariason.

Workers at Bremerton's Puget Sound Navy Yard are seen heading home on September 12, 1942. The war kept this yard booming, and several ferries, notably the Kalakala, brought workers from Seattle to work each day in the yard. Courtesy, The Seattle Times

MASON COUNTY

Population (1983): 33,600 (third least populated of the twelve Puget Sound counties)
Area: 961 square miles (eighth largest of the twelve)

Of all the Puget Sound counties, Mason leans heaviest on wood products, though this is changing because of a deep recession in such businesses. Manufacturing in 1980 accounted for nearly one-third of the employment in the county, governmental services for slightly more than one-quarter, followed by retail trade and services.

Mason County was carved from Thurston County in 1854 as Sawamish County, but this name was changed a few years later to honor Charles H. Mason, first secretary of Washington Territory, who served as acting governor for a brief period in the 1850s. Three-quarters of the county consists of mountainous terrain including the southern end of the Olympic National Forest. As early as 1892, three Mason County sawmills were producing 4.5 million board feet of lumber per year.

Shelton, the county seat, is the only incorporated city in the county. It was named for David Shelton, former fur trapper, Indian fighter, gold prospector, and member of the first territorial legislature, who homesteaded there in 1853. It was Shelton who requested the county be formed and later that it be named for Mason.

Shelton developed as a logging and milling center especially after the Satsop Railroad was built in 1884 to haul logs to Shelton.

Mark Reed of Olympia with others built a power house, saw, and shingle mills there for Simpson Logging Company. And he was instrumental in attracting Rainier Pulp and Paper Company to Shelton in the mid-1920s which merged with other mills as Rayonier, Inc. Their central laboratories in Shelton developed the finest sulphite book and bond papers, rayon silk, plastics, serviceable "cellophane," and other products.

The Washington State Correctional Center is located near Shelton.

Several historical unincorporated communities have developed in Mason County, among them:

Hoodsport, named for Hood Canal. Once a logging town, it is now a resort and tourist center and site of an Olympic National Forest Ranger Station.

Union, originally called Union City, was named by early settlers Willson and Anderson who opened a store there in 1858. It, too, was once a logging center.

Other historic geographical names include:

Lake Cushman, a man-made lake ten miles long which developed from dams built in the 1920s to furnish water for Tacoma's hydroelectric plant. The name honors Orrington Cushman, packer and interpreter for Governor Isaac Stevens during treaty negotiations in 1854. On its shores is a 581-acre state park.

Hartstene Island, named by Wilkes in 1841 to honor a member of his expedition, Lt. Henry S. Hartstein (Wilkes misspelled the name "Hartstene".)

Skokomish River (and Indian reservation of 5,804 acres), named for the Indian tribe there. The name means "river people."

Squaxin Island, named for an Indian band called "alone people." On the island is a 1,494-acre reservation and a 31-acre state park.

The timber grows tall in Mason County, which through the years has produced huge amounts of wood products. Courtesy, Special Collections Division, University of Washington Libraries

PIERCE COUNTY

Population (1983): 507,000 (second most populous county in the state)
Area: 1,675 square miles (seventh largest of the twelve Puget Sound counties)
Employment: More than one-third of the jobs are generated by governmental agencies including Fort Lewis, McChord Air Base, Western State Hospital, the State Soldiers' Home, and city and county governments. Various services employ about 19 percent, retail trade 15 percent, and manufacturing 12 percent of the work force.

In December 1852, the Oregon territorial legislature separated the county from Thurston and named it for newly elected President Franklin Pierce.

Forty years after its formation, Pierce County could boast of eighteen sawmills turning out 172 million board feet of lumber yearly. More than 46 million lath were produced and nearly 30 million shingles a year. These endeavors employed more than 1,200 men. Manufactured goods included plaster and cement, harnesses, mattresses, tents, flour and grain products, matches, boxes, machinery, cigars, railroad cars, wagons and carriages, and smelted ores. Meat packing and brewing were major industries.

Tacoma in 1880 became the county seat after it was named the terminus of the Northern Pacific Railroad. M.M. Carver had chosen the townsite in 1868 and soon James Steel and Lewis Starr joined him. The population jumped from 1,500 in 1883 to more than 47,000 by 1890 as a result of the arrival of the Northern Pacific.

Tacoma became a serious rival to Seattle. The battle to become the premier port on Puget Sound was waged between the two cities for decades, and in fact, has never ceased. The thirty miles between the two cities has gradually filled with residential and industrial areas.

Tacoma's population in 1983 was 158,400, making it the second largest city on the Sound and third largest in the state.

Other incorporated municipalities in Pierce County include:

Puyallup *(1983 population: 18,550; incorporated 1890)* The settlement was platted in 1877 by Ezra Meeker, who, with his father, introduced hop growing to the area. Meeker wrote many books of historical importance. The first post office was called Franklin, but there were numerous towns so named and the settlers sought a distinctive appellation. As Meeker wrote: "We agreed there would be but one Puyal-

lup." The name is said to mean in the Indian language "generous people." Here, in the fertile river valley, is located a Washington State University Agricultural research and Extension Center. In the spring, the valley is bright with daffodils and other bulb flowers.

Bonney Lake *(1983 population: 5,975; incorporated 1949)* This city is one of the newest municipalities in the region. In 1947, Kenneth Simmons platted the town after purchasing the lake and 1,000 adjacent acres for the purpose of founding this community located east of Puyallup. It is now the third largest incorporated city in Pierce County.

Fircrest *(population: 5,400; incorporated 1925)* Fircrest was first platted in 1907 by Edward J. Bowes, the famous host of radio's Amateur Hour which was broadcast nationally during the 1930s and 1940s. Major Bowes called it "Regent's Park" but development lagged. In 1925, in an effort to change its image, the town adopted the name of the adjacent golf course. Fircrest developed rapidly after World War II and today is nearly surrounded by metropolitan Tacoma.

Sumner *(population 5,130; incorporated 1891)* Sumner was platted by John Francis Kincaid on the banks of the Stuck River on the donation land claim of his father. The founder came to Puget Sound with that first wagon train that traveled over Naches Pass in 1853. He named the town for Charles Sumner, the Boston slavery opponent and famous senator.

Steilacoom *(1983 population: 4,990; incorporated, 1854)* One of Puget Sound's most historic towns, and the first to incorporate, Steilacoom is located on the site where John Work of the Hudson's Bay Company in his 1824 journal reported existence of an Indian village called "Chilacoom." Steilacoom was founded by LaFayette Balch in 1851 when he erected a trading post there. Many historic structures are maintained in the town.

Nearby was Fort Steilacoom, established in 1849 by the U.S. Army. The fort was abandoned in 1869 and five years later was donated to the territory as a site for a hospital for the insane, today's Western State Hospital.

Milton *(1983 population: 3,400; incorporated 1907)* The town developed around a sawmill. The name is a contraction of "Mill Town."

Buckley *(1983 population: 3,110; incorporated 1890)* Buckley was originally named "Perkins' Prairie" after an early settler. When the railroad came through, it was called "White River Siding" until in 1888 it was given the name of the superintendent of

the Ellensburg-Tacoma division of the Northern Pacific, J.M. Buckley. The Rainier State School for the developmentally disabled is located here.

Gig Harbor *(1983 population: 2,580; incorporated 1890)* The town was named in 1841 by explorer Charles Wilkes, who explained that the inlet had sufficient depth of water for small vessels such as gigs. First settled in the early 1880s by Dr. Alfred M. Burnham, the village flourished about a sawmill until the mill closed. A new town of the same name developed nearby which attracted Scandinavians and Slavs who developed a fishing community.

Fife *(1983 population: 2,390; incorporated 1957)* Fife is named for William Fife, a wealthy and well-known Tacoman who was instrumental in early development of the community.

Orting *(1983 population: 1,810; incorporated 1889)* was first settled by Daniel Verner in 1854. The townsite was platted in 1887 by F.E. Eldridge. Originally called "Carbon," the confusion with nearby Carbonado resulted in a name change in 1878. "Orting" is taken from an Indian word said to mean "prairie village." Since 1891, the state soldier's home has been located near there.

Eatonville *(1983 population: 1,075; incorporated 1909)* This city in the Cascade foothills was named for T.C. Van Eaton who platted the village in 1880. For a time it was an important lumber milling center.

Ruston *(1983 population: 620; incorporated 1906)* A tiny enclave surrounded by Tacoma, this town was named for W.R. Rust, one of the founders and president of the Tacoma Smelting Company which oper-

ated a smelter there.

Five other small towns in Pierce County have incorporated. **Du Pont** (incorporated in 1912) developed as a company town of the E.I. Dupont de Nemours Company on 3,600 acres which surrounded its explosives factory. It is on the site of old Fort Nisqually established in 1833 by the Hudson's Bay Company, the remnants of which, rebuilt, are on display at Tacoma's Point Defiance Park. **Carbonado** (incorporated in 1948) was named for the Carbon River on which coal was found in 1876, and was a company town operated by the Pacific Coast Coal Company. **Wilkeson** (incorporated in 1909) was named for Samuel Wilkeson, secretary of the Northern Pacific Railroad whose company began mining coal there in 1878. **Roy** (incorporated in 1908) was platted in 1884 by James McNaught who named it for his son. **South Prairie** (incorporated in 1909) was so named by first settler Paul Emery because it was south of Connell and Porter prairies. The village was established as Melrose in 1884, and platted by Frank Bisson in 1888 when its original name was restored.

Almost 60 percent (292,054) of Pierce County's residents live in unincorporated areas which include several major population centers such as **Parkland,** which grew up around Pacific Lutheran University; **Lakeview,** which began in 1896 as a railroad station near a small lake; **Lakewood Center,** planned as a shopping complex in a wooded residential area in the American and Gravelly lakes district; **Midland,** the midway station on the Tacoma-Puyallup electric rail line of the 1890s; **Summit,** the high point on the

Opposite: *This view of the Tacoma tideflats with Mt. Rainier in the background was taken from the old City Hall in 1897. (MOHAI)*

Right: *Tacoma's castle-like Tourist Hotel partially burned in 1896 while being built by the Northern Pacific Railroad. By 1906 the hulk had been transformed into Stadium High School. Four years later adjacent "Old Woman's Gulch" had been reconstructed as a magnificent natural stadium. On dedication day, seen here, 7,000 students danced before 25,000 spectators. Courtesy, Special Collections Division, University of Washington Libraries*

same rail line; **Anderson Island,** named by the 1841 Wilkes Expedition for the chief trader of the Hudson's Bay Company at Fort Nisqually; **Fox Island,** named by Wilkes for J.L. Fox, the expedition's assistant surgeon; **McNeil Island,** named by Wilkes for William Henry McNeill [sic], Boston-born captain of the *Beaver,* the Hudson's Bay Company steamer. In 1869, the U.S. Corps of Engineers erected a jail there and in 1909 the jail became a federal prison, and more recently a state institution.

Above: *The historic ship* Constitution *sailed around the country in the early 1930s. In June 1933, she stopped at Tacoma. Courtesy, Special Collections Division, University of Washington Libraries*

SAN JUAN COUNTY

Population (1983): 8,700 (the least populous of the state's thirty-nine counties)

Area: 179 square miles (smallest county in the state)

Employment: Services, government, and retail trade are the major employers. Tourists, yachters, summer and retirement dwellers provide much of the business. Some of the smaller islands are privately owned.

San Juan County, formed in 1873 from part of Jefferson County, includes 172 named islands and 300 tide-washed rocks, the tops of a submerged mountain chain. The highest peak is the 2,409-foot Mt. Constitution.

Three nationalities plus the Native Americans have named these islands. The Spanish explorer Lopez de Haro discovered the island group in 1791. He was under the command of Francisco Eliza, who sailed under the authority of the Viceroy of Mexico, one Señor Don Juan Vicente de Guemes Pacheco de Padilla Horcasitas y Aguayo. Eliza, with an eye to future patronage, named the chain "Isla y Archiepelago de San Juan." He and his colleagues, as they named the various islands, used portions of the viceroy's name, honored each other, or appended geographical descriptives.

The British arrived next. George Vancouver and the Hudson's Bay Company supplied such names as Strawberry Bay and Colville Island.

Then came Charles Wilkes, the U.S. Navy commander of the American Survey Expedition of 1841. Perhaps unaware of the Spanish charts, a worshiper of heroes of the War of 1812 and of the efforts to quell the Barbary pirates, he renamed the islands the "Navy Archipelago" and supplied each of the major ones with the name of a U.S. Navy hero.

In 1847, the British admiralty directed Captain Henry Kellett to rework the charts to clear up the confusion and the duplicate names. Kellett, as might be expected, dropped many of Wilkes' names and reinstated the original Spanish titles.

As a result, names in Canadian waters have an English-Spanish flavor; in upper Puget Sound (including San Juan County) the Spanish, American, and English influences are apparent; and in lower Puget Sound, the names display a predominantly American flavor along with many American Indian names.

The pioneers on the islands farmed, grazed animals, especially sheep, and logged the islands. At one time several sawmills were operating, producing in 1892 nearly three million board feet of lumber.

Friday Harbor *(1983 population: 1,203; incorporated 1909)* The county seat, Friday Harbor, is the only incorporated town in the islands. It was named by a British ship captain who stopped in the bay to ask an old Kanaka sheepherder in the employ of the Hudson's Bay Company the name of the inlet. The Kanaka indicated he did not know. The captain then asked him his name and he responded, "Friday." The captain thereby named the inlet "Friday Harbor."

Roche Harbor This unincorporated resort community at the northwest end of San Juan Island was named for Richard Roche who served under British Captain Henry Kellett in 1846. The Hudson's Bay Company established a trading post there in 1850. From 1882 to 1956 it was the site of the Roche Harbor Lime and Cement Company, at times the largest producer of lime west of the Mississippi. The town was developed by the company under John S. McMillan, a former Tacoma attorney who entertained many dignitaries, including President Theodore Roosevelt, at his Afterglow Manor.

Among the larger islands are:

Blakely, named in 1841 by the Wilkes Expedition to honor Johnston Blakely, American naval hero of the War of 1812

Clark, named by Wilkes after Midshipman John Clark killed in the Battle of Lake Erie during the War of 1812

Decatur, named by Wilkes for Steven Decatur, one of the most famous naval heroes of the War of 1812

Henry, named by Wilkes in honor of Wilkes Henry, his nephew, who was killed by natives while the expedition was in Fiji

James, named by Wilkes for Reuben James, a sailor who saved Steven Decatur's life by moving in front of his commander to receive the blow of a Turk's saber

Jones, named by Wilkes to honor Jacob Jones, naval hero of the *Wasp* in the War of 1812

Lopez, third largest of the islands, named for the Spanish explorer Lopez Gonzales de Haro, reputedly the discoverer of the archipelago

Matia, (pronounced MAY-shuh), really several islands which Eliza shows on his charts as "Isla de Mata" or "Brush Island"

Orcas, largest of the San Juans, takes one of the names of the Spanish viceroy and/or the name of a vessel in the Spanish fleet, "Boca de Horcasitas," with the "h" omitted. The mansion of Seattle shipbuilder Robert Moran is located on the island, as is 5,000-acre Moran State Park.

Patos means "duck" in Spanish. A lighthouse is located here, for this is the northernmost of the American San Juans.

San Juan, the second largest island takes the name given the archipelago by Eliza. Here the University of Washington Biological Laboratory operates. And the San Juan National Historical Park, established in 1966, marks the site of the English camp and the American camp during the years when the island's ownership was in question.

Satellite, named for the British ship of that name commanded by James Charles Prevost, British commissioner during the San Juan boundary dispute.

Shaw, named by Wilkes for navy captain John D. Shaw, who served prominently in the 1815 war against Algiers and the pirates.

Speiden, named by Wilkes for one of the expedition's pursers.

Stuart, named by Wilkes to honor Frederick D. Stuart, captain's clerk of the 1841 expedition.

Sucia, named by Eliza in 1791. The name in Spanish means "dirty" or "foul" in the sense that the word means "reefy" or "unsafe" for ships.

Waldron, named by Wilkes to honor either Thomas Waldron, captain's clerk on the ship *Porpoise,* or R.R. Waldron, purser on the *Vincennes.* Both vessels were on the Wilkes' expedition.

Unincorporated Roche Harbor on San Juan Island is seen as it appeared in 1920. Courtesy, Special Collections Division, University of Washington Libraries

SKAGIT COUNTY

Population (1983): 66,100 (seventh among the twelve Puget Sound counties)

Area: 1,735 square miles (sixth largest of the twelve counties)

Employment: The five major industries by employment percentage are government (local, state, and federal), 21 percent; retail trade, 19 percent; manufacturing, 16 percent; services, 16 percent; and agriculture, forestry; and fishing, 10 percent.

Skagit County was created out of southern Whatcom County in 1883 and was named for the river and the Indian tribe. The county includes Fidalgo and Guemes islands.

Incorporated cities include:

Mt. Vernon *(1983 population: 13,600; incorporated 1890)* The first settler was Joseph Dwelly in 1870-1871. The community developed in 1877 as a trading post on the Skagit River under proprietors E.C. English and Harrison Clothier; they named the settlement for the Potomac River estate of George Washington. Mt. Vernon was chosen the seat of government when the county was formed.

Anacortes *(1983 population: 9,425; incorporated 1891)* Located on Fidalgo Island, this city was originally called Snip Harbor. In 1876 the name was changed by Amos Bowman, who platted and promoted the town. He created a Spanish-sounding name based on the maiden name of his wife, Anna Curtis. Anacortes has oil refineries and pulp mills.

Sedro Woolley *(1983 population: 6,225; incorporated 1898)* The first settlers, David Batey and Joseph Hart, came to the area in 1878. In 1884 they sold forty of their acres to Mortimer Cook, who laid out a townsite which he named "Bug." The women of the town were horrified at the appellation and suggested the Spanish word "cedro" be substituted, meaning "cedar" for nearby Cedar Mountain. But they misspelled it as "sedro." The town prospered during a gold rush that followed, and in 1889 the Great

Northern Railroad established a junction north of Sedro. There P.A. Woolley developed a townsite bearing his name. The next year, the towns incorporated as Sedro-Woolley, though the hyphen was soon forgotten.

Burlington *(1983 population: 3,820; incorporated 1902)* In 1882 the town developed as a logging camp established by John P. Millett and William McKay. Washington State is a leading producer of flower bulbs—iris, tulips, and narcissus—most of them grown on the Skagit Delta about Burlington.

La Conner *(1983 population: 645; incorporated 1883)* This small community, which straddles Swinomish Slough, was started in 1867 as a trading post called Swinomish by Alonzo Lowe. In 1869 he sold out to John S. Conner, who named the post office La Conner after his wife Louisa Anne Conner, using the initials of her first two names and her last name.

Concrete *(1983 population: 570; incorporated 1909)* The first settlers in 1875 were two prospectors, Amasa Everett and John Rowley. The town was platted by Magnus Miller in 1890 and called "Baker" after a nearby stream. In 1891, Amasa Everett discovered the limestone deposits that developed into the town's major industry. For a time the village was known as "Cement City." This was changed to "Concrete" when the town was incorporated.

Lyman *(1983 population: 240; incorporated 1909)* The town received a post office in 1880, which was given the name of its first postmaster, B.L. Lyman. In 1884 the town was platted by Otto Klement.

Hamilton *(1983 population: 220; incorporated 1891)* The town was named for William Hamilton, the first settler, who arrived in 1877.

Fidalgo and **Guemes** islands both carry names supplied by the Spanish explorer Eliza in 1791.

This 1909 view is of La Conner from across Swinomish Slough. Courtesy, Special Collections Division, University of Washington Libraries

The school board of Anacortes met, in the early years of the century, in this room. Anacortes was originally called Ship Harbor, and remains to this day a small, working mill town. Courtesy, Special Collections Division, University of Washington Libraries

SNOHOMISH COUNTY

Population (1983): 360,900 (third most populous of the twelve Puget Sound counties)

Area: 2,098 square miles (third largest of the Puget Sound counties)

Employment: Manufacturing, much of it lumber, pulp paper, and aerospace, accounts for about 30 percent of employment. Retail trade employs 19 percent of the work force, all governments 17 percent, services 16 percent, construction 5 percent, and transportation and public utilities 5 percent.

The territorial legislature established Snohomish County in January of 1861 following receipt of a petition sent by Emory C. Ferguson and others to Olympia requesting the mainland portion of Island County be formed into a separate county. The name they suggested was that of the principal settlement, Snohomish City, which Ferguson had founded. The local Snohomish Indian tribe provided the name not only for the town but for the river and the county as well.

Incorporated cities in Snohomish County are:

Everett *(1983 population: 56,200; incorporated 1893)* Everett developed late but quickly became the county's largest city. Henry Hewitt, Jr., and Wyatt J. Rucker of Tacoma both had plans to develop an industrial city on Port Gardner Bay. They soon joined forces. Hewitt, the son of a Wisconsin lumber baron and himself a successful Tacoma lumberman with Eastern connections, quickly involved such investors as Walter Oakes, president of the Northern Pacific Railroad; Colgate Hoyt, a director of the Northern Pacific Railroad; Charles L. Colby, a New York banker, investor, and board member of the Northern Pacific (the town was named for his son, Everett); C.W. Wetmore, a New York capitalist and shipbuilder; and John D. Rockefeller, then the richest man in America. But in the recession of the 1890s, Rockefeller became disenchanted and sold his share of the holdings. James J. Hill, president of the Great Northern Railroad, then took over as the major developer. He sold 900,000 acres of railroad timberland to his St. Paul neighbor, Frederick Weyerhaeuser, who by 1903 had moved west and built a large sawmill on the Everett waterfront.

Today, Everett is home to not only sawmills but to several high-tech firms and a Boeing plant that employs more than 10,000.

Edmonds *(1983 population: 27,000; incorporated 1890)* Pleasant H. Ewell first settled in the area in 1866. He sold his claim to Frost and Fowler, merchants of Mukilteo, who sold to George Brackett. It was Brackett who in 1872 platted and named the town after Senator Edmunds of Vermont, but the handwriting was misread by the postal authorities who called the post office "Edmonds."

Lynnwood *(1983 population: 23,000; incorporated 1959)* This city, the third largest in the county, is one of the newest. Until after the Second World War it was merely a crossroads. Then, as surburbs began to sprawl north from Seattle, it blossomed. The name combines the first name of Lynn Oburn, wife of one of the promoters, with a suffix that indicates the sylvan surroundings.

Mountlake Terrace *(1983 population: 16,000; incorporated 1954)* This is another town that developed after the war as a rapidly expanding area of housing tracts. The name comes from the views of mountain and lake.

Marysville *(1983 population: 6,275; incorporated 1891)* The town's first settler was J.P. Comeford, an Indian agent on the Tulalip Reservation. He bought the land in 1872 and five years later was operating a store and wharf on Ebey Slough. Others who followed included James Johnson and Thomas Lloyd, who suggested that the new community be named for their former homes in Marysville, California.

Snohomish *(1983 population: 5,450; incorporated 1883)* This oldest of Snohomish County towns was founded in the early 1860s by E.C. Ferguson and E.F. Cady as a trading post on the river to serve both local settlers and the commerce flowing up and down the Snoqualmie and Snohomish rivers. At first called Cadyville, it was later called Snohomish City, then simply Snohomish. Until 1894, when Everett wrested it away, Snohomish was the seat of county government.

Mukilteo *(1983 population: 4,670; incorporated 1947)* Originally known as Point Elliott, the town was founded by J.D. Fowler and Morris H. Frost who were partners in a trading post and store. In 1862, Fowler was named postmaster and adopted as the name of the post office a variation of an Indian word meaning "good camping ground."

Mill Creek *(1983 population: 3,355; incorporated 1983)* This town is so new that it shows on few maps. It is a development of fine homes and condominiums around a golf course, clubhouse, and other amenities.

Arlington *(1983 population: 3,330; incorporated 1903)* Originally a logging community called "The Forks" for the confluence of the rivers near there, the first plat developed was that of Maurice Haller in 1883. He named it "Haller City" in honor of his father, Major Granville O. Haller. A competing village was laid out by J.W. McCloud, a railroad contractor, which he called "Arlington," an often used name in America which stems from Lord Henry Arlington, cabinet minister to Charles II of England. Later the Arlington investors bought out Haller.

Brier *(1983 population: 3,210; incorporated 1965)* One of the newer municipalities, Brier adopted the name of a street that ran through the community.

Monroe *(1983 population: 3,000; incorporated 1903)* In 1878, Salem Wood established a community called "Park Place." John Vanasdlen opened a store and applied for a post office, for which he submitted the name of "Monroe" after the President. The town later was moved about a mile in order to be adjacent to Great Northern tracks being constructed through the area. In so doing, Monroe supplanted a tiny settlement known as Tye or Wales. Monroe is now the site of the State Reformatory.

Lake Stevens *(1983 population: 1,720; incorporated 1960)* The lake was named for Governor Isaac Stevens in 1859. The town that developed took the name of the lake.

Stanwood *(1983 population: 1,660; incorporated 1903)* The city began as a trading post in 1866 on marshland near the mouth of the Stillaguamish River. The name of the community that developed, "Centerville," was changed in 1877 when merchant D.O. Pearson was named postmaster and rechristened the settlement with his wife Clara's maiden name.

Sultan *(1983 population: 1,656; incorporated 1905)* is named for the river, which was named for an Indian chief "Tseul-tud." The town developed in the early 1880s after gold was found in the river nearby.

Darrington *(1983 population: 1,020; incorporated 1945)* A logging community in the Cascade foothills, the city was named to honor an early resident whose name was "Barrington." But postal authorities misread the first letter of the name on the post office application, and it became "Darrington" instead.

Granite Falls *(1983 population: 890; incorporated 1903)* This quiet community was named for the falls in the nearby granite rock canyon of the Stillaguamish River.

Woodway *(1983 population: 860; incorporated 1958)* This new community of fine homes just south of Edmonds was named for its tree-lined roads and large forested lots.

Gold Bar *(1983 population: 850; incorporated 1910)* When gold was found on a nearby bar in 1869, the settlement received its name. The town was platted and formally named in 1900 by the Gold Bar Improvement Company.

Index *(1983 population: 135; incorporated 1907)* One of the gateway cities to Stevens Pass, Index was named for the neighboring peak, which resembles an index finger.

Everett's Port Gardner Bay is pictured here in 1899. Courtesy, Special Collections Division, University of Washington Libraries

This monument commemorating the landing of Captain George Vancouver was erected in 1915 by the Daughters of the American Revolution. It stands in Everett's Grand Avenue Park not far from the home of the late Senator Henry M. Jackson. Courtesy, Special Collections Division, University of Washington Libraries

THURSTON COUNTY

Population (1983): 133,500 (fifth largest among the twelve Puget Sound counties)

Area: 727 square miles (ninth largest of the twelve Puget Sound counties)

Employment: More than 40 percent of the jobs in Thurston County (location of the state capital) are in local, state and federal government positions. Services and retail trade each account for about 17 percent, manufacturing 7 percent, finance, insurance, and real estate together employ about 4 percent.

In April 1852, the Oregon territorial legislature established the first counties on Puget Sound. Thurston at first stretched from Pacific County to Canada and from the Cascades to the sea, and encompassed most of present Western Washington including all of Puget Sound. Originally to be called Simmons County for Michael Simmons, the first settler on the Sound, it was decided instead to honor the first delegate from Oregon Territory, Samuel Thurston, an anti-Hudson's Bay Company activist who died while on his way home after serving in the nation's capital. The next winter, Isaac N. Ebey, the only legislator from north of the Columbia, convinced the Oregon legislature to carve four new counties from north Thurston—Pierce, King, Jefferson, and Island. Their areas, too, were originally larger than at present and would be diminished as more counties were established.

Thurston County was the site of many "firsts" in the history of Puget Sound including the first American settlement, the first newspaper, the first and only location of the legislature, and for many years it was the most populous of Puget Sound counties. Settlers at the southern end of Puget Sound soon were harvesting the heavy timber, as did settlers elsewhere. Logging was for many years the major industry and in 1890 seven sawmills in Thurston County cut 36.5 million board feet and twelve shingle mills turned out 142 million shingles. Coal was dug from the earth in several places and limestone was quarried near Tenino. Shellfish were harvested in quantity including the succulent tiny Olympia oyster.

Olympia *(1983 population: 28,000; incorporated 1859)* Named county seat as well as state capital, Olympia was the largest city on the Sound for many years.

In 1846 Levi Lathrop Smith took a land claim on Budd Inlet while his partner Edmund Sylvester settled on Chambers Prairie. Two years later Smith died (he suffered from epilepsy) and Sylvester, by previous agreement, took over his claim. In 1850,

Sylvester had the township platted, then replatted, and it was named Olympia at the suggestion of Colonel Isaac Eby, though two others are also given credit in some of the history books. The name is said to originate from the Olympic Mountains and from a book Ebey had in his library by an author named Olympia Fulvia Morata. The Olympics, in turn, take their name from Mt. Olympus, so named by British Captain John Meares in 1778 after the ancient Greek home of the gods.

When Governor Isaac Stevens' wife and family came to Olympia late in 1854, they were not enthralled at what they saw. Their son Hazard later described the scene:

A low, flat neck of land, running into the bay; down it stretched the narrow muddy track, winding among the stumps which stood thickly on either side; twenty small wooden houses bordered the road, while back of them on the left and next to the shore were a number of Indian lodges, with canoes drawn up on the beach, and Indian dogs running about.

The Northern Pacific Railroad, as it built north from Portland, passed Olympia by; but the townsfolk, though it took them five years, built a ten-mile spur line to connect at Tenino.

Other incorporated towns in Thurston County are:

Lacey *(1983 population: 14,030; incorporated 1966)* This suburb of Olympia was originally named Woodland after Isaac Wood who settled there in 1852. By 1890, Lacey had two large sawmills, a resort hotel, and the region's biggest horseracing track. When a post office was requested, federal authorities refused the name Woodland since another town so named already existed. Wood's attorney, O.C. Lacey, who owned land in the area, then substituted his own name. The Catholic Benedictine Order established St. Martin's College there in 1893.

Tumwater *(1983 population: 7,050; incorporated 1869)* Located on the falls of the Deschutes River, Tumwater is the oldest American settlement on Puget Sound. The Indians called the falls "spa-kwatl" meaning waterfalls. The French voyageurs of the Hudson's Bay Company called them "deschutes" which means "falls" in French. Company Englishmen called them "Puget Sound Falls." Wilkes referred to them as "Shutes River Falls." Michael Simmons, leader of the Americans who settled there in 1845, called his settlement "New Market, " and later "Tumwater" which reflected the Chinook jargon word for the falls, which the Indians thought emitted a sound not unlike the throb of the human heart, "thum-thum."

Tenino *(1983 population: 1,400; incorporated 1906)* Tenino was established in the 1870s as a railroad construction camp. The name probably derived from an Indian word meaning "junction," for here an early military road forked from an Indian trail. Some say the name derived from an early railroad engine numbered 10-9-0. Nearby are the Mima or Tenino mounds. The origin of these thousands of gravel humps from six to seven feet in diameter is unknown, though the accepted theory is that they resulted from some sort of glacial activity.

Yelm *(1983 population: 1,390; incorporated 1924)* The name comes from an Indian word meaning "heat waves rising from the earth." James Longmire, who came over Naches Pass with the first immigrant train in 1853, settled near there.

Rainier *(1983 population: 992; incorporated 1947)* The town is named for nearby Mount Rainier.

Bucoda *(1983 population: 540; incorporated 1910)* Aaron Webster first settled in the area and built a sawmill in 1854. He sold out to Oliver Shead who named the village Seatco. Here the Territorial Penitentiary was located from 1874 to 1888. Samuel Coulter bought the site and involved Portland capitalist John B. David and railroad superintendent J.M. Buckley. The name was changed in 1890 to use the first syllables of their three last names—*Bu-Co-Da.*

In the temporary state capital at Olympia on November 18, 1889, Elisha P. Ferry was inaugurated as the first governor of Washington Territory. No newcomer to the position, he had served two terms as the appointed governor of the Territory of Washington. Courtesy, Special Collections Division, University of Washington Libraries

WHATCOM COUNTY

Population (1983): 112,100 (ranking sixth of the twelve Puget Sound counties)
Area: 2,125 square miles (second largest on the Sound)

Employment: More than 40 percent of the jobs are in retail trade and services. Manufacturing accounts for 18.7 percent and local, state, and federal government for 18 percent of all jobs. Construction, transportation, and public utilities; finance, insurance, and real estate; and agriculture, forestry, and fishing employ about 4 percent each.

Whatcom County's first settler was Captain William R. Pattle who, in 1852, while seeking spar timber growing near the water, found a seam of coal on the beach of Bellingham Bay. He and two companions, James Morrison and John Thomas, immediately staked out donation claims. That same year, Henry Hewitt, William Brown, Henry Roeder, R.V. Peabody, William Utter, and H.C. Page arrived on a San Francisco schooner intent on funding new homes on Puget Sound. Soon a mill was operating which at-

tracted others and the settlement that developed was called "Whatcom," after a Nooksack Indian chief whose name supposedly was translated as "noisy water."

Later settlements named Sehome and Fairhaven were established nearby, all to later consolidate as Bellingham.

The first territorial legislature in March 1854, created Whatcom County from part of Island County and originally included San Juan Island in the new county.

In 1857, the Fraser River gold rush brought tens of thousands of gold seekers through the area. San Francisco merchants flocked to Bellingham Bay to set up general stores and other supply centers, many

The town of Whatcom, shown in this 1888 sketch, later was incorporated as part of Bellingham. Courtesy, Special Collections Division, University of Washington Libraries

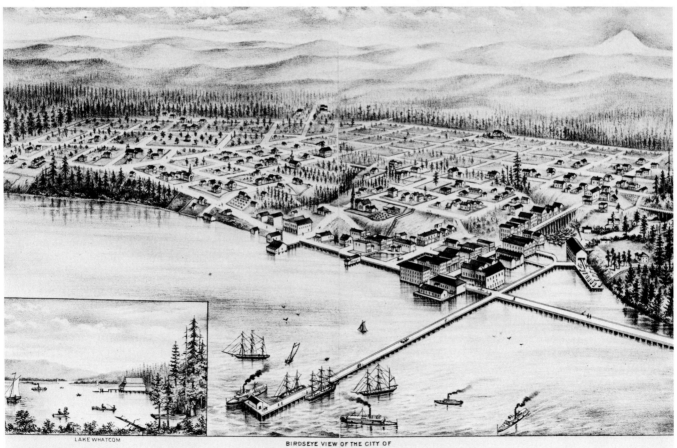

LAKE WHATCOM

BIRDSEYE VIEW OF THE CITY OF
WHATCOM, WASHINGTON TERRITORY.
1888.

The mills of Bellingham were busy in 1950 when this photograph was taken. Courtesy, Special Collections Division, University of Washington Libraries

of them in tents, to serve the miners. But gold was found only in small quantities and the rush fizzled out. The region, however, was so agreeable and promising that many of the prospectors decided to remain.

By the 1890s, this most northerly of Puget Sound counties was traversed by the Great Northern, a branch of the Canadian Pacific and the Seattle Lake Shore and Eastern railways, all three of which met at New Whatcom and Fairhaven. The county seat was established at New Whatcom, which boasted a population of 7,500. It is now part of Bellingham, which is still the seat of government.

Seven incorporated cities are located in Whatcom County.

Bellingham *(1983 population: 45,900; incorporated 1904)* In the half century following settlement of Bellingham Bay, several adjacent communities developed. At different times, as separate or consolidated entities, the towns were named Whatcom, Sehome, New Whatcom, Pattle's Point, Unionville, (Old) Bellingham, and Fairhaven. They were consolidated as

Bellingham in 1904.

Bellingham was named for the bay on which it is located which, in turn, was named by George Vancouver in 1791 for Sir William Bellingham, controller of the British Navy storekeeper accounts, who personally checked Vancouver's supplies prior to the expedition leaving England.

Ferndale *(1983 population: 4,390; incorporated 1907)* In 1872, after fifteen families had settled in the area, a schoolhouse was erected amidst a cluster of giant ferns. The schoolteacher, a Miss Eldridge, is credited with naming the school "Ferndale." The name was later picked up by the city.

Lynden *(1983 population: 4,220; incorporated 1891)* First settled in 1869, the town was named by Mrs. Phoebe N. Judson, the first white woman to live there, who recalled the poetic line by Thomas Campbell in his poem "Hohenlinden" which begins: "On Linden, when the sun was low. . ." She substituted "y" for "i" because she thought it looked prettier. Lynden is in the heart of a poultry raising and dairying region.

Blaine *(1983 population: 2,390; incorporated 1890)* Site of the Peace Arch Park, this border city was platted in 1884 as "Concord," but the following year its staunch Republican residents named it for James G. Blaine, who was Secretary of State under President Garfield and the unsuccessful Republican candidate for President the year of Blaine's incorporation.

Everson *(1983 population: 1,000; incorporated 1929)* The city was named for Ever Everson, first white settler north of the Nooksack River.

Sumas *(1983 population: 781; incorporated 1891)* Like Blaine, Sumas is an international boundary town. Its name is a Cowichan Indian word meaning "big level opening."

Nooksack *(1983 population: 503; incorporated 1912)* This town (and river) took the name of an Indian tribe which is said to mean "people who eat fern root."

Point Roberts The point, named by Captain Vancouver in 1792 for Captain Henry Roberts of the British navy, became the site of an unusual geographic occurance when the boundary was established between Canada and the United States. This small tip of a peninsula that extends down below the 49th parallel is actually part of Whatcom County, but is accessible only by passing through both U.S. and Canadian customs.

Lummi Island and **Lummi Peak** (1,650 feet high) are the ancestral homes of the Lummi Indian tribe whose reservation is on the adjacent mainland.

Mt. Rainier provides a dramatic backdrop for Gig Harbor on eastern Puget Sound. Discovered in 1841 on the Charles Wilkes expedition, Gig Harbor was pronounced an "excellent little Bay" by one of Wilkes' midshipmen. Later, Scandinavian and Slavic immigrants developed a fishing village of the same name. Photo by Rollin Geppart

Above: *Schoolchildren enjoy tours of Tacoma's Ft. Nisqually, earliest pioneer settlement on Puget Sound and outpost of the region's important fur trade. Photo by Rollin Geppart*

Right: *The Brigade Encampment, an annual event at Ft. Nisqually, re-creates the celebration held at the return of the fur brigades from their season of hunting. Photo by Rollin Geppart*

Opposite: *This historic home in Steilacoom was built by E.R. Rogers, one of the town's early merchants. The house was completed in 1891, but two years later Rogers was forced to sell it because of the financial crisis known as the Panic of 1893. Now restored and functioning as a restaurant, the home is listed on the National Register of Historic Places. Photo by Rollin Geppart*

Opposite, above: *Peace Lutheran Church in Silvana, the "Little White Church on the Hill," was completed by early settlers in 1890. It is the second oldest church building in Washington, and has been designated a state historical site. Photo by Rollin Geppart*

Opposite, below: *This recently restored home in Coupeville, known as the Kineth House, was built in 1887 as a retirement home for the John Kineth family, who owned a farm west of town. The home is located on Ebey's Landing National Historical Reserve. Photo by Rollin Geppart*

Above: *The Paradise Inn in Mt. Rainier National Park has provided lodging in this magnificent setting since 1917. Photo by Rollin Geppart*

Left: *The abundant waters of the Sound continue to reward the region's enthusiastic anglers. Courtesy, Seattle/King County Convention & Visitors Bureau*

Below: *Spectators watch as shells return from a race on the Lake Washington Ship Canal in Seattle. The University of Washington is a frequent contender in major crew competitions. Photo by Jennifer Schoewe*

Opposite: *The rivers of the Puget Sound region offer ample recreational opportunities. Here rafters prepare to take on the Skagit River, one of the principal streams that flows from the Cascades into the Sound. Photo by Rollin Geppart*

Above: *Back yards lead right to the water along Cooper Point, viewed here from Budd Inlet. Photo by Rollin Geppart*

Right: *Weekend windsurfers are drawn to the peaceful waters of Budd Inlet. Photo by Rollin Geppart*

Opposite: *Sailing the inland sea is a favorite pastime for Puget Sound residents, who claim the largest per capita boat ownership in the world. Photo by Rollin Geppart*

Left: *Deceptively tranquil Deception Pass at the north end of Whidbey Island is known for its narrow, intricate channel and treacherous tides. Photo by Rollin Geppart*

Opposite: *The late afternoon sun casts a warm glow over picturesque Hicks Lake at Lacey, a suburb of Olympia. Photo by Rollin Geppart*

Below: *On the islands and lowlands of Puget Sound the various native conifers form an undulating green sea. In the foreground is foxglove, an omnipresent perennial. Photo by Jennifer Schoewe*

Left: *A field of mustard in full bloom provides a dazzling foreground for this country church near Mt. Vernon. Photo by Rollin Geppart*

Below: *Tulip farms in the Skagit Valley create spectacular springtime color. The flowers are grown primarily for their bulbs, which are distributed throughout the United States. Photo by Rollin Geppart*

Above: Fresh-from-the-field flowers are sold at roadside stands in the Skagit Valley, a popular weekend destination for city dwellers. Photo by Rollin Geppart

Top: *Daffodils contrast brilliantly with tulips on this flower farm near Mt. Vernon, site of an annual tulip festival. Photo by Rollin Geppart*

Right: *The Tacoma Narrows Bridge, at 4,200 feet long, was the fourth longest suspension bridge in the world when it opened in October 1950 to replace "Galloping Gertie," the bridge that collapsed ten years earlier. Now part of State Route 16, the bridge connects Tacoma with the Olympic Peninsula. Photo by Rollin Geppart*

Below: *The Tacoma Dome, completed in 1983, has brought new vitality to Tacoma's city center. At fifteen stories high with five acres of space under its dome, the versatile structure features sports events, concerts, and exhibitions of all types, and has attracted many famous personalities from Bruce Springsteen to Billy Graham. Photo by Rollin Geppart*

Above: *The charming waterfront town of La Conner is situated on the eastern portion of the Swinomish Channel in Skagit County. Once a trading post, this historic community has in recent years become a weekend getaway for urbanites. Photo by Rollin Geppart*

Right: *A solitary fisherman finds seclusion beneath the graceful arch of Rainbow Bridge in La Conner. Photo by Jennifer Schoewe*

Above: *Besides being the state capital, Olympia is a deepwater port and still a vital commercial shipping center, particularly for the region's logging industry. Its location on sheltered Budd Inlet makes it an ideal spot for pleasure boating as well. Photo by Rollin Geppart*

Opposite: *The State Capitol at Olympia, with its landscaped grounds and impressive dome, is a year-round tourist attraction. Photo by Jennifer Schoewe*

Right: *The Old Capitol Building in downtown Olympia opened its doors in 1892 as the Thurston County Courthouse. It was purchased in 1901 as the state capitol, and was used until the present domed structure was completed in 1935. Still used for state offices, the recently refurbished Old Capitol Building is listed on both the state and national registers of historic places. Photo by Rollin Geppart*

Above: *Seattle's Pioneer Square and its adjacent park are favorite attractions for Seattleites and tourists alike. Courtesy, Seattle/ King County Convention & Visitors Bureau*

Left: *The University of Washington Arboretum displays native Northwest ornamental plants as well as numerous exotic species. The Japanese garden is a favorite feature of the Arboretum, which is open to the public year round. Courtesy, Seattle/King County Convention & Visitors Bureau*

Above: *The Museum of Flight, which is devoted to the history of aviation, is located at the south end of Boeing field. Pictured here (center) is the Stearman PT-13A, built in 1937. At left is the Boeing Model 100-P12, built in 1929. Photo by Rollin Geppart*

Left: *The opening day of boating season is celebrated in Seattle each May with crew races, fireworks, and a gathering of over 2,000 boats on Lake Washington and the locks. Many celebrate the day in appropriate costume. Photo by Jennifer Schoewe*

Opposite, top: *Volunteer Park is home to the Conservatory and the Seattle Art Museum. Here a woman sits in front of a sculpture titled "Black Sun" by Isamu Noguchi. Photo by Jennifer Schoewe*

Opposite, bottom: *Montlake Bridge in Seattle opens to make way for a passing sailboat. Courtesy, Seattle/King County Visitors & Convention Bureau*

Left: *The Seattle Center is the scene of annual events such as the Bumbershoot Festival featuring arts and crafts and entertainment, and the Folk Life Festival, which celebrates the city's diverse ethnic cultures. Courtesy, Seattle/King County Convention & Visitors Bureau*

Opposite: *Seattle's skyline takes on a luminous quality at dusk. Courtesy, Seattle/King County Convention & Visitors Bureau*

Below: *The Pickle Family Circus, originally presented as a benefit, has become a popular summertime event held on the grounds of St. Mark's Episcopal Cathedral in Seattle. Photo by Jennifer Schoewe*

The Seattle Center, legacy of the successful Century 21 Exposition held in 1962, has become a symbol of vitality and progress in the Puget Sound region. Pictured here is the International Fountain with the Space Needle in the background. Photo by Rollin Geppart

9 Partners in Progress

The following pages provide a fleeting synopsis of the men and women who gambled their futures on the promise of boundless opportunity in the vast, untamed wilderness of the Puget Sound.

From the womb of this unforgiving land, these hardy pioneers established the businesses from which this entire region has based its past, its present, and its future. These individuals created the stimulus for the ongoing growth and development that makes the Puget Sound an exciting and dynamic place.

Establishing this area's economic base was not an easy assignment. The first entrepreneurs to settle on the Sound were courageous and enduring people. Many a young pioneer saw his dream end there at the edge of the Pacific Ocean. Those who were defeated often returned to their homes with much thinner wallets. However, just as many pioneers saw their dreams become reality in this new land. Those people stayed on in triumph and watched their fortunes grow through hard work and determination.

Pioneer businesses faced an endless array of challenges. Indian wars, a civil war, and foreign wars tore at the fabric of the new communities. Difficult transportation routes, poor communication, and crude technology made progress slow and cumbersome. Devastating financial busts and great depressions assailed the very foundations of the new ventures. Only extraordinary determination and undying hope could provide the strength required to tame the Puget Sound.

Slowly the businesses took hold and turned each battle into a victory. Roads were cut through thick wilderness. The shipping industry boomed, and the railroads arrived. The territory became a state, and a legal system was established. Schools and churches were founded in ever-increasing numbers. People poured into the area. Some were on their way to the Alaskan goldfields, others were simply striving to find a better life for themselves. All found that a new life and unlimited opportunity awaited those who remained on the shores of the beautiful Puget Sound.

This influx of people brought additional industries and the expansion of those already established. As businesses multiplied, Puget Sound became an economic force, and its cities grew at unprecedented speed.

Today on the Sound there is a new breed of business. Many local companies are national or international in scope. Some have histories that date back to those early days, while others have just begun. Whatever their story, common threads of determination and dedication still remain intricately entwined in the foundation of every one.

The organizations whose stories are detailed on the following pages have chosen to support this important literary and civic project. They illustrate the variety of ways in which individuals and their businesses have contributed to the area's growth and development. The civic involvement of Puget Sound's businesses, institutions of learning, and local government, in cooperation with its citizens, has made the region an excellent place in which to live and work.

MUSEUM OF HISTORY AND INDUSTRY

The Seattle Historical Society came into being on November 13, 1911, when Mrs. Morgan Carkeek invited some of her friends to lunch, during which they discussed preservation of local heritage. Emily Carkeek, raised in Bath, England, had always admired the museums of her home country and believed the time was ripe for Seattleites to begin preserving their history. Since the city had been founded only fifty-nine years previously, some of the original pioneers were still alive. The artifacts, memorabilia, and photographs of the earliest days were available in great quantity.

On January 8, 1914, the historical society was incorporated and immediately the historical objects began to arrive. Soon thousands of items were stored in boxes in attics, garages, empty offices, and elsewhere. Obviously a museum building was needed.

Morgan Carkeek, when he gave the original Carkeek Park to Seattle, had stipulated the museum

The Museum of History and Industry was started by this group of women who attended the first Founder's Day celebration at Emily Carkeek's home on November 13, 1911. Courtesy, the Museum of History and Industry

should be built there. But in 1926 that property was taken over by the Navy and became the site of Sand Point Naval Air Station. Carkeek then donated property farther north, the city park that today bears his name. Because it seemed far from downtown, the historical society board began to look for a site nearer the city center.

The Carkeeks' daughter, Mrs. Theodore Plestcheeff, who served as society president for many years, and a couple of her friends discovered the present site of the museum on the edge of the arboretum. Several businessmen, including H.W. McCurdy, joined in the effort to raise the funding for a

building. And on February 15, 1952, the first section of the Museum of History and Industry opened. Before it was completed, the facility was too small to provide all the storage needed and also house exhibits. Wings were added through the years and the collections continued to grow. The museum now preserves more than half a million photographic images and half a million individual artifacts and items of memorabilia. Many items are, of necessity, stored off the museum grounds.

The present board of trustees of the society, now called the Historical Society of Seattle and King County, is facing the problem of growth and studying site alternatives. Today, as Washington nears its centennial of statehood, its regional heritage is receiving increased attention. The Museum of History and Industry faces the future with renewed confidence and with dreams of becoming one of the nation's premier historical museums.

SOURCE NORTHWEST, INC.

Laron Olson was set to pursue his dream of becoming an Air Force pilot when nature intervened during summer break and a growth spurt put him over the Air Force's height restriction. Forced to reconsider his future, Olson began studying business and economics at the University of Washington and working for Saco Sales, a local wholesale distributor.

During that time Saco Sales went from a prosperous distributorship to a company on the verge of bankruptcy. Olson decided that the time was right to launch his own distributorship. To begin his venture Olson agreed to buy some of his employer's inventory. However, he needed a $150,000 loan to get the business started, so he turned to the banks.

Olson's business venture was not an inordinately risky one because he already had backing from several customers and vendors. However, Olson's background was risky. He was only twenty-five years old and, except for a few odd jobs, Saco Sales was the only place he had ever worked. The conservative banking community looked dubiously upon his lack of business experience, and he endured numerous rejections of his loan applications. Finally, one impetuous banker agreed to take a chance on the venture, and Olson finally secured his loan.

In August 1978, with $150,000 and seven employees, Source Northwest, Inc., made its debut. Because of the firm's limited resources, Olson decided that he would have to sacrifice some sales in order to provide good service. With that philosophy in mind, Source distributed to Ernst Home Centers, an ex-Saco client, nearly exclusively. That dedication to service paid off, and the company's list of clients grew with its resources.

Then, in September 1984, Olson made a decision that drastically altered the direction of his business. At the urging of Ernst, Source added the manufacture of mini blinds and pleated shades to its repertoire. The move was a rather sudden one, and the entire operation was put together in just three months. Its goal was to manufacture thirty blinds per day, and Source added five additional employees to handle the work load.

That estimate soon proved to be far too modest. After just three months, production had increased from 30 to 100 blinds per day, and the number of employees had grown substantially. After just one year of operation, production exceeded 300 blinds per day.

Source's burgeoning manufacturing branch, as well as the continued success of the distributorship, has left Olson in a happy quandary. Source Northwest, Inc.,

Laron Olson, founder and president.

which expanded to its Woodinville location in 1982, is once again outgrowing its space, and Olson is forced to contemplate yet another move. The little distributorship, which was begun by a novice just seven years ago, now employs more than forty people and grosses over eight million dollars per year.

Source Northwest, Inc., began in August 1978 with seven employees. Today the distributorship and mini blind and pleated shade manufacturer employs forty people, most of whom have gathered for this photo in front of Source's Woodinville location.

NORTH STAR CASTEEL PRODUCTS, INC.

The iron and steel industries have been part of Seattle's life-style for decades. Generations of steel workers made a living working in the fiery foundries of the past. Today the industry has dwindled from a robust thirty foundries to only six or seven. Those that survive do so through expertise and the use of modern technology.

North Star Casteel Products, Inc., is one of those modern, surviving foundries. It is a steel foundry, but its roots are in the iron industry. The buildings that are now part of North Star were once an iron foundry, vintage early 1900s. They were converted to handle steel on May 1, 1972, when William Gibb launched North Star Casteel on a shoestring.

Gibb had the expertise a modern foundry needs. His thirty-two years as an engineer in other foundries and his metallurgy degree from the University of Washington more than qualified him for success in his new venture. What he needed was financing. That he found through the faith of four partners who were willing to stake their money on Gibb's expertise.

North Star's first customers were clients of the foundries where Gibb had previously worked. The rest were the result of maintaining a reputation for quality and service. Within the first couple of months of operation, Gibb was able to increase his staff from the original seven employees to fifteen. Within two years North Star purchased back the stock interests of three of the partners. Today the company is owned by Gibb and minority partner Jerry L. Barton.

When North Star began it averaged about 3,000 pounds of steel pour per day. In 1985 the firm poured over 16,000 pounds per day. North Star manufactures trailer hitches for trucks, parts for the food industry and pulp mills, and a variety of custom-made pieces for a number of industries nationwide. It specializes in pouring manganese steel; manganese metal is not mined in the United States and must be imported. There are only about ten foundries in the United States that specialize in pouring manganese steel.

North Star has kept up with modern technology by computerizing many of its efforts and maintaining a state-of-the-art laboratory in order to perform chemical analyses of the metals. In 1984 the

William K. Gibb founded North Star Casteel in 1972.

firm diversified with the acquisition of the Viking Chain Company, which specializes in the manufacture of link chain for sawmills and industrial plants. The new acquisition further increased its work force until today the company employs nearly fifty people.

Gibb has made a special effort since he began his business venture to contribute to the betterment of the Seattle area by employing numerous university students during the summer to help them meet their tuition expenses. Many of those students have returned to the foundry every summer during their college years. Gibb provides for his regular employees as well by offering them a profit-sharing plan.

The future of North Star Casteel Products, Inc., is in the hands of the second generation of the Gibb family. Gibb's son, William Jr., is now being groomed to run the company by working as a superintendent at the foundry.

Foundry employees use huge vats of molten steel to form products for a variety of clients.

DOUG FOX TRAVEL

Doug Fox, founder and president of Doug Fox Travel from 1945 to 1978.

Doug Fox was an amazing entrepreneur who took an idea and built a business that is known throughout the Northwest as an innovative, risk-taking agency and a national leader in the travel industry. His ceaseless energy played a major role in making his company, Doug Fox Travel, one of the largest travel agencies in the United States.

Prior to going into business for himself, Fox performed a variety of jobs for Pacific National Bank and then was employed by Northwest Airlines for three years. As a result of his experience with Northwest Airlines, Fox developed a zeal for the travel business. In 1945 he opened his first travel agency in the White-Henry-Stuart Building in downtown Seattle.

During the early years business for the new travel agency was anything but brisk. Total sales for the first month amounted to only $300. However, Fox persevered, and business slowly grew. Fox was the sort of man that friends and employees alike described as honest, fair, and considerate. He was a man who understood service. For his first customers, Fox not only made travel arrangements and wrote tickets, he also hand delivered them. It was these qualities that helped him increase his business over the years through satisfied customers who returned again and again and referred their friends to him.

In 1953 an opportunity presented itself for Fox to acquire his first branch office in downtown Bremerton; it was the only travel agency on the entire peninsula down to Tacoma. That same year he opened a second branch office in the Northgate Mall, the nation's first travel agency in a shopping mall.

During the next thirty-two years Doug Fox Travel flourished. Thirteen branch offices were opened during Fox's tenure as owner of the agency, and he employed more than 150 people throughout the Puget Sound area.

In 1978 Doug Fox decided to retire from the day-to-day operations of the company and sold an interest in the firm to its four senior executives. However, he never did fully retire from the business. He remained active as a consultant with the company until September 16, 1980, when he died suddenly of a heart attack while on a fishing trip in the North Cascades.

Today Doug Fox Travel's annual sales have grown to over eighty million dollars. The firm currently employs more than 325 people at its twenty-eight branches located throughout Washington, Oregon, and Alaska. Doug Fox also acquired the first travel agency to be located on airport property in the United States. This office is open twenty-four hours a day and operates an airport parking lot for customer convenience. A nationwide toll-free number is also provided to handle customer problems and needs.

Susan Fox, Doug's widow, and George Mason oversee the firm's direction as co-chairpersons of the board, and Jack Nichols holds the position of president of Doug Fox Travel. These individuals and the rest of the organization's management staff are responsible for having kept Doug Fox Travel on an innovative track through continued expansion, additional options for travelers, and a commitment to service and customer satisfaction.

CONTINENTAL INCORPORATED

In 1921 a small group of forward-thinking men from the University District in Seattle organized what was to become the largest independent mortgage banking firm in the Pacific Northwest—Continental Incorporated. The founders' original plan was to develop a pool of funds by selling stock in the firm and then using these funds to make loans to local businesses. The concept was a good one, but the early years were rocky. One of the tiny company's first loans was to a local sawmill that burned to the ground. The mill, it was discovered, had no fire insurance, and Continental had to bear the loss.

Other such losses followed, and the future seemed bleak for the mortgage bank. Then in 1924 the board of directors decided on major management changes in an effort to save the operation. It appointed as operating head of the firm W. Walter Williams, a World War I veteran in his twenties who had been working for the company since its early days. With his new title, Williams inherited the job of guiding the company's destiny.

The new management changes proved to be the shot in the arm

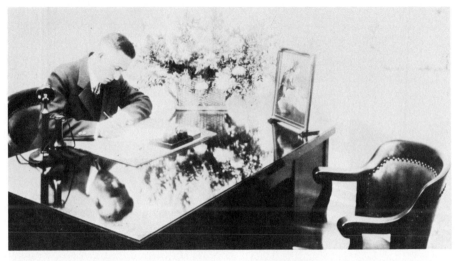

Continental needed, and things began to pick up. By the late 1920s the firm was lending to a variety of concerns, and business was on the rise. Williams was appointed president of the corporation in 1927 and held that title for the next thirty-one years.

However, cloudy skies were approaching for the mortgage company as well as for the rest of the business community. The 1930s brought the Great Depression. Businesses closed their doors, banks

W. Walter Williams, president of Continental Incorporated from 1927 to 1958, shown at the company office located in the University District in the 1920s.

failed, and bread lines formed, but Continental rode out the storm. As a result of those years, the firm diversified into new lending activities.

These activities came following the formation of the Federal Housing Administration in the 1930s. Home mortgage lending became an increasingly important part of Continental's business. Today the corporation services over one billion dollars of such mortgages, and these comprise a major part of its current mortgage servicing portfolio.

During the postwar period, the company moved into real estate development. This resulted in the building of shopping centers such as Northgate and University Village, as well as apartment houses, self-storage warehouses, and residential subdivisions.

Then, in the 1970s, Continental began a major expansion program, opening branches throughout the Puget Sound area, as well as in Honolulu, Hawaii, and Portland, Oregon. Today the corporation has a total of eleven offices.

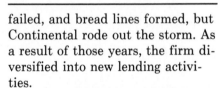

The interior of Continental's first location. Shown are two of the firm's first employees.

CAPITAL INDUSTRIES, INC.

As a purchasing agent for a prime military contractor during World War II, Dave Taylor realized that there was a demand for efficient and service-conscious metal fabricators to fulfill the military spare-parts needs after the war. As a result he was the successful bidder on various government contracts, and launched a tiny business literally from his kitchen table. There the company's name, Capital Industries, was facetiously conceived in that the new little enterprise did not have any—capital, that is, only industry.

Taylor's first business problems were fundamental. He needed employees, space, equipment, and financing. However, he had unflinching determination, a trustworthy personality, a sense of business acumen, and many friends. It took these attributes to commence the initial contracts that were completed—with family labor, in a rented garage, with borrowed equipment, and with financial backing from people who believed in his abilities.

Within a few months Capital was able to lease a larger facility

Dave Taylor, Sr., the entrepreneurial spirit behind Capital Industries, Inc.

on Poplar Place, a few blocks from that first garage. From there the firm began to expand its customer base into the private sector, with the fabrication of railroad car, truck body, and O.E.M. truck components. Throughout the 1950s Capital continued to service the military's needs through subcontracts with prime government contractors.

By the mid-1960s the Rainier Valley plant, having been expanded several times, was bursting at the seams. The company moved again, this time to a newly constructed 40,000-square-foot building in the Georgetown District. This expansion preceded Capital's introduction into the markets of industrial refrigeration, the providing of refuse containers for the solid-waste industry, and participation in the Boeing Everett plant

development in the late 1960s.

From the early days of the business' inception until his retirement in 1972, Taylor was ably assisted by Roy Erickson. Erickson served Capital as its vice-president and chief estimator, responsible for preparing many successful bid proposals.

In 1969, after graduating from college, Taylor's twin sons, Ron and Dave Jr., joined their father in the business. Through judicious plant expansion and equipment acquisition, Capital was able to maintain a strong and diverse customer base in the 1970s and 1980s. Capital was postured to share in the growth of the construction, fishing, boat-building, electronics, and oil industries. Today Capital products are scattered from the oil fields of Alaska, to the plains of Montana, to the shores of Hawaii.

During the early 1980s Dave Sr. retired from active involvement in the day-to-day operations of the firm, and his two sons assumed its management. Today Capital is owned by the Taylor children, Ron, Dave Jr., and Candace. The company has received numerous honors in its 35-year history, the most notable being the 1984 SBA Region X Subcontractor of the Year.

The 1980s have brought increased economic pressure to the metal fabrication industry. However, Capital Industries, Inc., due to its commitment to quality, service, and diversification, has continued to grow. The company currently employs more than 100 people, and its Georgetown plant now consists of four buildings and 100,000 square feet of manufacturing space.

Truck-mounted turret enclosure manufactured by Capital for a prototype missile weapons system.

215

KARR, TUTTLE, KOCH, CAMPBELL, MAWER, MORROW & SAX
A PROFESSIONAL SERVICE CORPORATION

In 1904 Day Karr and George W. Gregory established a small law practice in the growing city of Seattle. Today that firm is one of the oldest, largest, and most respected law practices in the Pacific Northwest.

When it began, the firm of Karr & Gregory specialized in litigation and business law. Work was lean during its early years. The practice of law in Washington State was still an infant profession, and the two young lawyers had yet to establish reputations. Therefore, in order to supplement their incomes, the partners took second jobs. Karr clerked in a cigar store, and Gregory coached football.

The partners complemented each other's style. Karr, a graduate of the University of Kansas Law School, was a quiet, reserved man, with a penchant for perfection and detail. Gregory, a graduate of the University of Michigan, was robust and extroverted. He was known for his fun-loving sense of humor and was often referred to as "Dad" Gregory. Despite their marked dif-

ferences, the two were good friends and spent much of their free time together pursuing their mutual interest in hunting.

Karr and Gregory gradually built their practice through long hours, good work, and determination. The firm's first office was in the Georgetown district of Seattle. Within a few years it moved into the heart of downtown Seattle.

In 1932 the development of the modern firm began when Payne Karr joined his father's practice, just four months after Gregory's untimely death. Howard Tuttle began his tenure with the firm in 1936, Carl Koch joined the firm in 1940, followed by Clarence Campbell in 1946. Campbell had been associated with the firm on a part-time basis since his graduation from law school in 1930. In 1953 Muriel Mawer joined the practice, and eventually became the firm's first female partner. Together these individuals would control the destiny of Karr, Tuttle for the next several decades.

The firm incorporated in 1977,

The law office established by Day Karr and George W. Gregory in Seattle in 1904.

and "P.S." was added to its name. In 1986 the firm merged its practice with Sax & MacIver. Together, these firms represent over a century of service to their clients and the community. Karr, Tuttle has grown from a two-person office in an outlying district of Seattle into one of the Northwest's major firms capable of representing the complex and diverse interests of major corporations and the personal legal needs of individuals.

Today Karr, Tuttle, Koch, Campbell, Mawer, Morrow & Sax, P.S., employs nearly eighty attorneys. It has both a main office and a branch office in Seattle, as well as a branch in Bellevue. The firm has experienced tremendous growth and considerable change over its eighty-plus-year history, but it has managed to retain the easy working relationship among its lawyers and the attention to detail that was first established by Day Karr and George Gregory.

THE CALLISON PARTNERSHIP, LTD.

In 1960 Anthony Callison entered the private practice of architecture working from the attic of a house he rented in Seattle. For the next thirteen years the firm experienced a diversity of successes and failures, seldom knowing what the future held. From that humble beginning one of Seattle's most successful architectural practices has emerged, with a current staff of 140 and billings exceeding eleven million dollars annually.

In 1973 a phone call to another local architectural partnership, Erickson and Hobble, set one of the cornerstones of the firm's future success. Callison had known both Bud Erickson and Bob Hobble professionally and personally for some time, and realized they possessed skills and capabilities his firm lacked, and vice versa. Therefore, through a timely phone conversation, they discussed the possibility of a merger, only to learn they both shared the same goal. The merger was consummated in 1973 under the new firm name of Callison, Erickson, Hobble.

As with any other business, the client base becomes the lifeline of an architectural practice. Shortly after the merger, Bud Erickson was contacted by Nordstrom regarding the interior design of a renovated building Nordstrom was considering occupying in Spokane. It was not a question of if the firm could do the work, but how soon it could start.

The Spokane project was a great success, completed on time and within budget, and the design was well received by the Nordstrom family. As a result of the company's performance on that first project in Spokane, Nordstrom commissioned it to do additional work. Since 1974 the firm has been responsible for all of Nordstrom's

major installations on the West Coast. This commitment of service to the client, hard work, and a quality product has brought success to both concerns.

However, during those first few years of the new partnership, business was somewhat cyclical, with the number of employees fluctuating dramatically from quarter to quarter. In addition, just two years after the partnership had begun, Erickson was offered a position within Nordstrom as director of store planning, and the firm once again changed dramatically. It was during this restructuring that the venture acquired its current name, The Callison Partnership. In order to add professional depth and management expertise, two new partners were named, David Lindsey and Charlene Nelson.

It became evident that the firm needed additional quality clients if it was to be a dynamic, growing organization capable of attracting high-caliber staff and mitigating the economic fluctuations it had experienced in the past. As a result, in 1981 The Callison Partnership made a commitment to develop a more diversified practice. Six new markets were identified, including hotels, office buildings, high-tech facilities, retail facilities (shops and shopping centers), financial institutions, and a combination thereof. In addition, services such as computer programming, space planning, and tenant improvement work were added.

Today The Callison Partnership has achieved its diversification goal, with 50 percent of the firm's work being done outside the state of Washington. A national clientele

Principal members of The Callison Partnership discuss a project at the firm's original offices on Sixth Avenue in the Regrade area of Seattle.

has been identified, contributing to the more than 200 projects The Callison Partnership designs annually. Eighty percent of the firm's work is generated by repeat and referral clients. To respond to this growth, the firm has installed an in-house, state-of-the-art, computer-assisted design and drafting system and a data- and word-processing computer system. Also, the firm recently named additional principals: Gerry Gerron, Dave Olson, and Mike Whalen. The Callison Partnership looks to the future with enthusiasm, and is committed to further expanding its client and geographical base by providing the same high-quality professional service that successfully brought the firm to the position it enjoys today.

Seattle's Park Place office building is an example of the fine architectural design work that helped establish The Callison Partnership's current reputation for quality.

WRIGHT SCHUCHART

Wright Schuchart's roots in the Puget Sound area can be traced back over 100 years to a 24-year-old Canadian carpenter named Howard S. Wright. Wright heeded the call to go west and by 1885 moved to the bustling frontier town of Port Townsend, Washington Territory.

There the burgeoning lumber and shipbuilding industries provided ample opportunity for the industrious craftsman. By 1889 the town's busy harbor ranked second only to New York City as the largest U.S. shipping port clearing marine craft. Business for the young carpenter was good.

The little town continued to prosper for the next several years, and men like Wright prospered as well. Then the financial backing for the Port Townsend-Southern Railroad failed. Plans for the railroad were changed so that it would stop in Everett instead of Port Townsend, and the opportunities were suddenly available across the Puget Sound in the community of Everett.

Wright, who was married and

Part of the changing skyline of Seattle are high-rise buildings constructed by Wright Schuchart: (left to right) First Interstate Center, 1111 Third Avenue Building, Seattle-First National Bank Building, and Columbia Seafirst Center.

had two children, moved his family across the Sound to seek his fortune in the new little city. The move was a prudent one; at the time Everett was a community with access to unlimited and unexploited natural resources. Combined with its designation to become the western terminus for the expanding transcontinental rail lines, the area was attracting millions of dollars and hundreds of enthusiastic businessmen.

Wright was inundated with contracting work following his arrival in Everett. He built the city's two-story brick Foabes Building, the Hodges Building, and many houses. One, at 2112 Rucker Avenue, became his family home and is considered one of the finest variations of colonial revival classic box style found anywhere.

Wright's son, Howard H., went to work for his father in 1923 at the age of twenty-four. At about that same time his brother-in-law, George J. Schuchart, also joined

the firm at the elder Wright's urging. By the late 1920s a company office was opened in Seattle.

However, the stock market crashed just one year later, and construction projects dwindled to none. To keep the company operating, new construction contracts were bid on the basis of what each employee said he would need to be paid during the job. The organization then bid projects as the total of the salaries plus costs.

As the country shook off the devastating effects of the Great Depression, business gradually increased for the struggling construction company. By the mid-1930s Wright was building again, this time all over the state of Washington. The firm completed the Everett Savings and Loan Building, built Seattle's Gainsborough Hotel on First Hill, constructed Waller

The Hood Canal floating bridge drawspan installation on Puget Sound.

Hall on the Washington State University campus in Pullman, and erected Cascadian Hotel in Wenatchee, along with numerous other projects in Aberdeen, Grand Coulee, Anacortes, and Tacoma. The elder Wright agreed to sell the company to his son and son-in-law. Shortly afterward, Wright Schuchart was awarded a construction contract for the Puget Sound Pulp and Timber Company. This was one of the first million-dollar projects undertaken by a private construction company in the Northwest.

Wright and Schuchart had an exceptional partnership that contributed to their well-managed business. Wright ran the Seattle office and concentrated on commercial projects, while Schuchart maintained the Everett office and managed the industrial contracts.

During World War II the firm became involved in military contracts, providing housing at Port Orchard, a torpedo storage depot at Keyport, and an Army base at Pasco. A large part of the city of Richland was also constructed by the firm for the then-secret Hanford atomic project.

By the 1950s the company was

Pipeline construction, North Slope, Alaska.

heavily involved in numerous major commercial and industrial construction projects. Wright Schuchart built Northgate Shopping Center, the first suburban shopping mall in the United States. Since then it has literally shaped the Seattle skyline as we know it today.

However, Wright Schuchart's influence extends beyond Seattle and indeed beyond the state of Washington. During the 1950s the firm completed major industrial construction projects in Alaska and Idaho.

In the 1960s the company was called upon to build the most unusual and most visually significant project in its history. The 1962 Seattle World's Fair was fast approaching, and Wright Schuchart was asked to construct the Space Needle, the symbol of the fair and now the most well known of Wright Schuchart's creations.

This seminal Seattle high rise is now one of a list of other such structures Wright Schuchart has had a hand in building. During the

1960s the company branched even further from those original Port Townsend roots with projects from California to Maine. As the 1980s approached, the firm continued its diversification with the acquisition of such firms as General Construction Company.

Wright Schuchart's tallest project is Seattle's Columbia Seafirst Center. The 76-story structure, with its 1.5 million square feet of office space, is the tallest building in Seattle and the tenth tallest in the United States.

Today the company is under the third-generation direction of Howard S. Wright and George S. Schuchart. It continues to diversify with acquisitions such as Frontier Companies of Alaska and its group of subsidiaries.

As Wright Schuchart continues to grow, its business philosophy of building "on time and within budget" is increasing its reputation as a quality-conscious construction firm with an ever-expanding expertise in virtually all aspects of the construction business.

The North Slope process plant module fabrication, Tacoma.

BEN BRIDGE

In 1912 Samuel Silverman combined his entrepreneurial spirit and his skills as a fine guild watchmaker to establish a jewelry store on Third Avenue in the small but growing community of Seattle. That first store enjoyed success, and Silverman delighted in providing his fellow citizens with the latest in jewelry. Watches in those days were made only for the pocket, and customers purchased watch mechanisms and watch cases separately.

As a shopkeeper, Silverman wanted to provide more than just a commodity; he also wanted to provide service. Customers in 1912 enjoyed complimentary jewelry checking and polishing as well as watch-time adjustments as they shopped at Silverman's, and the

Sam Silverman and his wife (behind the counter) converse with customers in their first shop in 1912. The glass case contains watch cases, which customers bought separately from the mechanism.

Sam Silverman (left) and an unidentified friend outside the first Silverman's jewelry store on Third Avenue.

Ben Bridge awaits his first customer of the day at the store's new location at Fourth and Pike. This was the first store bearing the current name, Ben Bridge. Photo circa 1926

firm has retained that tradition.

However, unbeknownst to Silverman, his business was about to become a partnership. World War I was over, and a young sailor named Ben Bridge, fresh from his tour of duty with the Navy, came home to Seattle to work for Schwabacher Bros., where he was a department head and protégé of Nathan Eckstein. He met Silverman's daughter,

Sally, and the couple married. Following the wedding Silverman convinced Bridge to go into partnership with him, and the store became Silverman and Bridge. Eventually Silverman was advised by his doctor to move to California. Bridge purchased his father-in-law's interest in the store in 1926 and renamed the company Ben Bridge. The store retains that name today.

Ben and Sally Bridge had two sons, Herb and Bob. Both boys worked in the store throughout their childhood, and Herb was trained as a watchmaker at the store, which was now located at Fourth and Pike.

Following four years of service during World War II, Herb returned to Seattle to rejoin the firm. Bob, who served in the Navy during the Korean War, rejoined the business in 1954. True to family tradition, both men remained active as officers in the Naval Reserve through their retirement, Herb as the senior Naval Reserve rear admiral.

When Ben Bridge was ready to retire in 1955, his sons purchased his interest in the business. The firm began to expand by the 1960s when it went into the discount jewelry business for a period of five years and subsequently into an association with a major department store, just as that company

was expanding into full-line department stores. In 1968 Ben Bridge also opened its first mall store at Southcenter.

The late 1970s and early 1980s marked a time of tremendous growth for the firm as store after store opened in Washington. Then, on July 31, 1981, Ben Bridge relinquished its seven department store outlets to devote itself to stores under complete company control.

Today Ben Bridge has twenty-six stores in Washington, Oregon, and California and has more stores planned for 1986 and beyond. Herb and Bob Bridge still head the firm, but the next generation of Bridges has joined the staff and is being groomed to take the helm.

The fourth generation is well qualified to lead in that Herb's son, John, is an attorney and a Naval Reserve officer, and Bob's son, Ed, is a graduate of the University of Washington School of Business and an accountant.

LEASE CRUTCHER AND LEASE KISSEE CONSTRUCTION COMPANIES

Howard Lease grew up in the construction business in Great Falls, Montana. His father, N.T. Lease, had started as a carpenter in Cascade, Montana, in 1883 and moved to Great Falls in 1884. There N.T. Lease was a charter member of the United Brotherhood of Carpenters and Joiners of America. N.T. Lease and various partners were responsible for building projects throughout Montana, including the Cascade County Courthouse.

When his father died in 1929, Howard Lease continued in the family business and took over his father's interest in a partnership with H.S. Leigland. Times were tough for the two new partners. The Depression gripped the nation, and construction work was scarce. Despite the adversity the little firm managed to survive. Today it is credited with many of the commercial building projects that were constructed in Great Falls prior to 1939, as well as projects in Helena and other Montana communities.

Pastures looked greener in Seattle and the firm moved there in 1939. It took with it a single-entry bookkeeping system and a supervisor, C. Howard Walden, C.P.A. The press of war work was such that there was no chance to revise the bookkeeping system, and the accountant believes that Lease and Leigland did more construction work than any other firm in America using Howard Lease's single-entry bookkeeping system.

In July 1942 Ernie Kissee joined Lease and Leigland. Kissee was an extraordinarily capable and hard-driving construction superintendent. He managed several large construction projects in Oregon and Washington for the firm. Then, in 1953, Kissee's abilities were challenged when he opened operations for Lease and Leigland

The Cascade County Courthouse in Great Falls, Montana, was constructed by N.T. Lease and partner T.C. Richards between 1900 and 1903.

in the frozen northland of Alaska. The projects Kissee managed in that unforgiving land were often under the most arduous circumstances.

In 1955 the Lease and Leigland partnership was dissolved, and Lease continued to expand his operations in Washington and Alaska under the name Lease Company, Inc. Kissee remained associated with Lease and continued to control the Alaska operations. Today one can look in any direction in Anchorage, Alaska, and see structures that Lease and Kissee built.

In 1957 Jim Crutcher, Lease's son-in-law, joined the organization and began to learn every phase of the operation. In the early 1970s Kissee and Crutcher formed their own construction companies and began working in partnership with Howard Lease. Eventually, Kissee became manager of construction in Alaska, with Crutcher holding the same position in the Pacific Northwest.

William Lewis, Howard Lease's grandson, joined the firm in 1978 to continue his family's tradition of dedication to the construction business. Lease died in 1983, leaving Kissee to continue operations in Alaska, and Crutcher and Lewis to continue Lease Crutcher Construction Company's projects in the Northwest.

Construction and business operations today are far different from the firm's beginning. It no longer has a single-entry bookkeeping system, but continues to operate under the same full-time philosophy of satisfying clients and recognizing the importance and needs of its employees.

A more recent Lease Crutcher Construction Company project, the Pacific Northwest Bell Telephone Company building in Bellevue, Washington, was completed in May 1983.

ADAMS NEWS CO., INC.

Adams News Co., Inc., was founded in 1927 by George L. Adams in a small facility on Battery Street in Seattle. There he began a wholesale periodical distribution business that has grown from 17 magazine titles to over 2,400 today.

George's son, Jay, began working in the business in 1929, sweeping floors and "swamping" on delivery trucks.

Jay enrolled at the University of Washington, received his bachelor's degree in 1937, and then struck out to explore the world. Jay's experiences included serving as a deck hand on an Alaskan cannery tender, working on two ships to the Orient, selling for Fawcett Publications in the upper Midwest, as well as selling advertising while pursuing his M.B.A. from the University of Washington. Jay served in the Transportation Corps during World War II.

After the war Jay returned to Adams News and assumed the position of general manager. He proved to be an exceptional man-

ager, and the firm's real growth occurred under his direction.

Following the death of his father, Jay bought into the business with Lawrence Riches. In January 1949 the name of the firm was changed to Riches & Adams, Inc., to reflect the new partnership. Together the pair propelled the company toward further expansion in keeping with Jay's commitment to make Riches & Adams the most effective, efficient, and service-oriented periodical and book whole-

George L. Adams

saler in the industry.

For the duration of the partnership the business grew dramatically because of the pair's dedication and hard work. This extra effort brought about several moves for the firm, resulting in the need for more space, as it steadily expanded its list of titles and product lines.

In 1968 Lawrence Riches, who had been president of the firm

This 1947 photo shows Adams News Co.'s sales and delivery personnel in front of the office and warehouse at 309 Wall Street.

Jay B. Adams

Jay B. Adams—circa 1930.

since 1948, passed away. Jay, upon assuming the role of president, brought in two new business partners, Norman Bay, Jr., of Bay News Company in Portland, Oregon, and Jack Drown of Drown News Agency in Westminster, California. For the next several years the business flourished under its new management team and Jay's competent leadership.

It was Jay's wish, before his passing, to change the name back to Adams News Co. On January 1, 1980, the change officially took place. Mrs. Inez M. Adams (Jay's somewhat silent business partner for many years) is now president of Adams News Co., Inc.

As president, Inez has continued to plot a course of controlled growth for the business. She worked for years alongside Jay and, as a result, has brought considerable experience and expert business savvy to the corporation's management team.

Through the years Adams News Co., Inc., has expanded into five basic product categories. They include magazines, comics, paperbacks, reference books, and children's books and games. It has been the company's pleasure to sell over 17 million units of reading and related merchandise annually, providing a basis for the company's service to retailers, institutional accounts, and publishers.

Adams News Co.'s goal is to provide each retailer with the correct product selection, the appropriate service, and the proper marketing support.

Today the business that started with just a few employees and 17 magazine titles has grown to serve over 1,000 retail and more than 300 institutional customers, with one of the most advanced computer-tracking systems in the industry.

In 1986 Adams News Co., Inc., marked fifty-nine years of service to the greater Seattle/King County area. Despite its continued growth and ever-increasing sophistication, the firm clings to Jay Adams' basic business philosophy. He was a man who was always concerned about the future of the distribution industry and a firm believer in the fairness of government. Today Adams News Co., Inc., maintains that same spirit.

A portion of Adams News Co.'s sales and delivery fleet at the current office and warehouse facility at 1555 West Galer Street.

PEMCO FINANCIAL CENTER

Above left
Robert J. Handy, founder.

Above
Stanley O. McNaughton, president, chief executive officer, and chairman of the board.

PEMCO Financial Center sprang from Robert J. Handy's dream and a borrowed five-dollar bill.

The young Broadway High School math and journalism teacher studied credit union-enabling legislation. If he opened and ran such an organization, he thought, perhaps he could augment his meager salary and provide fellow teachers with a "safe place to save and a good place to borrow."

A friend lent Handy five dollars to pay the application fee for a credit union charter. When it was granted May 1, 1936, Handy struck a deal with University National Bank that would give Seattle Teachers' Credit Union

the capital it needed to finance borrowers.

Seeking a $200 loan, the credit union's first customer found Handy's "office"—a tiny rent-free cubicle in the Fourth and Pike Branch of Seattle First National Bank. Handy approved the loan, wrote the first check, then raced to University National Bank to borrow enough money to cover it.

The fledgling credit union occupied five addresses before settling into the structure Handy built for it in 1949 on Eastlake Avenue. A 1952 merger enabled the credit union to broaden its membership to teachers across the state, and Seattle Teachers' Credit Union be-

came Washington Teachers Credit Union.

In 1973 the name was changed again to Washington School Employees Credit Union when services were extended to all employees in accredited schools and colleges.

Handy, who also was well acquainted with the insurance business, thought teachers deserved low-cost auto coverage. Records showed they were better-than-average drivers whose losses were a good deal less than their auto insurance premiums. This observation led him to found Public Employees Mutual Insurance Company in 1948-1949, PEMCO Insurance Company in 1950, and PEMCO Life Insurance Company in 1963.

In 1969 PEMCO Corporation, a data-processing and leasing firm, provided support services to its first customers, Washington School Employees Credit Union and PEMCO Insurance Companies. Two years later Teachers State Bank (now EvergreenBank) opened its doors for business and joined PEMCO Corporation's customer list.

EvergreenBank was the first bank in Washington to offer "single-statement banking," and its Clearing Services Department consistently ranks among the top five nationally in number of credit union share drafts processed.

Stanley O. McNaughton, chief spokesperson and policymaker for PEMCO Financial Center, joined the organization in 1961. His primary task was to chart a course for the future of the growing firms. In 1970 he was elected president of the insurance companies and later became chief executive officer and chairman of the board.

Today PEMCO Financial Center's seven companies occupy a state-of-the-art structure housing nearly 700 employees. It covers the entire block on which the first small credit union facility was built. For efficiency, these separate and distinct center firms share several common functions such as purchasing, personnel, marketing, data processing, and communications. This results in economy of scale—an economy that enables the center to offer its services at low rates. Together, the companies provide comprehensive financial services to more than 300,000 Washington customers.

Just five decades after Bob Handy borrowed five dollars to start Seattle Teachers' Credit Union, PEMCO Financial Center companies claim nearly $500 million in combined assets.

PEMCO Financial Center.

KING COUNTY MEDICAL BLUE SHIELD

Depression bread lines, a desperate need for affordable health care, and innovative thinking by physicians all played a role in the development of King County Medical Blue Shield.

In 1933 local physicians banded together to form a corporation to serve the community's medical needs during the Great Depression. Participating doctors each donated ten dollars to cover the start-up costs of the organization. However, that capital was quickly depleted, and King County Medical began with a deficit.

Initially established for low-income workers, King County Medical was a nonprofit corporation. Subscribers chose their doctors and prepaid the corporation in small payments, originally one dollar per month. Subscribers' medical expenses were paid out of these funds to the 400 physicians and seven hospitals participating in the plan. During its first year King County Medical paid $25,000 in medical claims, and its membership numbered 10,000. By 1940 it had 40,000 members and was off to a solid start.

By that time prosperity had returned to Seattle, but World War II loomed on the horizon. Seattle was a boom town during the war, with a flood of workers coming to the area for employment in the shipping and aircraft industries. Doctors and hospital beds were in

short supply. King County Medical again came to the citizens' aid by building Doctors Hospital in 1943.

The corporation continued to grow after the war. In response to stiffening competition, King County Medical began offering additional types of coverage. In 1947 it raised rates to $3.50 per month. By its twentieth anniversary King County Medical covered 170,000 people with a variety of plans for higher-income as well as low-income workers.

King County Medical also experienced the changes of ever-advancing technology and the increasing costs of that technology. Throughout the 1950s and 1960s it faced those changing times and costs with its own increased technology and an assortment of new health plans.

During the past twenty years changes have occurred at an accelerated pace. In 1966 the firm be-

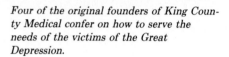

Four of the original founders of King County Medical confer on how to serve the needs of the victims of the Great Depression.

gan processing Medicare Part B claims and offering its own Medicare supplement plan. More products were developed, introducing dental and vision plans, a million-dollar major medical plan, and life and disability coverage. Insurance brokers began selling its plans, and the marketing area expanded into Yakima and Lewis counties.

By 1982 family health insurance had risen to nearly $200 per month. To combat the rising cost of health care, the company improved internal controls and automation, coordinated benefits with other insurers, and offered new, low-cost health plans. These efforts allowed ninety-two cents of every premium dollar to be returned as claims payments.

Today King County Medical Blue Shield serves 646,000 people with the cooperation of 2,600 participating doctors. It paid $300 million in claims in 1985, a figure that is 12,000 times the amount it paid in 1933.

The medical claims and customer service departments were located in the same room in 1935. Today both departments occupy several floors.

WASHINGTON DENTAL SERVICE

Legend has it that the colorful and often forceful Alfred Renton "Harry" Bridges was the instigator behind Washington Dental Service program, a prepaid dental plan. As the story goes, Bridges, who was a leading activist in early labor disputes and head of the International Longshoremen's and Warehousemen's Union during the 1930s, made it his business in the 1950s to obtain proper dental care for the children of ILWU members. Bridges first approached the Washington State Dental Association with a plan to form a group that would provide 100-percent coverage of dental care for ILWU members' children. However, the WSDA rejected the idea, and Bridges was sent on his way without the dental care plan he desired.

Now Bridges was not the sort of man who gave up easily, and this time was no exception. He continued to press the WSDA about the program until one day, after he had threatened to establish a program independently, the WSDA agreed to give the idea a try.

The new organization, called Washington Dental Service, first began in 1954 with a membership of 4,000 ILWU members' children. Under the initial program, member dentists performed dental services on a fixed-fee basis, and the children had 100-percent coverage for all dental procedures except orthodontics. This program included only children because the thinking of the day was that adults were destined to have dentures anyway.

As the program caught on, the first step was to become an independent organization with a director separate from the WSDA's. As the program began to grow, attitudes toward adult dental health care changed and the corporation began to add a variety of subscribers with varying levels of coverage

Claims representatives offer advice and assistance with dental service insurance claims for members.

to its growing rolls.

For a while WDS provided emergency dental services to welfare recipients under state contract. Later the firm developed a statewide dollar-per-year program for schoolchildren that covered treatment for dental accidents

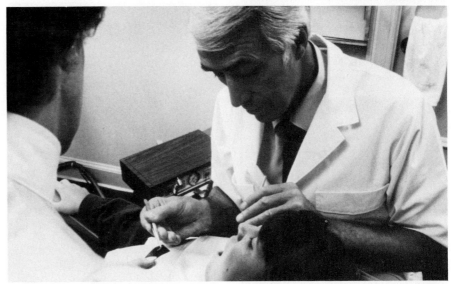

A member dentist performs routine dental care on a patient with Washington Dental Service coverage.

twenty-four hours a day.

However, WDS's most dramatic growth took place in 1964, when the company introduced an incentive dental coverage program that covered every member of the family. Under this program, the firm encouraged preventive dental care by paying higher portions of a covered family's bill if they visited their dentist at least once a year.

Today ILWU members' children still receive coverage, but WDS has expanded from the original 4,000 subscribers to over 421,000 adults and children, involving nearly 95 percent of all the dentists practicing in the state. And WDS pays ninety cents out of every dollar it receives for dental care, keeping only ten cents on the dollar for

day-to-day operations. Member dentists receive payments on a modified scale that is designed to provide the fairest coverage as well as the most appropriate payments for patients and dentists alike.

In 1985 Washington Dental Service expanded its subscriber coverage to include retired teachers. Never before had the program been able to provide coverage for retired individuals. However, WDS, in its constant quest to increase its level of dental coverage, has forged ahead into yet another untested area with the addition of this latest group of subscribers.

SEATTLE UNIVERSITY

Quality education was in short supply in Seattle's early days. The Puget Sound area was growing rapidly with the addition of railroads, city improvements, and vastly increasing business interests. However, the new state's great educational institutions were still small, struggling facilities.

As a result, two Jesuit priests, Victor Garrand, S.J., and Adrian Sweere, S.J., set out to improve the quality of both education and religious training for the young citizens of Washington State. The two founded a school at Sixth and Spring streets in Seattle in 1891. The new institution, named Im-

James B. McGoldrick, S.J., served as a teacher and friend to Seattle University students for fifty years.

maculate Conception, moved three years later to an expansive campus on the "eastern outskirts" of the city at Madison and Broadway streets.

The campus consisted of nine lots, which represented the better part of a city block. The Jesuits

had purchased the land from Arthur Denny for the grand sum of $182.83. Initially, the new institution was a Catholic boys' preparatory school. It was officially incorporated in 1898 as Seattle College and began offering its first college-level courses two years later.

It was not until 1909 that the school held commencement ceremonies for its first class of gradu-

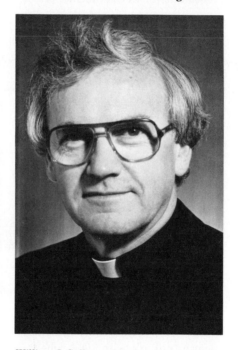

William J. Sullivan, S.J., became president of Seattle University in 1976.

ates. Even though that special day had been years in the making, the ceremony did not last long. The entire graduating class consisted of just three students.

For the next several years Seattle College expanded at a steady pace. The last of the grade school classes was moved out of the institution in 1916. The school then settled in to its commitment to teaching high school and college-level young men a solid curriculum coupled with religious training. In 1919 Seattle College High School

A.A. Lemieux, S.J., served as president of Seattle University from 1948 to 1965.

moved to a new campus on the north side of Capitol Hill.

During World War I college-level courses were briefly suspended, and then reinstated in 1922. The institution's total enrollment that year was sixteen students. By 1928 the college and high school were formally separated, with Seattle College moving to separate quarters at Tenth Avenue and Roanoke Street.

In 1931 Seattle College was able to return to the Broadway campus after Father Joseph Piet, S.J., Jesuit Provincial for the Pacific Northwest, gave five Jesuits a mandate to reopen the campus. The institution began life anew with an opening day enrollment of thirty-five students.

One of those first five Jesuits was James B. McGoldrick, S.J. Seattle College was his first teaching assignment, and it was to be his last. McGoldrick remained at the institution for more than fifty

Some of the institution's first students discover the rigors of higher education.

years. To many, his name is synonymous with Seattle University. A lively Irishman with an iron will and a quick wit, McGoldrick looked beyond tradition and applied his own rules of common sense and uncommon virtue to each and every situation.

In 1932 McGoldrick brushed aside a prevailing belief and a 400-year tradition that prohibited women from attending American Jesuit colleges. As a result, thirty women enrolled in special afternoon courses and McGoldrick invoked the ire of Jesuit authorities in Rome. However, he tactfully diffused the situation and eventually revolutionized Jesuit education in America. Because of his foresight, Seattle College became the first Jesuit school in the country to admit women to bachelor of arts degree programs.

McGoldrick's enthusiasm for the school went beyond revolutionizing traditions. He had a vision for the

institution, and he worked tirelessly toward achieving the greatness he knew it deserved. When the college had barely reopened and money as well as students were scarce, McGoldrick enthusiastically exclaimed, "This is just the beginning of a great university!" He passed away on April 27, 1983, and today a bust of dean emeritus McGoldrick stands in the school's library bearing the inscription "an

institution is the shadow of a man."

From the 1930s through the 1980s the college expanded and changed in unprecedented ways. Complementing the tradition of a liberal arts education, the School of Education was established in 1935 and was accredited by Northwest Association two years later. The School of Nursing was opened in 1940, and the following year brought the School of Engineering. In 1945 the Business School was established.

In 1948 Seattle College became Seattle University, and A.A. Lemieux, S.J., became president of the institution. Lemieux's term lasted for the next seventeen years, and he had a profound influence on the direction, integrity, and quality of life at the university. Under his direction, the institution established a reputation for quality that spanned the nation. Lemieux instigated so many new construction projects during his tenure as president that he has often been referred to as "the builder."

The Garrand Building was the first building to be constructed on the Seattle University campus. It is still in use today and houses the school's biology department.

Seattle University's Liberal Arts Building.

However, by the late 1960s Seattle University began experiencing financial difficulties. The tenure of Lemieux had passed, and the ensuing years were tumultuous. The early 1970s produced three presidents in five years. From 1966 to 1976 the institution endured budget deficits for nine of these ten years. There were rumors that the university would have to close, enrollment dropped, and the staff received no pay raises during part of that period. Then, in 1976, Father William J. Sullivan, S.J., was named president of the institution. Sullivan was a bright, visionary man who was vitally concerned with continued academic excellence and the financial well-being of Seattle University. He immediately set to work to regain the institution's financial stability and reputation for quality in the Northwest.

Today, after ten years under Father Sullivan's leadership, Seattle University's endowment has reached twenty-two million dollars. This represents almost five times the amount of the fund when Sullivan became president in 1976. The institution is now the largest independent university in the Northwest.

In 1983 the school launched a three-year campaign that represents the first comprehensive fundraising effort in its history. The campaign's goal is to raise twenty million dollars for new buildings and an endowment to further the quality and scope of the school's academic offerings. The campaign has proven to be a success and is nearing its goal. With the funds already raised, new construction has begun and more is scheduled. Two new buildings are planned, which represent the first construction to take place on the Seattle University campus in eighteen years.

Tuition costs, like all costs, have changed considerably over the course of the university's history. In 1985 students paid $6,120 in annual tuition expenses, compared to just $100 in 1935. Today Seattle University's 4,400 students may choose from sixty-six undergraduate and thirteen graduate degree programs. In recent years Seattle University has begun several new programs including the Institute of Public Service in 1974, Matteo Ricci College in 1977, and the nation's first graduate program in computer software engineering in 1979.

Matteo Ricci College is a unique concept in education. It is a cooperative effort between Seattle Preparatory School and Seattle University that allows high school students to participate in an integrated program that eliminates much of the work that is repetitive between the senior year and the freshman year. It also enables students to obtain a bachelor's degree in six years from the time they enter high school, instead of the traditional eight years.

Seattle University also has a new program, established in 1985, called the Institute for Theological Studies, which is designed to provide theological education to lay men and women who wish to work in positions of ministry in the community.

Over its long and productive history Seattle University has endured both good times and bad. It has faced near financial disaster and won, but through it all it has built a reputation for academic quality for which any institution could be proud. Today it looks toward 1991, its centennial year, with great optimism and continued aspirations for educational quality and service to the community.

Today Seattle University students can choose their courses from a wide variety of specialized programs.

CAREAGE

In 1959 Gene E. Lynn, then an engineering representative for Harstad Engineers, was assigned to do a study of the nursing home industry for a client who was interested in developing a retirement facility. The Hearthstone, located near Green Lake in Seattle, is the result of that study.

However, for Lynn that study was just the beginning. As a result of that project he saw a need for a business that could focus its attention on the state of nursing homes and care for the aged and make some positive changes in that field. Lynn found the statistics astonishing and the industry ill prepared to handle the future challenges.

According to the demographics, the 65-plus age group was and is the fastest-growing age group in the nation. The number of men and women in that group was increasing at a rate of five times that of the general population. Since 1950 the annual death rate in that age group has dropped 25 percent, and the life expectancy after reaching age sixty-five has increased by nearly three years. The health care industry, however, was not keeping pace.

With those facts in mind, Lynn entered the field of health care development. In May 1962 he quit his job and launched a company designed to be an investor, developer, designer, contractor, and operator of nursing homes.

Lynn first established his business as a partnership with Willis E. Campbell. Together they formed Campbell-Lynn. From 1962 to 1966 the Campbell-Lynn partnership flourished. The firm developed and leased twenty-four nursing

homes in the Northwest. In addition, the pair developed and constructed eight additional nursing homes through third-party contracts.

Those first innovative projects helped lead the transformation of the nursing home industry. Rundown facilities that lacked proper care could be replaced by homes designed for the comfort and protection of people who needed 24-hour care.

In 1966 the partnership dissolved, and Lynn began developing health care facilities alone as CAREAGE, a name he had coined during his first year in the nursing home business. In 1967 Lynn formed his second alliance, this time with Safecare, a division of Safeco Insurance. That relationship lasted until 1969 and was responsible for the development of twenty new nursing homes in just twenty-six months.

However, in 1969 Safeco wanted to purchase CAREAGE, and Lynn decided not to sell. The joint venture was dissolved, and CAREAGE once again began developing health care facilities on its own. The organization is solely owned by Lynn, who enjoys the freedom that brings.

Since its inception CAREAGE

William J. Sullivan, S.J., president of Seattle University, and Gene E. Lynn, owner and president of Careage, in front of Seattle University School of Nursing's Gene E. Lynn Building.

has had a hand in designing, constructing, equipping, and managing nursing homes, medical offices, clinics, and hospitals. Lynn now has decided to concentrate CARE-AGE's efforts solely on nursing and retirement home development. That decision is the result of Lynn's belief that developing proper nursing and retirement home facilities requires not only knowledge and expertise, but also love. He believes that CAREAGE possesses all three of those qualities in abundance.

Residents of a Careage retirement home enjoy a well-planned, nutritious meal in the beautiful surroundings of Bellevue, Washington.

231

WASHINGTON MUTUAL SAVINGS BANK

It was September 21, 1889. Seattleites possessed the spirit and determination to rebuild their city after the devastating June fire, but money was a scarce commodity. Many proprietors were housed in tents among the blackened blocks that had once represented a booming business community. That evening, however, five men met and founded the Washington National Building Loan and Investment Association, which would one day be called Washington Mutual Savings Bank.

The new lending institution was established with just $5,000 and a commitment to provide safety for savings and service to home owners. With those funds and that commitment, the institution was responsible for funding several projects during Seattle's reconstruction period.

Washington Mutual's founding fathers were Robert Moran, James Hamilton Lewis, E.O. Graves, Dr. P.B.M. Miller, and I. Hill Case, all Seattle luminaries and experienced businessmen. Graves, a banker and civic leader, was elected president of the new institution.

One of the organization's first acts was an innovative one. The founders were responsible for making the first monthly installment home loan on the Pacific Coast. However, that type of loan was to become a standard banking practice over the next twenty years.

The savings and loan grew rapidly during its first few months in business. Its initial financial statement listed assets of $19,615.58 and dividend payments of $337.47.

However, just four years after its establishment, the savings and

Washington Mutual Savings Bank's forerunner first received its charter on September 25, 1889, before Washington had been accepted for statehood.

loan faced a financial crisis during the Panic of 1893. Bank deposits overall decreased by one-third, and fourteen of King County's original twenty-three banks closed their doors. Washington Mutual's forerunner, however, remained steadfast and reliable, and a brisk business eventually resumed. In 1907 a second panic hit the nation, and still more businesses failed. Again the savings and loan survived, instilling greater confidence among its customers.

By 1897 Herman Chapin had succeeded Graves as president. The bank had already made several moves, each time because it had outgrown its previous location. That trend was to continue for several years.

Even in its early days Washington Mutual was an aggressive, forward-thinking institution. It led a long campaign to establish sav-

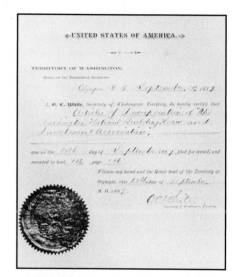

ings and loan and then mutual savings bank legislation in Washington. In 1915 the Mutual Savings Bank Law was passed. Those efforts were led by the institution's vice-president and manager, Raymond R. Frazier, who succeeded the retiring Chapin as president during that same year. In 1917 another piece of legislation was passed that allowed savings and loan associations to become mutual savings banks, and the institution

From the firm's office at 810 Second Avenue, Washington Mutual Savings Bank provided a multitude of innovative banking services for early Seattleites.

This building, at Second Avenue and Cherry Street in downtown Seattle, was one of many "homes" of Washington Mutual Savings Bank during its early years.

converted in September of that year.

World War I brought numerous war-related activities to Seattle, and Washington Mutual put its heart into the war effort. The bank set records for bond sales during the war and assisted veterans with filing claims in the postwar years.

By December 31, 1929, deposits had grown to fifty-one million dollars, and interest payments exceeded two million dollars. During that period of growth the bank contin-

Raymond R. Frazier instigated numerous early changes within the banking industry. He was elected president of Washington Mutual Savings Bank in 1915 and was later appointed chairman of the board.

ued to provide additional services to its customers. At the request of school administrators, Washington Mutual launched the Seattle Public Schools Savings Program in March 1923. That program lasted for the next fifty years and taught hundreds of thousands of schoolchildren the value of saving money. Many of those students eventually used those childhood funds to finance their college educations or launch careers.

The 1930s brought devastating financial trouble to banks throughout the nation. The Depression had the country in its grasp, and the grip was tightening. Banks across the nation failed, and customers' savings were wiped out. Washington Mutual, however, rode out the financial storm. As one financial institution after another closed its doors forever or put its customers on notice, Washington Mutual bravely opened its doors for business each banking day and paid every withdrawal request in full. In addition, the bank saved many of its customers from losing everything they owned by using every possible means available to avoid foreclosing on its customers' homes.

However, those years were not

easy ones for the bank, as deposits plummeted and surplus funds dwindled. Then, in 1933, Dietrich Schmitz was elected president of the institution. He was an outstanding financial leader, and as the Depression lifted he worked to reestablish Washington Mutual's solid foundation. Soon, business was again on the rise, and surplus funds were robust once more.

During World War II Washington Mutual again aided the country with an aggressive savings bond campaign. In addition, the institution opened its first branch office, which was a merger with Coolidge Mutual Savings Bank. By the 1960s Washington Mutual had established branches throughout the state.

In 1958 Stuart C. Frazier succeeded Schmitz as president. He served until his death in 1960, at which time Harry G. Baldwin was elected president. Anthony I. Eyring replaced Baldwin in 1963, and C.W. Eldridge was elected to the presidency ten years later. In 1981 Louis H. Pepper, a recognized authority on banking and real estate law, was elected chief executive officer. Pepper had served as bank counsel and as a trustee for over twenty-five years.

Today the institution that began with just $5,000 and an invincible pioneer spirit has over four billion dollars in assets and several subsidiaries. Washington Mutual Savings Bank has expanded its service to represent more than just a bank and now provides a wide variety of financial services including full-service security brokerage, insurance, and pension administration for its customers.

CH2M HILL

In 1945 Holly Cornell, who had recently returned from World War II, and Fred Merryfield started the now-nationwide professional engineering firm of CH2M HILL in a small bedroom office in Corvallis, Oregon.

Cornell, a structural engineer, and Merryfield, a professor of civil engineering at Oregon State College, were joined in 1946 by Jim Howland and Burke Hayes, two classmates also just returned from the war. The four formed a partnership and called their new venture Cornell, Howland, Hayes & Merryfield.

The firm concentrated its efforts in the growing field of consulting engineering. By 1947 the partners had already completed their 200th project. The following year two new partners, Ralph Roderick and Archie Rice, joined the company. Business was on the rise, and the firm began the first of its expansion efforts with the opening of its Boise office in 1950. That same year it adopted the name CH2M. No one remembers exactly how the CH2M abbreviation first came to be. Rice claims the acronym was the result of a word game. Hayes says it was a client's idea. However it came about, the name took some time to catch on. The firm continued to use Cornell, Howland, Hayes & Merryfield for some time because the founders believed CH2M did not seem professional enough in those more straight-laced days. However, despite the company's initial efforts to ignore the catchy name, it prevailed. CH2M was officially incorporated in 1966. Five years later the firm merged with Clair A. Hill and Associates, and the name CH2M HILL was adopted.

In 1960 the firm opened an office in Seattle. The Seattle regional office, now located in Bellevue, has the largest professional staff of any of the firm's offices. CH2M HILL is the largest consulting engineering firm in Washington State. Two of CH2M HILL's recent growth areas are solid waste management and toxic and hazardous waste management. The Seattle regional office is one of the main centers for this work.

Since CH2M HILL opened its Seattle office, it has been responsible for a number of notable water supply, wastewater-treatment, and industrial projects in Washington. The first was the Normandy Park Creek drainage study and design, which triggered the opening of the Seattle office. In addition, the firm has completed major projects for Boeing, the Lakewood Water District, the Puget Sound Naval Shipyard, and the City of Seattle, as well as many other well-known area clients. Its projects range

Bremerton Wastewater Treatment Plant, one of many projects CH2M HILL has designed to improve water quality around Puget Sound.

from multimillion-dollar, ultracomplex engineering assignments such as the Yakima-Tieton Irrigation District Rehabilitation Project, to a multitude of smaller projects throughout the state. CH2M HILL gets nearly two-thirds of its work from current clients who look to the company whenever they have new or additional projects.

In 1968 CH2M HILL acquired the Seattle office of H. Zinder and Associates, a firm of economists. That acquisition allowed CH2M HILL to further diversify its expertise and add breadth to its operations.

CH2M HILL's Seattle office employs nearly 325 people—a figure that has doubled over the past five years. Charles V. "Tom" Gibbs is manager of the Seattle regional office. Gibbs is a Seattleite who completed his bachelor's, master's, and predoctoral work at the University of Washington. Before joining CH2M HILL, Gibbs was active in

the local community and held a number of positions with Seattle Metro, including seven years as executive director.

A community-minded spirit is part of the CH2M HILL business philosophy. Employees are encouraged to become involved in activities that will benefit area citizens. As a result, many of the Seattle office staff are heavily involved in such projects as the Food Bank, Municipal League, the United Way, and various chambers of commerce.

CH2M HILL is an employee-owned firm. At the time of its incorporation in 1966, the partnership was dissolved in favor of sharing the company with the men and women who are ultimately responsible for its success. CH2M HILL has found that this policy not only improves the firm's product quality but substantially lowers employee turnover.

Today CH2M HILL is active in

a wide variety of projects for public and private clients, including environmental studies, facilities planning and design, urban and regional planning, site development, and a host of other related activities. It employs engineers, planners, economists, scientists, and support personnel.

CH2M HILL has won numerous national and regional awards for excellence, and it looks forward to many more in the future. The Seattle regional office is ready to help Washingtonians tackle and conquer the environmental and engineering challenges the future will bring to the state.

CH2M HILL's early soils investigation equipment, as shown here, has evolved over forty years into state-of-the-art laboratory and technical facilities to meet the engineering needs of the firm's public and private clients.

ROFFE, INC.

Samuel Roffe founded Roffe, Inc., almost by accident back in 1953. At the time Roffe was a fabric cutter for Seattle Woolens, a clothing manufacturing company. However, Seattle Woolens was sold to Pete Manzi after it had filed for bankruptcy. Manzi changed the factory's emphasis from uniforms to men's sport and top coats, dropping the firm's old commitment with Pacific Outfitters. With these changes, Roffe saw an opportunity and chose to go into business for himself.

So he began—with one lone power machine operator as his employee, a rental agreement from Pete Manzi for the use of his factory during off-hours, and the company's discarded uniform accounts as his customer. Roffe, who could not afford to quit his regular job as a fabric cutter, pursued his new business venture at night and on weekends.

The business struggled along for two years. Then, in 1955, the manager of the University of Washington Bookstore, who knew of Roffe's penchant for perfection and quality, asked him to make ski pants to sell in the store. Soon, Roffe ski pants were being distributed to ski specialty stores in the West. By 1956, through innovative experimentation, the company became the first in the United States to manufacture stretch ski pants.

As Roffe's reputation grew, so did his business. In 1958 the firm gave up its rental agreement and moved into space of its own. Roffe was finally in business entirely for himself.

In those days the ski business itself was an infant industry. Growth was slow until the 1960 Winter Olympics at Squaw Valley. Roffe's reputation for fine-quality skiwear had earned the firm the honor of outfitting the U.S. Olym-

pic Alpine Ski Team that year. As a result of those televised Olympics, skiers became national sports figures, and thousands of Americans took to the slopes for the first time.

Throughout the 1960s skiing experienced a large increase in popularity, and Roffe grew with the sport. The company's once-tiny western distribution business exploded, and Roffe ski pants appeared in specialty shops nation-

In addition to his fabric-cutting job at Seattle Woolens, Sam Roffe also modeled for the company "because he happened to be the right size." Photo-ad circa 1929

wide.

By 1967 parkas were added to the Roffe line, and the uniform business was abandoned. However, while Roffe was known for its high-quality, functional items, it lacked fashion savvy. Sam Roffe realized he needed to concentrate on this if he was to compete with the more fashion-conscious European skiwear manufacturers. As a result, he hired the company's first

designer.

Roffe's newly redirected emphasis on creative efforts and technological advancements marked the beginning of its transformation from basic skiwear-manufacturing company to a fashion leader.

By 1976 Roffe was ready to begin looking toward international expansion. That year it signed its first agreement with Mitsui & Company of Japan. The firm has since extended its distribution to Canada, Australia, South America, and Europe.

Today Roffe, Inc., employs approximately 275 people. It still manufactures its product exclusively in the United States with union labor, and Sam Roffe is still in charge. He can still be seen, aproned, with scissors in hand, working on the latest fashion line. As an employee once characterized him: "He isn't an executive. He's a cutter . . . who happens to own a multimillion-dollar skiwear company.

Sam Roffe still spends most of his time on the cutting floor of his skiwear factory. He is shown here with two of his firm's models.

PRUDENTIAL BANK

Prudential Bank, FSB, first became part of Seattle's financial community when it was incorporated under the name Union Savings and Loan Association on June 1, 1916. However, the institution lasted under that name for only thirty days. Then, on June 30, 1916, the board voted to change its name to Prudential Savings & Loan Association. Fortunately, that name satisfied the board, and it endured for many years.

Business for the savings and loan during its first eleven years of operation was far from brisk. Although the bank's board members were among the community's influential luminaries, they were not aggressive bankers. As a result, the fledgling institution recognized almost no growth, and resources fluctuated between $300,000 and $400,000.

Then, in 1927, major board and office personnel changes altered the bank's floundering fortunes. The new managers launched a vigorous advertising campaign to attract additional shareholders. The aggressive stance worked, and assets soared from $400,000 in 1927 to nearly $2.5 million by December 31, 1930.

Prudential's good fortune was short-lived, however. The 1930s brought the Depression and, like the rest of the country's financial institutions, Prudential found itself in deep financial trouble. Loan defaults were increasing at alarming rates, and long lines of shareholders were withdrawing their funds. Prudential was unable to bear up under the financial burden, and it was forced to suspend customer withdrawals. During that period the association was also not permitted to accept deposits of savings, and business languished.

In an effort to save the institution, another management change

Stephen S. Selak, currently a consultant to Prudential Bank, served as president and manager for many years.

was made. In 1932 Stephen S. Selak was hired as assistant secretary and given the mandate of resolving the "frozen" loans that were being held by the organization. His hard work and innovative planning paid off, and Prudential received approval for FSLIC insurance and had its full business operations restored by 1936. Selak went on to become president and manager of the now financially sound institution in 1944. Today he serves in an advisory capacity for Prudential Bank.

In March 1949 the board of directors converted the association into a mutual savings bank, and its new name, Prudential Mutual Savings Bank, reflected that change. Over the next three decades the institution enjoyed increased profits and growth. Then, beginning in 1979, Prudential again suffered at the hands of a volatile economy. Like many of its fellow institutions, it experienced three years of unprofitability in the early 1980s.

However, in January 1983 Patrick F. Patrick was named president and chief executive officer,

Prudential Bank operated out of this tiny office for several years before the building was replaced by the current headquarters.

and the bank took yet another management approach. This new approach reorganized the institution, changing it to a public company and then to a holding company, and profitability was restored. Today Prudential Bank's assets are in excess of $300 million.

Erected in 1971, the fourteen-story Northern Life Building houses Prudential Bank's corporate offices. The institution's offices have been at this location since 1928.

J.M. McCONKEY & CO., INC.

J.R. "Mac" McLean and his wife began growing bulbs in the backyard of their home in Elma, Washington, in 1932. Mail-order and local sales grew, and what began as a supplemental income to help support a Depression family soon became a prosperous business. McLean found that to operate the young business he needed more land for growing bulbs and a warehouse for handling them. As a result, he moved to the Puyallup Valley, the bulb-growing capital of the United States.

The bulb business was seasonal, and McLean was soon importing many different bulb varieties from Europe to round out his offerings. In what was the first of many innovative moves, McLean became the first importer of quality tulip bulbs from Japan following World War II. By that time McLean was also selling his product nationwide to wholesale greenhouse operators who would grow the bulbs for holidays and for cut flowers.

These growers needed products other than bulbs to supplement their businesses. Soon McLean added a few supply lines to his offerings. And, in his farsightedness, he saw a future in plastic pots. McLean was a pioneer in the introduction of plastic flower pots for greenhouse growers and of plastic nursery containers for field growers of nursery stock.

By the 1960s the McLeans were ready to retire, and Mac suggested that Jack McConkey, then a salesman for a Seattle agricultural firm, buy him out. Jack and Elaine McConkey did just that and became the new owners in 1964.

Jack McConkey had enjoyed a career as an innovative salesman, and the future of plastics in horti-

Jack McConkey (right), president, and his wife, Elaine, who serves as secretary/treasurer.

culture became immediately apparent to him. Greenhouse growers were using heavy clay pots that were difficult for workers to handle and to transport, and nurseries were using second-hand metal cans that were unsightly and dangerous to handle.

However, getting an industry to change is always difficult. Yet a positive change will occur when presented properly, at the right time, and by a positive company. The McConkeys were the major force in accomplishing that positive change in the horticulture industry. By being able to send their products to market in attractive, safe-to-handle plastic containers, growers could serve their customers on a year-round basis. Gardening was no longer a seasonal pleasure—landscapers and home owners could plant and create natural beauty year-round.

The firm was no longer just a supplier of bulbs; in fact, bulbs

were later dropped from its product line. The McConkey name soon became familiar throughout the country, and in 1969 the firm's name was changed to J.M. McConkey & Co., Inc. That same year McConkey bought a plastic pot production plant in Tacoma and another in Inglewood, California. Soon injection-molded plastic pots were being manufactured twenty-four hours a day, seven days a week to keep up with the growing demand. A fleet of truck tractors and semitrailers was and is busy year-round delivering to growers

The Sumner, Washington, headquarters of J.M. McConkey & Co., Inc.

The McConkeys opened this 64,000-square-foot facility in Garden Grove, California, to accommodate the giant nursery market that exists there.

throughout the West.

With the plastic pot division well under way, the McConkeys turned their attention to other areas of the horticulture industry. This began the company's evolution from a bulb farm to the largest manufacturer and distributor of horticultural products in the West.

In 1974 the business was moved from Puyallup to a 72,000-square-foot facility the company had built in Sumner, Washington. That same year the company also built and moved into a 64,000-square-foot structure in Garden Grove, California, to better serve their prime market in that state.

J.M. McConkey & Co., Inc., has had a knack for predicting changes in the horticulture business and then being prepared to provide new and innovative products for the industry. This knack has led to the publication of a 100-plus-page catalog in order to display all of the products the company either manufactures or distributes to thirteen states throughout the West, including Alaska and Hawaii, and to British Columbia. The firm also has ventured into the international market with sales to Australia, Saudi Arabia, and a number of other foreign countries.

McConkey's search for new and better technology for the horticulture industry did not stop with plastic pots. In 1967 he decided it was time for the industry to mechanize. He toured the country but found no equipment other than what a few growers had built for themselves. He did discover Gordon Gleason, whom he calls an

"innovative nurseryman with a genius for designing and building equipment." At McConkey's urging, Gleason began developing machines commercially, and J.M. McConkey & Co. became the distributor for what is today Gleason Industries, Inc., of Clackamas, Oregon. There is now equipment to mix growing media, automatically fill pots, plant seeds, convey plants into greenhouses or into the field, and water and fertilize them. The McConkey/Gleason team changed horticulture worldwide, for today it is an industry with mechanization rather than manual labor.

In the late 1970s McConkey launched a wire division with hanging basket wires as the primary product. His timing was perfect. The nation was soon hit by a hanging plant craze, and McConkey found himself the only manufacturer in the United States set up to mechanically produce the various wires to hang all the different pots. The wire division operated twenty-four hours a day, seven days a week, and the company enjoyed windfall profits. Since then the firm has added the production of wire rings for use in making Christmas wreaths, and ships the product nationwide. More recently the company added brown kraft sleeves to its product line. Produced by the millions each year, these paper sleeves are designed to

protect plants during shipment.

The McConkeys speak with pride of the relationships they have built over the years with businesses that manufacture products that their firm distributes. These companies range from local firms to a number of *Fortune* 500 corporations.

A relationship was recently established between J.M. McConkey & Co. and General Electric. GE produces a new greenhouse covering that should lower greenhouse heating bills by about 40 percent, and J.M. McConkey & Co. has been selected as its exclusive West Coast distributor.

J.M. McConkey & Co., Inc., has grown from a backyard bulb farm to a corporation that employs over 150 people and has had a profound effect on the modernization of the horticulture industry in general. Today the firm is still family operated. Jack McConkey serves as president, and his wife, Elaine, is secretary/treasurer. In addition, the McConkeys' two sons, Edward and Trenton, are both involved in the business. The McConkeys hasten to add that the firm is blessed with top management that assures a positive and expanding future. There is a feeling of "family" throughout the organization to support the McConkeys' statement that it has taken everyone in the company to make it a success.

PACIFIC LUTHERAN UNIVERSITY

The Reverend Bjug Harstad arrived in the West in October 1890 with a mandate from the American Lutheran Church to establish an educational institution in the Pacific Northwest. He worked quickly. By December of that year Harstad had found a location and formed a corporation called the Pacific Lutheran University Association. The site Harstad chose for his school was called Parkland. It was lush prairie located ten miles south of downtown Tacoma, and he delighted in the hard, rocky soil that served as a fond reminder of his Norwegian homeland.

However, Harstad also had some sound economic reasons for choosing Parkland. In order to build his school, Harstad needed both people and funds. There were still only seven Lutheran congregations in the entire Northwest, and the school project had not been provided with any funds from the church. As it happened, Ward T. Smith had arrived in Parkland just prior to Harstad and, like Harstad, had decided to stake his future in the beautiful little community.

The Reverend Bjug Harstad, founder.

Smith purchased a large amount of land in the area and intended to divide the land into small plots and sell them to launch his real estate career. Now all he needed were clients.

Since Harstad needed funds and Smith needed people, it was only natural for their interests to merge. Harstad would attract Norwegians from the Northwest, Midwest, and East to help build the school. Smith, in return for clients, would give 10 percent of his proceeds from the sale of $100 lots to finance the school's construction. In addition, Smith agreed to donate 100 acres for the new campus. Smith donated the 100 acres, but the sale of the lots was disappointing.

To reach his fellow Lutherans, Harstad began *The Pacific Lutheran Herald,* a Norwegian-language newspaper. The paper was a literary and social monthly, but also served as a practical means for enlisting supporters.

Funds for the school's first building were largely from churches and individuals contacted by Harstad. Construction began in March 1891, just five months after Harstad had arrived in the area. Old Main, now called Harstad Hall, and listed as a National Historic Site, was dedicated in October 1894. At the dedication, a visiting bishop from Iowa called the building the "Miracle Castle."

The new Pacific Lutheran Academy, with Harstad as its president, had an enrollment of thirty students and a staff of ten that first year. By 1896 the academy published its first catalog, which announced tuition of one dollar per week. Instrumental music, typing, and shorthand, however, were extra. The academy continued as a high school for the next four years. Then, in 1898, the institution became Pacific Lutheran Academy and Business College, and the first strains of higher education began for the school.

The academy's first years were lean. The faculty existed on paltry, and sometimes no, wages. Two faculty members kept cows on cam-

Pacific Lutheran Academy's first faculty consisted of (bottom row, left to right) Meyer Brandvig, Mrs. Carlo Sperati, and Miss Sophie Peterson. In the top row (left to right) are the Reverend Ballestad, the Reverend Carlo Sperati, T.C. Satra, the Reverend T. Larson, the Reverend N. Christiansen, W. Shahan, and the Reverend B. Harstad.

pus to provide their families with dairy products. Many others depended on the generosity of the local stores to extend them credit so they could feed their families.

In 1917 the fledgling institution could no longer survive, and the doors to the Miracle Castle were closed. However, the school that was built on vision, dedication, and faith would not die. Two years later, in 1919, PLA merged with Spokane and Columbia Colleges, two other struggling Lutheran schools, and the academy was reopened.

The school's name was changed again in 1921 to Pacific Lutheran College, when it added a junior college and a two-year education program. In the early 1930s the institution was organized into a three-year normal school that became a four-year college of education in 1939, and a college of liberal arts two years later.

The 1920s and 1930s brought many changes to the tiny school, and many quality programs were founded during that era. However, it was not until the university's

second half-century that it began to experience the growth that enabled it to attain regional, national, and even international prominence. During the first fifty years of its existence, only two campus buildings were constructed, but for the next twenty-five years nearly one major structure a year was added.

The college's growth can be linked to the arrival of president Seth Eastvold in 1943 and the flood of GIs returning from World War II. Alumni who graduated during the postwar period have made names for themselves in varied endeavors and have helped put the school on the map worldwide. For example, Dr. William Foege, a 1957 graduate, spearheaded the worldwide eradication of smallpox and later directed the Center for Disease Control in Atlanta, Georgia. Dr. Isaria Kimambo, a 1962 graduate, became chancellor of the 20,000-student University of Dar Es Salaam in Tanzania. Lute Jerstad, member of the class of 1958, was one of the first Americans to climb Mount Everest.

Finally, in 1960 the school became a full-fledged university and took back its original name, Pacific Lutheran University. When Robert Mortvedt took the helm as president in 1962, he continued the emphasis on expansion and concentrated on academic programs. He continued to build a faculty that has achieved an outstanding reputation. Several national texts now rank PLU among the nation's elite academic institutions.

President Eugene Wiegman began his term in 1969, during the height of nationwide campus un-

Pacific Lutheran University's 1985 graduating class.

rest. He brought to the institution a new sense of community and social awareness coupled with activism. Since 1975, when current president William Rieke began his administration, the university has raised more than twenty million dollars through gifts and grants for capital construction and renovation, including a $7.5-million science complex that bears Rieke's name.

The modern version of the Miracle Castle boasts the largest undergraduate enrollment among both Northwest independent colleges and American Lutheran Church-affiliated colleges nationwide. During the past fifteen years the alumni rolls have doubled and now exceed 20,000. In addition, Pacific Lutheran University has become active in international relations. PLU has exchange programs with universities and study-abroad programs in the People's Republic of China, Taiwan, West Germany, France, Denmark, Sweden, Hong Kong, Spain, England, Mexico, Tanzania, and Norway. Students from all over the world study on the PLU campus.

Pacific Lutheran Academy's original campus consisted of one building, Old Main (now Harstad Hall), which still serves as an active center of campus life.

241

EDGEWATER INN

On April 21, 1962, President John F. Kennedy opened the Seattle World's Fair with a gold nugget key and much pomp and circumstance—but without Seattle's now legendary Edgewater Inn.

The inn, which is the only hotel property in the West built entirely over the water, was plagued by a number of problems during its construction. As a result, the hotel that was supposed to open in time for the fair opened room by room after the fair had begun.

The onslaught of tourists in Seattle to see the fair made accommodations of any kind premium items that roomless visitors were willing to pay nearly any price to secure. However, the Edgewater Inn's developers steadfastly refused to take advantage of the shortage by overpricing their accommodations. Therefore, rooms at the Edgewater ranged from a reasonable nine dollars to sixteen dollars per night depending on the occupancy and location, and hotel employees made special efforts to accommodate as many desperate lodgers as possible.

The rooms were literally rented

The Edgewater Inn offers Seattle visitors a unique experience in accommodations. The hotel is built entirely over the water and the management encourages guests to fish from their room windows.

the very day they were completed. As a consequence, many of the hotel's first guests slept on rollaway cots in unfurnished rooms. Those guests were served a continental breakfast in the hotel lobby because the dining room had not yet been built.

The Edgewater Inn finally held its belated grand opening in November 1962. Since that time the hotel, which provides its guests with equipment for fishing from their windows, has become an established Seattle landmark. Its giant neon "E" has been used by ships in the bay as a directional beacon. During the 1964 earthquake the hotel was deemed one of the safest places in town because it stands on pilings that are better able to absorb shock.

This uniquely constructed building is supported by steel-reinforced cement pilings that have been sunk forty feet to bedrock and reinforced by 45-degree, three-foot-slab, steel-reinforced cement pilings extending eighty feet into the bay. In 1968 a fourth story was added to the building by constructing it in sections across the street and lifting them by crane onto the hotel.

A number of famous entertainers have stayed at the Edgewater, and many have tried their hand at fishing from its windows. The hotel has played host to such luminaries as the Dave Clark Five, Pearl Bailey, Johnny Carson, and George Carlin. It has survived the onslaught of frenzied fans seeking a glimpse of guests such as the Beatles, the Rolling Stones, Alice Cooper, and David Bowie. It even served as the inspiration for a Frank Zappa tune entitled "Mud Shark," presumably the result of a less than successful window-fishing experience.

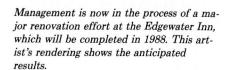

Management is now in the process of a major renovation effort at the Edgewater Inn, which will be completed in 1988. This artist's rendering shows the anticipated results.

WRIGHT RUNSTAD & COMPANY

Wright Runstad & Company was born over breakfast in Boston in the fall of 1970 when Howard Wright and Jon Runstad first discussed the venture that actually came together by 1972.

Wright brought nearly eighty years of his family's expertise as general contractors to the new firm, as well as a belief that real estate development should be completely separate from contracting because it requires completely different skills.

Runstad brought to the firm an outstanding education beginning with two undergraduate degrees from the University of Washington and an M.B.A. from Harvard. He also had experience in major commercial real estate development from his job with a Boston developer. In addition, Runstad had a strong desire to return to Seattle, his family's home for four generations.

With this combination of experience and love for Seattle, Wright Runstad set out to develop projects that would affect the very nature of Seattle and, ultimately, the city's liveability. The firm set about its purpose with the compassion that comes from understanding the awesome responsibility developers have to maintain an area's standards and the caring that comes from a sense of roots in the area.

The first group of projects did not begin until 1974, a full two years after the formation of the company. However, since those first projects began, Wright Runstad has become increasingly involved in Seattle's future, and it has established itself as a quality developer with an eye toward improving the city's business district.

The firm began as an outgrowth of the Howard S. Wright Construction Company, which celebrated 100 years of service to the Seattle area in 1985. However, today Wright Runstad is a distinct and separate organization with separate management, ownership, and operating objectives.

Over the past thirteen years, since its inception, the company has expanded geographically to Bellevue, Anchorage, Los Angeles, Portland, and Boise. Wright Runstad has made a commitment to the development of Bellevue's

The First Interstate Center, which was developed by Wright Runstad, is one of Seattle's finest examples of architectural design. Photo by Bischoff & Associates, Incorporated

A study model of Wright Runstad & Company's newest project in downtown Seattle, 1201 Third Avenue, a 55-story building of classical design that will set yet a new and higher standard for the city.

downtown district, and, true to that commitment, is now one of the most active developers in that area.

Since its formation, more than five million square feet of commercial space has been created by the firm. Over 70 percent of the company's development projects have been located in the Puget Sound area, with the majority centered in Seattle and Bellevue. Wright Runstad developed Seattle's First Interstate Center, the 1111 Third Avenue Building, and other landmark projects. It is currently developing its most ambitious project yet, located on Block 5 in the heart of Seattle's financial district. In Bellevue, the firm is responsible for such buildings as One Bellevue Center, Rainier Bank Plaza, and the Microsoft corporate headquarters.

As a long-term investor in the buildings it develops, Wright Runstad & Company provides ongoing professional property management services with special emphasis on strong long-term relationships with its tenants.

243

ROTHSCHILD AND COMPANY

Can you imagine 128 years of one family continuously serving the transportation industry of Puget Sound? This story commenced in Port Townsend, Washington Territory, in 1858 when David Charles Henry Rothschild carefully selected Port Townsend, the then-premier American seaport of Washington Territory, as his business and family home.

Henry Rothschild, 1863-1938

"DCH," born in Sulzbach, Germany, in 1824, attended a mercantile school until he was nineteen years old and then promptly came to America. He briefly returned to his home in January 1849, relating to his family his knowledge of the United States. In April he left again to seek adventure and opportunity in the world.

DCH traveled to San Francisco, arriving there by sailing ship in November 1849. The news of the great California gold discovery was the magnet. Between then and 1858 he worked in San Francisco, Sacramento, and Nevada City; visited New York City and Germany; sailed three years in the Pacific as a supercargo visiting China, the East Indies, Australia, and Tahiti; and finally worked for a few months in Whatcom, Washington Territory. In August 1858 he settled in Port Townsend, thus completing his goal of adventure at the "old" age of thirty-four.

Port Townsend, located just at the mouth of Puget Sound, offered a magnificent harbor for sailing vessels, which then carried all the commerce to and from the Washington Territory. Ships needed service when in port, and DCH purchased central waterfront property and commenced a mercantile and ship service business that later included stevedoring. He constructed two stores on his fifty-five feet of main street frontage. They backed to the harbor and served the small boat he used to go to and from the ships at anchor.

Opportunity meant facing the business challenges of the moment and resulted in his good reputation, blended with modest success. DCH's first child was Henry, born in late 1863 in the living quarters above his store. DCH moved his family in 1868 into a newly built home overlooking the harbor and business area. Today the home is a state museum. DCH's five children included three sons. It was Henry who carried on after his father's death in 1886. Under Henry the company's activity became solely stevedoring. Business fortunes of the family were at a very low ebb, but over time Henry's skills and dedication nurtured the business and expanded its good name.

Henry's sister, Regina, married William J. Jones in 1891. William joined in Henry's business in the late 1890s and opened and managed the first branch office, in Tacoma, in 1900. Bill moved to Seattle in 1904 and repeated the success. Then, in 1908, Bill and Henry expanded the business into the Columbia River district through the purchase of Brown and McCabe Stevedoring Company, which Bill supervised from Seattle until 1910

Clayton Rothschild Jones, 1894-1956

when he moved to Portland.

Henry's marriage was childless while Bill's produced a son, Clayton, born in 1894.

As a result of a business disagreement regarding Bill's management of the Oregon operation, Bill separated from Henry in the business in 1913. Bill opened a competing firm. Soon Henry moved to Portland, leaving Rothschild and Company in the good care of president Albert Bartlett.

JONES WASHINGTON STEVEDORING COMPANY

Through most of the 1920s Fay Miller was president of Rothschild and Company due to the death of Albert Bartlett. Fay opened sister stevedoring companies in Everett, Anacortes, Bellingham, and also in Vancouver, British Columbia. Business success did not match ambition.

In the Columbia River district, Clayton Jones, son of Bill, succeeded to ownership of Bill's new company upon the early death of Bill in 1921. Rowland Clapp, hired by Bill prior to Clayton's return from World War I, and Clayton made an effective team, and that business prospered.

In late 1929 Henry, at sixty-six years of age, elected to retire. He reached an agreement with his nephew, Clayton, and the family business was rejoined. Several weeks later the stock market crash occurred. Business during the early 1930s was difficult.

Rowland moved to Seattle as president of Rothschild and Company—to face adversity and to achieve great success. Clayton remained in Portland, where the just-purchased Brown and McCabe business was amalgamated into Clayton's company, W.J. Jones and Son, Inc.

Rothschild's expansion of the 1920s was reversed by the sale of the sister companies; however, in late 1935 a powerful Oregon and Washington competitor, controlled in California, elected to sell, and the International Stevedoring Company business was obtained.

The firm adopted the name of Rothschild International Stevedoring Company, which continued in use until 1971. The present name, Jones Washington Stevedoring Company, was adopted in 1974.

Clayton R. Jones, while heading W.J. Jones and Son, also became head of a family—William, born in

Rowland C. Clapp, 1890-1967

1922, and Clayton Jr., in 1926. Upon completion of his education at the New York State Maritime Academy, followed by the Wharton School of the University of Pennsylvania, young Clayton joined Rothschild in 1950. He served in various capacities until assuming the presidency upon Rowland Clapp's retirement in 1963. As young Clayton's father died in 1956, the "Jr." now is seldom used.

In 1958 Rothschild celebrated 100 years of service. DCH, in choosing not only a truly wondrous location but also recognizing the enduring necessity of joining the producers with the consumers of the world through the medium of transportation with its service requirements potential, has given lasting opportunity to his descendants and all those associated with them in furthering the business DCH so wisely started. Clayton commented that the next 100-year celebration would be the responsibility of others still to come, a

view that typifies the very long-range attitude of this pioneer business.

Twenty-eight of the second hundred years are finished. The company's head office is in Seattle, with operational offices in Tacoma, Everett, Aberdeen, Port Angeles, and Olympia. The necessary lift trucks, specialized stevedoring gear, and equipment is owned, transported, and maintained on

Clayton R. Jones, Jr., 1926-

company premises by company employees. Activities in Oregon involve the business of Jones Oregon Stevedoring Company, headquartered in Portland, whose president is Clayton R. Jones III, familiarly known as "C-3," fifth-generation family manager of DCH's "opportunity."

This story cannot be told without the expression of the sincerest thanks of the family owners to all who have worked with the Rothschilds and the Joneses and to the families of these dedicated and appreciated people.

RAINIER BANCORPORATION

Brothers Robert and Oliver Spencer await their first customers of the day at the National Bank of Commerce office on First Avenue and Yesler Way in Seattle's downtown.

Newcomers to Seattle in 1889 inhaled an exciting mixture of frontier optimism and faith in the future. No longer an outpost on the Pacific, Washington Territory was on the road to statehood, and land speculators in Seattle promised the choicest lakeview lots for less than $600. Several new banks were organized that year to finance this expansion, and two of them, the National Bank of Commerce and the Washington National Bank, would provide the base for the present Rainier Bancorporation.

Strong men have long been the hallmark of banking. Robert S. Spencer, founder of the National Bank of Commerce, and Manson Backus, who organized Washington National, were men with a sure eye to the promise of the future and a cautious, steady hand on the financial means to achieve it. In a time when banking deals were decided by an individual's character and a handshake, Spencer and Backus enjoyed reputations as solid and careful judges of character. Their similar banking philosophies led to the merger of Washington Trust into the National Bank of Commerce in 1906.

As Seattle grew and prospered in the first decades of the twentieth century, so did the National Bank of Commerce. But the structure of banking was beginning to change, and a new generation of bankers was shaping the industry. Andrew Price, a young Seattle financier and banker, grew increasingly frustrated with regulations limiting expansion of banks throughout the state. As a result, he formed a holding company for his Marine bank group and coined a new word in the process, creating the Marine Bancorporation in 1927. The following year Price bought the National Bank of Commerce of Seattle, which became the flagship operation of the Marine Bancorporation.

Andrew Price, once labeled the *enfant terrible* of Seattle bankers by *Fortune* magazine, earned a reputation as a salesman, innovator, and corporate builder. With the National Bank of Commerce as the anchor, Price and Rainier Bancorporation acquired numerous local Washington banks that became the precursor to today's branch banking.

In 1948 Maxwell Carlson succeeded Price, and at forty-two, became one of the youngest major bank presidents in the nation. Carlson continued to expand on Price's vision of a "department store of finance," broadening the bank's retail, consumer, and mortgage loan services and opening over seventy new branches. Carlson saw that Seattle, strategically situated at the edge of the Pacific Rim, offered spectacular potential for business in Asia and Alaska. He established an international division with offices in Tokyo and Hong Kong and encouraged greater participation in the financing of Alaska's growth.

Current chairman and chief executive officer G. Robert Truex, Jr., came to Rainier in 1973 from Bank of America in San Francisco where he was an executive vice-president and held several senior-level positions.

Changes in state and federal banking laws in the late 1960s and early 1970s and the "Boeing Recession" ushered in a transitional period in which banks sought new paths to a stable future. Truex reorganized the departmental structure of the bank, improved its computer services, and regionalized the branch system. He also gave local managers more autonomy, and led the way for an increased role in commercial banking. In addition, he orchestrated a change in corporate name from Marine Bancorporation and National Bank of Commerce to Rainier Bancorporation and Rainier National Bank. The change announced the arrival of a modern financial organization as did the opening of Rainier Bank Tower, the striking forty-story building on the Metropolitan Tract designed by Japanese-American architect Minoru Yamasaki.

By 1986 Rainier Bancorporation had become one of the fifty largest bank holding companies in the nation, with assets of over $8 billion, a far cry from the original $1.25 million that capitalized the Marine Bancorporation nearly sixty years earlier.

The Rainier Bank Tower at Fifth Avenue and University Street in Seattle.

DARIGOLD, INC.

In the days following World War I the dairy industry in the Puget Sound area, as in the rest of the country, was in turmoil. Local dairy farmers with their perishable products were at the mercy of an often fickle market where large milk-processing companies might or might not buy their farm-fresh milk. Relief from those chaotic conditions was gained when the federal government, through the Capper-Volstead Act of 1921, allowed individual dairy farmers to join together into local cooperative organizations which through group effort and planning considerably reduced milk-production risks and stabilized marketing conditions.

In the following years, as the cooperative movement grew in the Pacific Northwest, local independent cooperatives further organized together as the United Dairymen's Association to develop more efficient milk product processing and marketing programs. At one time in the early 1940s this umbrella organization represented as many as 47 local, independent cooperative groups and nearly 50,000 small dairy farmer members in Washington, Oregon, Idaho, and western Montana.

In recent years, through consolidation and merger, the previously large number of small, local cooperative groups has consolidated down to one major cooperative dairy farmer umbrella organization, the Northwest Dairymen's Association, with a membership of 1,500. Although the number of members is less than it was four decades ago, individual farms are much larger and total milk production is greater.

As producing milk on the farm is a full-time operation in itself, dairy farmers found little time for milk product processing and marketing. In the late 1920s the

The Darigold plant in the early 1940s on Elliott Avenue West in Seattle, where Darigold products (butter, cheese, evaporated milk) were processed.

United Dairymen's Association purchased the Seattle-based Consolidated Dairy Products Company to act as a product processing and marketing agency for all its independent local members. "Darigold," a name selected in a dairy farmers' member contest, was trademarked and used as the marketing brand

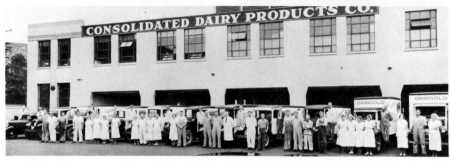

In 1936 Consolidated Dairy Products (now Darigold) employed—as it does now—laboratory specialists, administrative personnel, and distributors to help the dairy farmer bring his product to the marketplace.

name for products processed by Consolidated and other United Dairymen's Association member organizations licensed to use it. Over the years the Darigold name had become so well known and respected throughout the Northwest that Darigold, Inc., replaced Consolidated Dairy Products as the firm's official corporate name.

Currently the overall cooperative organization consisting of Northwest Dairymen's Association, the milk producing part of the organization, and Darigold, Inc., the product processing and marketing arm, is headquartered on Elliott Avenue West in Seattle. Production and distribution plants are located throughout Washington, Oregon, and California. Hawaii

and Alaska are serviced through brokers and distributors.

In the beginning Darigold was primarily a marketer of bulk fresh milk and manufactured dairy products such as cheese, butter, and evaporated and dried milk. In 1952 fresh milk and ice cream products were added to the product line, followed in 1969 by farm animal feed.

Today Darigold represents more than 1,500 employees. Yearly sales of approximately $650 million rank it 69 in the top 100 food processors in the country. Its modern milk-drying operation at Lynden, Washington, is one of the largest in the world. Through its insistence on quality from its members' farms to the final consumer and its interest in research, community participation, and complete sales and customer service programs, Darigold, Inc., has earned the loyalty and respect of Puget Sound consumers as a supplier of fine dairy products.

MANSON CONSTRUCTION AND ENGINEERING COMPANY

Manson Construction and Engineering Company has been a part of the Pacific Northwest's marine tradition since its inception in 1905. The corporation's founder, a young Swedish-born adventurer named Peter Manson, first encountered the beautiful Northwest when he jumped ship in Portland, Oregon, to sign up with a pile-driving crew.

For a time the ambitious young man toiled at his newfound profession. However, Manson longed to own his own company. He was able to scrape together extra funds from his monthly wages and used the money to purchase parts to build his own pile driver. After he successfully completed the rig, he began picking up extra jobs to fill his spare time.

Vashon-Maury Island Lyon Drydock and Shipyard—the birthplace of Manson Construction and Engineering Company. Photo circa 1905

Then, in 1905, the Dockton Shipyard & Drydock fell on hard times, and crew members were laid off. Manson saw this depression as an opportunity to launch his business on a full-time basis. Manson Construction's first jobs in the watery domain of Puget Sound included driving piles for steamship docks, fish traps, and log-booming grounds.

Soon Manson moved his burgeoning company from its first home on Vashon Island to Seattle.

The original Manson derrick (No. 1) and pile driver (No. 4) working on the west pier of Indian Island Bridge in 1951.

There, with his first tugboat and a second pile driver, he gradually became a dominant force in the early development of the Puget Sound waterfront.

The 1920s were prosperous years for the firm. Manson's son, Harry, a recent engineering graduate, joined the business during that time and added his engineering expertise to the company. The father-son team soon expanded the business to the new and exciting Alaskan frontier.

However, the 1930s brought the Depression, and Manson Construction came under financial pressure. The future looked bleak, but Peter and Harry had the sort of pioneer determination that such hard times demand, and they hung on. Gradually, the nation's economy began to rebound, and Manson Construction rebounded with it.

By 1939 the company was again prosperous. By that time, however, Harry had died, and Peter was ready to retire. The business was then turned over to Elmer Edwards. Edwards, who was Harry's brother-in-law, guided the firm for the next forty years. During that

time Manson Construction added dredging as well as the building of everything from breakwaters and marinas to bridges to its repertoire. By the 1970s Manson was the leading heavyweight marine construction company in the area, and had built some of the most sophisticated equipment in the field.

Today the firm is directed by the founder's grandson, Peter Haug, who succeeded Edwards in 1979, along with general manager Glenn Edwards. Haug instituted the company's white-with-red-trim color scheme that has made Manson equipment easily identified by everyone in the industry. Haug made the colorful change because the reflection of the previous gray paint made distinguishing the equipment on a job site next to impossible from afar. Haug and Edwards currently oversee approximately 200 Manson Construction and Engineering Company employees and are responsible for complex marine projects from Alaska to Mexico.

BOGLE & GATES

In 1891 the Puget Sound area could still be considered the wild and woolly West. Washington had been a state for little over a year, and its legal system had just begun to be defined.

Those were exciting times for lawyers who hoped to help form the legal base on which Washington would rely for generations to come. Judge W.H. Bogle and Charles Richardson were two young gentlemen who would later be responsible for many aspects of that base through their practice during that period of change and refinement. During that time the two opened a law practice in the frontier town of Tacoma. The firm specialized in admiralty law and was involved in many landmark marine cases.

The two partners practiced together for some time until Bogle moved to Seattle in the late 1890s. There he formed a partnership with Tom Hardin and Charles Spooner under the name Bogle, Hardin & Spooner. In 1906 Bogle's son, Lawrence, joined the firm following graduation from school and a short stint at another law firm.

From the early 1900s until 1926

the firm grew and evolved, changing its name several times in the process. It gradually branched out from its admiralty law specialty into other areas, but admiralty law remained its major field of expertise.

In 1926 the predecessor to today's modern firm of Bogle & Gates emerged. That year Cassius Gates joined W.H. and Lawrence Bogle, and the firm's name was changed to Bogle, Bogle & Gates. W.H. died just one year after Gates joined the firm, leaving Lawrence Bogle and Cassius Gates to guide the practice.

The two partners were a complement to each other because of their vastly differing personalities, and the practice flourished under their leadership. Bogle, Bogle & Gates litigated cases such as the "Strath Allyn-Virginian," which eventually went to the Supreme Court and helped establish signal guidelines for ships. The firm also represented many clients who profoundly affected Washington's future. Some of those clients included Canadian Pacific Railway Company, Kennecott Copper Corporation, Alaska Steamship Com-

The law firm of Bogle, Bogle & Gates in 1951 on the occasion of its twenty-fifth anniversary under that name.

pany, Seattle Construction & Dry Dock Company, and the Oregon and Washington Railroad and Navigation Company.

In 1965 the firm's name was changed to Bogle, Gates, Dobrin, Wakefield & Long. It was shortened for simplicity's sake in 1974 to Bogle & Gates. Today it is one of the largest and most successful law firms in the Northwest. It has expanded its practice in corporate and commercial matters and in civil litigation to such a degree that admiralty law has become a relatively small portion of the firm's overall practice.

Bogle & Gates' principal office is in Seattle, but it has also opened branch offices in Bellevue, Anchorage, and Washington, D.C., in order to better serve its clients. Today the firm that began in the frontier town of Tacoma when Washington's legal system was a mere skeletal frame has over 140 lawyers within its practice.

THE SEATTLE TIMES

On August 10, 1896, Colonel A.J. Blethen published the first 3,500 copies of his tiny four-page newspaper. Those first papers signaled the beginning of *The Seattle Times'* rise to a publication of national stature and journalistic acclaim.

Blethen had purchased the paper, then called *The Press-Times,* and its Associated Press franchise from a printing company that had been publishing the paper "as a mere incident of a job-printing business." The first issue under the new ownership carried an an-

Alden J. Blethen, 1896-1915

nouncement that "Colonel Alden J. Blethen of Minneapolis, 'a journalist of wide experience and acknowledged ability,' henceforth would edit the paper." Blethen had ambitious plans for his new venture, but the task before him was great. The previous publisher's lackadaisical attitude had evoked apathy in the citizenry, and the paper's circulation languished at 5,000, out of Seattle's total popula-

tion of 45,000.

However, Blethen was used to challenging adversity and winning, and he set out with that same determination in his newspaper venture. He had many ideas for improving the publication. He began a campaign to increase circula-

C.B. Blethen, 1915-1941

tion by reducing subscription rates from sixty cents to fifty cents per month.

Just fourteen days after Blethen's first issue, he announced plans to move the paper from Yesler Street to more suitable quarters, at Second Avenue and Columbia Street. Blethen also changed the content of the paper. He gave more prominence to local news and developed a society page, a theater page, and "The People's Forum," the first generation of letters to the editor. He obtained more national news through broadened Associated Press reports. Those changes, along with Blethen's poignant and lively journalistic style, put the little evening paper on the

Elmer E. Todd, 1941-1949

road to success. Just one and a half months after Blethen assumed control, the circulation had grown from 5,000 to 6,931. Within eight months it reached 8,215.

By 1898 Blethen's efforts to revitalize *The Times* were rewarded. Thousands of fortune seekers were pouring into the area on their way to the Alaska goldfields, and *The Times'* circulation jumped to 17,267. That growth required larger quarters, so the paper moved to Second and Union. There, on February 9, 1902, the paper published its first Sunday edition.

Then, on February 13, 1913, disaster struck. Three newsboys sitting on the steps of the Times Building noticed that the structure was on fire. Damage was extensive. *The Times* found temporary quarters at 1324 Fourth. However, the paper did not miss a day of publication thanks to one of Seattle's other dailies, *The Post-Intelligencer,* which shared its printing facilities.

In 1916 the paper moved to Times Square, which became the center of activity for news-hungry Seattleites. *The Times* had a giant reader board outside its building that displayed up-to-the-minute news on everything from election results to World Series scores. However, *The Times* again outgrew those facilities and moved in 1931 to its present location at

Fairview Avenue North and John Street.

C.B. Blethen, who in 1915 had succeeded his father, A.J. Blethen, died in 1941, at which time Elmer Todd became the first non-Blethen publisher. Todd handed the job to W.K. Blethen in 1949. At the time of W.K. Blethen's death in 1967, John A. Blethen was named publisher. From 1982 to 1985 W.J. Pennington published *The Times.* Today Frank A. Blethen is publisher and chief executive officer. John A. Blethen has continued as the company's chairman of the

John A. Blethen, 1967-1982

W.K. Blethen, 1949-1967

board since turning over his duties as publisher in 1982.

For several years circulation for both *The Times* and *The Post-Intelligencer* grew, and competition heated up. However, the evening *Times* steadily pulled away from the morning *Post-Intelligencer,* and by the early 1970s *The Times* had emerged a clear-cut winner. *The Post-Intelligencer* was losing money. For many years the citi-

zens had enjoyed the luxury of two major news and editorial voices— now the luxury was threatened. As allowed by the Newspaper Preservation Act, the two newspapers negotiated a joint operation, which consolidated much of their operations. Under that agreement each paper is allowed to maintain sepa-

W.J. Pennington, 1982-1985

rate editorial and news operations.

After extensive public hearings and court actions, *The Times* and *The Post-Intelligencer* entered into the Joint Operating Agreement in May 1983. As a result, Seattle's two editorial voices have been preserved. About twenty cities have similar joint operations.

The Times, with a daily circulation of 227,844 and a Sunday circulation of 477,307, is now recognized as one of the nation's best daily newspapers. It won its third and fourth Pulitzer Prizes in the early 1980s, has been cited for ex-

Frank A. Blethen, 1985-

cellence in design and use of color, and frequently is honored for its innovative feature sections.

The Times is one of the dwindling number of family-controlled newspapers in the United States. Frank A. Blethen, publisher and chief executive officer, is the fourth generation of his family to direct the company. *The Times* has 2,000 employees and also owns the *Walla Walla Union-Bulletin.*

OVERALL LAUNDRY SERVICES, INC.

Howard F. Keeler used his ingenuity and penchant for perfection as the catalysts for founding Overall Cleaning and Supply Company in 1920. The firm's name was changed to Overall Laundry Services, Inc., in 1970. Keeler first began his business by convincing a very dirty shipyard worker to let him have the man's heavily soiled clothes cleaned and returned to the shipyard.

Keeler's first customer was delighted with the laundry service, and he spread the word to his fellow workers. Soon Keeler was accepting laundry from a number of clients. For each one, he arranged to have the laundry cleaned, mended, pressed, and returned to the customer. For several years Keeler operated his tiny, one-man laundry operation, faithfully building his client base and slowly developing a reputation for quality service. By 1927 Keeler had enough business to justify expansion, and he built his first laundry plant on Yale Avenue in Seattle.

However, by the mid-1930s Keeler had another idea for his business. He decided to alter its course by offering to rent as well as service work clothing. He realized that there was a market for such a service because clothing was an expensive business cost for industries that were notorious for the heavy soiling of clothing. Keeler could see that renting such work clothing was an economically sound answer for those businesses, as well as an opportunity for Overall Laundry Services.

The company's first rental products were coveralls, shop coats, shop towels, and overalls. Over the past sixty-five years Overall Laundry's rental offerings have been greatly expanded. Today the firm is a complete rental supply service, providing products for uniform rentals, linen service, wiping towels, dust mops, floor mats, and restroom services.

However, it took many years for Overall Laundry to become the successful business it is today. Its growth years really began during the economic boom that followed the Great Depression. During that period Overall Laundry grew at an astonishing rate.

By 1937 the firm reached a sales volume of $2,000 per week. The Keelers were overjoyed and celebrated the company's phenomenal success. However, that spurt of growth was just the beginning for Overall Laundry. By 1946 the business had more than doubled its sales volume and was still growing rapidly.

Today Overall Laundry does a sales volume of over $300,000 per

Howard F. Keeler founded Overall Laundry Services in 1920. The business began as a tiny, one-man laundry service and has since grown into a regional rental supply firm.

week. It has two plants: a greatly expanded facility at the original location and a plant in Tacoma. Its laundry service centers cover western Washington from the Canadian border to Portland, Oregon. The company does over 250,000 pounds of laundry per week using 180,000 gallons of water per day.

Howard F. Keeler died in 1972 after spending nearly fifty-two years in the laundry business. He left the management of his company to his two sons, Mason "Beebs" and Travis Keeler. Beebs joined his father in the business in 1935 and is now retired. Travis started working part time for the company in 1955. He joined the firm on a full-time basis in 1962 and holds the title of president.

Today a fleet of Overall Laundry trucks service customers throughout the region.

Overall Laundry's first trucks provided delivery service to the Seattle area.

SAM'S TIRE SERVICE, INC.

Sam Pupo began his career in the tire business when he was just fifteen years old. From that tender age, and throughout his career, he built a reputation for friendliness and quality that eventually carried him through thirty-three years in the business and continued to play a part in the success of Sam's Tire Service, Inc., long after his death.

After a few years of working for other tire firms in Tacoma, Pupo opened his own small shop in 1940. That first shop specialized in commercial truck tires and a few passenger tires. Pupo had little money with which to begin his business, but he did have a good customer base as a result of the many long-time friends and associates he had accumulated over the years. Gradually he built his clientele, expanded the services his firm offered, and increased its number of employees until he was able to completely renovate and expand his business in 1960.

The expanded company had 24,000 square feet of floor space and employed fifteen people. In addition, it offered far more than just truck tires. The new plant included a modern recapping center where Sam's Tire Service recycled tires of all sizes. Other new services included brake and front end work and tires for most varieties of both commercial and passenger vehicles.

In 1962, just two years after the grand opening of the new plant, Sam Pupo died suddenly. Following his father's death, control of the business was passed to 24-year-old Frank Pupo. However, Frank was hardly a rookie. He had worked for his father after school and during summers since he was thirteen years old and was the company's retail manager when Sam died.

Frank soon began to build on the strong foundation that had been laid by his father. It took him nine years before he was able to open a second branch of the business, in Puyallup. However, under Frank's astute business management, growth since 1971 has been rapid. The company has burgeoned at the rate of about one new branch per year. Today there are sixteen Sam's Tire Service branches located throughout Washington.

In addition, Frank has expanded a host of other aspects of the business. In 1981 he moved the recapping plant into the old Heidelberg Brewery building, which gave the firm a 26,000-square-foot retread plant and a 64,000-square-foot warehouse. Four years later the corporate offices were moved into the building, which is located just

An architect's rendering of the new Sam's Tire Service facility at Port of Tacoma Road and Pacific Highway East, Fife.

blocks from the company's original Tacoma site. Recently the business became international in scope under the name STS International, and began importing and exporting tires worldwide.

Today Sam's Tire Service, Inc., employs over 200 people throughout the state. Its recapping plant is capable of retreading widely varied sizes of tires in addition to providing an extensive variety of services for both commercial and passenger vehicles. Frank Pupo is still in charge of the firm's day-to-day operations. He has five children, and while his daughter is not directly involved in the company, his four sons all work for Sam's Tire Service, Inc., in some capacity.

Frank Pupo, owner and president.

PUGET POWER

When the electric utility industry came to the Pacific Northwest, it was made up of many tiny, inefficient companies, each serving its own small circle of customers in Seattle. The early days of the business were chaotic, and service was very different from what we know today.

Puget Sound Power & Light Company emerged in 1912, growing over the years to keep pace with the increasing energy demands of the region. As more people moved to the Pacific Northwest to take advantage of its beauty and prosperity, new businesses and industries appeared. It wasn't easy for the fledgling power industry to consolidate and meet this challenge. Independent business people had to admit the limitations of their own small companies and, therefore, unite to provide efficient electric service.

Puget Sound's electric power industry got its start with the generation of electricity in local lumber mills. Scrap lumber was used to fuel early steam generators. It wasn't until 1885, with the founding of Puget Power's earliest predecessor, Seattle Electric Lighting Company, that electricity was used to light homes and businesses.

Over the next ten years nearly thirty privately owned electric companies were created. In just a few years minor mergers, poor financing, and bad management eliminated most of these early utilities. Clearly, the young industry was facing serious difficulties. Inexperienced management and inefficient machinery made electric power expensive and unreliable during this pioneering period.

A construction crew for the Snoqualmie Falls hydroelectric plant. The plant, which was completed in 1898, still provides power for Puget Sound customers.

Linemen in the late 1920s did not have the assistance of a "bucket truck" to lift them to overhead wires. Here, two linemen work on wires near Seattle's waterfront when Puget Power served the city.

The situation became critical in 1899 when a sudden surge of activity, brought on by the Alaska Gold Rush and the demands of rapidly growing businesses, forced companies to look for new sources of power. Just one year after the gold rush began, the power of flowing water was put to work with the completion of the Snoqualmie Falls hydroelectric plant, the first large hydroelectric plant in the Pacific Northwest. Electron, Nooksack, and White River hydro projects also became a vital part of the generation resource.

By the time this project was finished, the Pacific Northwest had changed from a number of small, scattered communities to a group of thriving cities, and industry pioneers saw that small, competing electric utilities would no longer be able to provide the service their customers desired.

This realization moved five electric companies to join forces in 1912. They merged their power, light, and railway services to form Puget Sound Traction, Light & Power Company, marking the beginning of electric service on a territorial basis. During the next eighteen years 129 more firms merged to form Puget Power's present integrated electric system.

As World War I got under way it brought increased business, industry, and a demand for more power in the Northwest. Puget Power's resources felt the strain of this demand. Men and materials were directed toward the war effort, and as a result, the company concentrated on expanding existing resources. However, the situation was remedied in 1916 when Puget Power engineers successfully pioneered the development of equipment to burn coal mine tailings—a black grimy sludge previously considered useless.

Following the war the corpora-

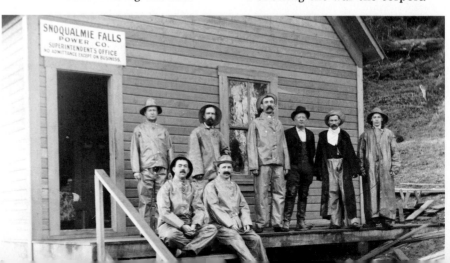

tion flourished. Puget Power strung new lines; built new substations; standardized wires, poles, and construction techniques; and replaced lines and equipment in some areas. The result was an interconnection of lines and power plants that made it possible, for the first time, to balance distribution. When the power demand of one area was small, surplus power could be used elsewhere.

Puget Power was also a pioneer in rural electrification. In the early 1900s the company had recognized the need for electricity in the rural areas of the state. The first power line in the nation to be used strictly for rural areas was put up in Lynden by a predecessor company in 1909. By 1927, when only 3 percent of the farms in the country were using electricity supplied by power companies, 63 percent of the farms in Puget Power's service territory were hooked up to company power lines.

Power plant development continued, and by 1930 the firm completed both the Lower Baker dam, located in the mountains east of Bellingham, and the Shuffleton steam plant near Renton.

While this fast-paced expansion slowed when the Depression began, it did not come to a standstill. Optimism continued as the firm was able to provide jobs in the construction of the first dam to span the Columbia River—Rock Island, near Wenatchee. The work began in 1930, and by 1933 the project was producing the state's largest block of hydroelectric power. On the heels of Rock Island came construction of the federally funded Bonneville and Grand Coulee dams.

In the pre- and post-World War II era Puget Power was forced to sell 60 percent of its property and distribution system, causing it to lose half of its customers. This was brought about by passage of a state law allowing for public takeover. But the company maintained its integrated electric system and some major generating plants.

During the war years both the corporation and the Pacific Northwest region experienced growth. The war effort had spawned new industries, new urban centers, more people, and a greater demand for power. To meet that demand, in 1942 Puget Power and other utilities in Washington, Oregon, Idaho, Montana, and Utah interconnected their lines and power plants and pledged mutual aid and cooperation toward meeting this challenge. This coordination of facilities was called the Northwest Power pool and was one of the first and most successful interties in the world; the Northwest Power Pool is still in operation today.

To ensure electricity for the growing region, Puget Power enlarged the Snoqualmie Falls plant, built the Upper Baker dam, and expanded the generating capacity of the Lower Baker dam. Additional low-cost power was provided when the corporation joined Chelan, Grant, and Douglas counties in a major mid-Columbia construction project. Four major dams—Wells, Rocky Reach, Priest Rapids, and Wanapum—were constructed between 1957 and 1967. Puget Power customers continue to receive power from these projects through long-term contracts with the Public Utility Districts (PUDs) that own them.

The 1970s and 1980s brought more growth, and the dams built during the previous twenty years were inadequate to supply needed power. In response to this dramatic growth, Puget Power embarked on the largest construction program in its history by creating a new and diverse mix of power re-

Puget Power's general office building on the corner of Seventh and Olive in Seattle was built in the early 1900s. In 1956 the general offices were moved to the present facility in Bellevue.

sources to complement the existing hydroelectric generators.

Conditions also improved as coal was developed as a clean, reliable, and economic resource. The Centralia coal plant and the Colstrip project in southeastern Montana—four coal-fired plants in which Puget Power has part ownership—are now important sources of power.

The company emerged as a leader utilizing conservation as an energy resource. Many programs have been implemented by Puget Power as a way of stretching the region's energy resources and customers' energy dollars.

Today Puget Power and its customers don't face the hardships that were common in the early days of electric power. The company has grown into a unified electric power network, serving more than 1.4 million customers in eight western counties, and one in central Washington. It continues to adapt to meet new challenges. Through its diverse mix of power resources and high technology, Puget Power is a reliable source of energy to the people of the Pacific Northwest.

FIRST INTERSTATE BANK OF WASHINGTON

First Interstate Bank of Washington, now the third-largest commercial bank in the state, has its roots in the vision and perseverance of the Northwest's pioneer bankers.

One such courageous individual, a successful New York banker, tempted fate and moved to Washington State over 100 years ago to found the Pacific National Bank of Tacoma in 1885. That young pioneer was Charles Masterson, who began his Puget Sound banking endeavor with just $50,000 in capital. Today that charter remains the founding document for the First Interstate Bank of Washington.

At first Masterson's venture was a smashing success. Tacoma's population grew from 7,000 to 36,000 by 1890, and the bank grew with the city. However, the country's economy was a volatile one, and Pacific National endured several financial panics over the next few years. The bank relied heavily on Masterson's financial prowess and sound management skills to see it through those dynamic years that proved fatal to many other banks throughout the area.

In 1895 Masterson orchestrated the first of many mergers when his bank joined with Citizens National Bank, another Tacoma institution. In 1905 Lumberman's National Bank also merged with that organization. Pacific National eventually became one of two major financial institutions in Tacoma, the other being the National Bank of Commerce, under the leadership of Chester Thorne. In 1913 those two organizations merged to form the National Bank of Tacoma, which boasted over one million dollars in assets.

The newly formed financial institution, with Thorne as its chairman, grew to be one of the most important banks in Washington.

In 1985 employees of First Interstate Bank of Washington marked the bank's centennial of service to the people of the state.

After Thorne died in 1927, the bank survived the Great Depression thanks to the extraordinary leadership and financial savvy of R.R. Mattison, who served as the institution's president during that period.

In 1935 the bank's name changed again. In that year it was purchased by Transamerica Corporation, which changed the name to the National Bank of Washington. Transamerica Corporation, a holding company with banks throughout the West, was the brainchild of A.P. Giannini, a San Francisco banker who had built a financial

Employees of the National Bank of Washington celebrated its fiftieth anniversary in 1935.

empire from a tiny bank designed to serve California's poor immigrants. Later Transamerica created Western Bancorporation to oversee the operations of its banks throughout the West.

When Washington legalized instate branch banking in 1933, it allowed the National Bank of Washington to move into an aggressive expansion campaign. That campaign resulted in the acqui-

Today First Interstate Bank of Washington's headquarters are located in this distinctive skyscraper in downtown Seattle.

256

sition of several smaller institutions throughout the state.

During World War II the bank participated in various activities including bond drives, scrap drives, and ration coupon distribution. Sadly, the bank's employees' contributions included the lives of four staff members who had been serving the war effort abroad.

In the postwar years National Bank of Washington experienced renewed growth, extensive renovations, and additional mergers. The 1960s saw continued growth and additional mergers make the bank truly a statewide organization. A 1970 merger with Pacific National

The lobby of the Tacoma main branch of the National Bank of Washington in 1947.

Bank of Seattle, which had been founded in 1928 by William E. Boeing and other business leaders, brought major changes to the bank.

The merger also resulted in a name change, to Pacific National Bank of Washington. The new institution immediately became the third-largest commercial bank in the state. With its new strength in both retail and commercial markets, the bank acquired fifteen additional branches in the Puget

Sound area and seven more in Spokane.

During the 1980s the bank made two additional merger arrangements that proved vitally important to its future. The first of these mergers involved the Spokane-based Fidelity Mutual Savings Bank. By 1982, when it became part of Pacific National, Fidelity had established itself as a well-known financial force in its own right, with its highly visible red rose corporate logo. The Fidelity merger added twenty-two branches to Pacific National's growing chain.

Olympic Bank was another important acquisition made during the 1980s. That institution, which was established in Everett in 1902, added twenty-one branches to the bank's coverage of the rapidly growing northwestern section of the state.

By that time the bank was known as First Interstate. Western Bancorporation, the holding company for Pacific National, had changed its corporate name to First Interstate Bancorp in 1981. The move was designed to enable customers to readily identify institutions affiliated with the parent company. As a result, Pacific National became First Interstate Bank of Washington and the other banks throughout the West also adopted the First Interstate name.

Today First Interstate Bank of Washington enters its second century of service as the fastest-growing full-service bank in the state. It has over 100 branches across Washington, and its affiliation with the First Interstate system affords its customers numerous interstate banking privileges.

The Pacific National Bank of Tacoma was first housed in this building on the corner of Twelfth and Pacific in downtown Tacoma. The bank shared the facility with the local chamber of commerce.

SELLEN CONSTRUCTION COMPANY, INC.

John Sellen founded John H. Sellen Construction Company as a sole proprietorship in December 1944. However, he was far from a novice in the construction field when he began his business.

Sellen, who was a native Seattleite, first entered the construction business in 1934 as a timekeeper for the Seattle firm of J.W. Bailey Construction. For the next six years Sellen patiently worked his way through the ranks as estimator, project manager, superintendent, and, finally, partner.

From 1940 to 1944 Sellen and Bailey constructed a number of military facilities for the United States Navy and the U.S. Army Corps of Engineers during the World War II years. In 1944 Bailey retired from the construction business, and Sellen bought him out. Included in that buyout was the office building at 228 Ninth Avenue North. Sellen Construction still maintains its headquarters at that original location. However, growth over the years has required numerous expansions and renovations, as well as the acquisition of additional property in the neighborhood.

Just three weeks after Sellen established his new business, he was low bidder on a project for The Boeing Company. That bid marked the beginning for Sellen Construction, and business has grown steadily since that initial project. In addition, that job, a $33,000 project installing hangar doors, established an ongoing relationship between Boeing and Sellen Construction that endures today. Over the years Sellen has performed scores of construction projects for The Boeing Company.

Sellen maintained as a business philosophy that a company is only as good as its people. Therefore, he was perpetually concerned with

John H. Sellen, founder.

Sellen Construction has completed significant building projects for every major hospital in the Seattle area including the Swedish Hospital Medical Center, shown here.

hiring and keeping people who were the best in their field. He was known to say that his business success was due to the fact that he always surrounded himself with people who were smarter than he was.

Because of that philosophy, Sellen began a rather unique business plan early in his firm's history. The plan has helped create longevity records for many of his employees that are highly unusual in the often-transient construction in-

dustry. His plan involved the establishment of Sellen Construction Company, Inc., a privately held corporation with active employee stockholders.

The first step toward this diversification of ownership came in 1952. That year the company moved from a sole proprietorship to a partnership, and, finally, to a corporation. The first incorporation of the firm listed Sellen, John Hansen, and William Scott as the original stockholders.

Since 1952 additional employees have been offered the opportunity to buy Sellen Construction stock, and today's ownership is spread among some dozen individuals. The stock is all privately held, and all stockholders are active working employees or officers of the firm. The fact that all shareholders are active employees makes for a very strong esprit de corps among company people.

Today the stockholders that are in charge of the management of Sellen Construction all have an impressive number of work years devoted to the business. Hansen, Sellen's initial partner and close friend, retired in 1972 after twenty-six years with the firm. William Scott is currently serving as chairman and chief executive officer and has thirty-five years of experience with Sellen Construction. Richard Redman is the company's president. Redman is Sellen's stepson and the only family member remaining on the firm's management team. Robert S. Magnusson first became a stockholder in 1956; today he is vice-chairman of the board and has been with Sellen Construction for thirty-seven years. The founder, John Sellen, died in November 1983.

During its first years Sellen Construction was an active bidding contractor, and its annual dollar volume grew from $500,000 in 1945 to $4.5 million in just ten years because of its skillful bidding practices. However, the company

The firm won a "Build America Award" in 1982 for the excellent workmanship in the renovation of the Four Seasons Olympic Hotel.

has evolved into primarily a negotiating-type contractor with a large percentage of its work coming from repeat business and referrals.

Sellen Construction has remained a local firm with virtually all of its business concentrated in the Puget Sound area. It has, however, ventured occasionally into eastern Washington, Oregon, and Hawaii for select clients.

The firm is credited with the construction of many fine Puget Sound area projects. Sellen Construction has completed a number of significant building projects for every major hospital in the Seattle area, including a number of jobs for Providence Hospital. Sellen was particularly proud of his company's work at Providence as he was born in that hospital, and he was happy to be able to make a contribution to the facility.

In addition, Sellen Construction has built numerous other prominent Seattle facilities including the Safeco office building, several Uni-

versity of Washington structures, the Peoples National Bank headquarters, Swedish Hospital Medical Center, and Prescott's Century Square, as well as many projects at Cornerstone's waterfront center. The firm also handled the renovation of the Four Seasons Olympic Hotel. This project won the firm a "Build America Award" in 1982 for its excellent workmanship. Sellen Construction began that project in November 1980, and the hotel opened in May 1982 after thirty-five million dollars had been spent on this special renovation project.

Sellen Construction Company, Inc., has grown steadily over the past forty years. Its annual volume now exceeds $100 million. The firm takes special pride in its growth record because its steady upward trend indicates growth with careful control by a conscientious management team.

The Skyline Tower in Bellevue.

AVTECH CORPORATION

In 1964 Avtech Corporation was a floundering audiovisual manufacturing company. However, that same year Robert Hancock and Richard Klein joined Avtech and turned the company around.

The pair, who both had extensive backgrounds in engineering, began changing the firm's direction. Hancock and Klein realized that the failing business needed an immediate cash surge, and they turned from the development of audiovisual equipment to job shopping. Hancock and Klein also staked their futures on Avtech by taking stock in the firm in lieu of wages for several years. That was a brave move considering the company's past fortunes, but the pair was confident that they could make Avtech profitable.

As a job-shop firm, Avtech produced printed circuit boards, provided high-precision sheet metal, and painted control panels and other items. By 1969 Avtech had acquired 80 percent of the printed circuit board business in the Northwest.

With the cash-flow problem under control, Hancock and Klein turned their attention to their first love and the true direction they wanted Avtech to take. The firm, which by then had twenty employees, began designing and manufacturing aircraft parts. Its first sales were for lighting ballasts and water-gauging systems for Boeing 747s and audio systems for Cessna Citations and Lear jets.

The shift into aircraft parts proved to be the right choice. Business began to boom, and Avtech moved from its 15,000-square-foot Magnolia location to the old Grandma's Cookies plant in Wallingford, which had 35,000 square feet of floor space.

In 1971 Avtech was essentially reborn. That year the company dropped its job-shop work and focused entirely on the design and manufacture of aircraft equipment. By the following year Avtech had grown from 35 to 120 employees.

During the next few years the firm added more employees, bought additional plant space, and added sophisticated computer equipment to its inventory. In 1978 Klein, who remains a major stockholder, withdrew from active management of the firm, leaving Hancock to oversee the business.

When the firm acquired the old Grandma's Cookies plant in Wallingford, and shifted its emphasis from job-shop work to the design and manufacture of aircraft equipment, Avtech was reborn.

By 1980 Avtech had 150 employees, and its relationship with Boeing had grown to such an extent that Boeing sales represented 41 percent of Avtech's business. Then disaster struck. Boeing cut back production of 747s and sharply reduced its orders with Avtech, which quickly responded to the crisis. Marketing efforts were stepped up, and orders from non-Boeing sources increased 23 percent by 1981. That year Avtech set a sales record of $4.7 million. The company's reputation for quality was firmly established. More and more airlines began to request Avtech parts, and sales to Boeing stabilized at one-quarter of the firm's total sales volume.

Today Avtech Corporation, the company that was born out of the gambled wages of two experienced engineers, looks forward to a future of unprecedented expansion and escalating sales figures.

TOUCHE ROSS & CO.

Touche Ross was formed in 1947 as a result of the merger of three large accounting firms: Touche, Niven, & Co.; George Bailey & Company; and Allen R. Smart & Co. The new organization, Touche, Niven, Bailey & Smart, was formed on September 1, 1947, and in 1969 changed its name to Touche Ross & Co.

As a result of that merger, Seattle's certified public accounting firm of Allen R. Smart became part of the Touche Ross organization. Smart had opened the Seattle office in 1935, when John Yeasting moved from Los Angeles. The one-man office soon added Ed Tremper and his practice to the company, with Tremper assuming responsibility for the practice when Yeasting joined The Boeing Company. Tremper went on to become one of the founding partners of Touche, Niven, Bailey & Smart and served as the partner in charge of the Seattle office until 1962 when he retired.

Growth has been steady for the now-international accounting and business consulting firm and has required several moves to accommo-date the growth in the Northwest over its fifty-year span. Continued growth has spurred the opening of additional branch offices in the area. In 1971 the Northwest Practice established an Anchorage, Alaska, office, and in 1983 it opened the Bellevue, Washington, office. Today those three offices are considered the Northwest Practice, with Seattle the designated center.

Touche Ross has continually expanded its services in order to better serve its clients' needs. It has added specialty divisions such as its management consulting services and tax consulting divisions as well as expertise in a wide variety of industry and service areas including aerospace, retail, food, health care, high technology, real estate, and specialty assistance to emerging companies. These additions char-acterize the firm's capacity to respond to change within the accounting industry in both a dramatic and creative way.

Although it is part of a national organization, the Northwest Practice office has had only three partners in charge during its entire history. All three of these partners are native Washingtonians and graduates of the University of Washington. The office takes pride in the fact that all of the partners in the Northwest Practice have been promoted from within the local ranks.

This home-grown spirit helps promote the community-minded attitude that prevails with the Northwest Practice offices. Touche Ross professionals have a real sense of community spirit because the Northwest truly is their home.

Today the Northwest Practice of Touche Ross totals approximately 300 staff members. Over the past fifty years Touche Ross has developed a tradition of excellence toward its clients, its professionals, and the community.

Three generations of leadership and tradition are represented with (left to right) senior partner Gerald E. Gorans (managing partner from 1962 to 1982), founding partner Edward P. Tremper (from 1937 to 1962), and current managing partner William A. Fowler. These three men have guided the firm in Seattle since its founding.

TOUCHE, NIVEN & CO.
ALLEN R. SMART & CO.
GEORGE BAILEY & COMPANY

announce the formation of a partnership to merge their practices as

— CERTIFIED PUBLIC ACCOUNTANTS —

on September 1, 1947 under the name of

TOUCHE, NIVEN, BAILEY & SMART

NEW YORK · CHICAGO · DETROIT · ST. LOUIS · PITTSBURGH
CLEVELAND · MINNEAPOLIS · LOS ANGELES · SEATTLE · DAYTON
SEATTLE
1411 Fourth Avenue · *Telephone:* Elliott 3935
AUGUST 20, 1947

The merger of three accounting firms to form the Touche, Niven, Bailey & Smart partnership was announced in The Seattle Times *on August 20, 1947.*

261

WASHINGTON NATURAL GAS COMPANY

Citizens of Tacoma turned urgently to their city council. It was the 1880s, and better street lighting was essential. Kerosene lamps failed too often to ensure safety on the city's muddy, ungraded streets. And important business could be lost to rival Seattle, which had introduced gas lighting for several street lamps and a few private customers some ten years prior.

Tacoma's leaders moved quickly. Within weeks, parts arrived for a plant to manufacture gas from coal. Townspeople cleared roots and stumps to make way for the wooden gas mains.

Only a handful of customers were served in Tacoma at first, but gas soon illuminated almost every business and residence in town. Some stores boasted huge gas chandeliers.

Gas was used solely for lighting until the 1890s, when the first

A display in the early 1950s announces the route of the proposed natural gas pipeline—and introduces the gas refrigerator, the first to make ice cubes and put them in a basket automatically.

griddles, and gas irons and oyster stewers were on the market, hastening the modernization of the early twentieth-century home. Gas assumed a central place in the region's energy picture.

A new era in gas service opened in 1956, when the cleaner, more potent, natural form of gas replaced the manufactured variety. Natural gas flowed into the state through major new pipelines linking Puget Sound consumers with vast gas fields in the American Southwest and Canada. Just one year prior, Washington Natural Gas Company had been formed to distribute the new fuel.

Residential customers welcomed natural gas. It also proved a boon for Puget Sound industry. One of the most easily controlled sources of energy, natural gas became a major commercial and industrial fuel. Local companies still use it for everything from firing furnaces and kilns to forging, cutting, hardening, drying, purifying, fabricating, processing, curing, and shaping materials.

The impact of natural gas on the region's advancement was dramatized in 1962, when the Seattle World's Fair became a showcase

One of Seattle's first street lamps lights the way for courageous travelers after this 1880s snowstorm. Courtesy, Washington State Historical Society

for the fuel. For a decade to follow, a forty-foot gas flame atop Seattle's Space Needle remained in service as a symbol of the gas industry's contributions to the progress of western Washington.

Washington Natural Gas today is a subsidiary of Washington Energy Company, with four sister companies engaged in energy conservation, exploration, and development. Washington Natural serves 266,000 residential, commercial, and industrial customers in Snohomish, King, Pierce, Thurston, and Lewis counties. Providing more energy each year than any other utility in the state, Washington Natural Gas continues to fuel the vitality of Puget Sound and her people.

A turn-of-the-century display of gas equipment.

gas ranges in the region began to relieve much of the drudgery of housework. With gas there was no more kindling to cut and carry, and no soot or dirt. Newspaper ads advised, "If you love your wife, buy her a gas range."

Soon gas water heaters, gas room heaters, gas steam radiators, gas

SUNDSTRAND DATA CONTROL

Today Sundstrand Data Control employs over 1,500 people at its headquarters in Redmond and at other sites throughout the country. However, this giant corporation, which has become a leader in its field, had a humble beginning. The firm's first office consisted of the basement of the home of one of its founding engineers.

The company was formed in 1947 when four ex-Boeing engineers established a partnership under the name United Control. The partners' expertise and penchant for invention quickly catapulted the firm to profitability and new quarters in the Union Bay area of Seattle. There, United Control completed its first contract to build windshield temperature controllers for the Boeing B-47 Stratojet.

This contract solidified the company's relationship with Boeing, and for the next several years United Control functioned almost exclusively as a supplier of various data-related devices to Boeing. As a result of that relationship, the firm's business burgeoned. By 1959 United Control was ready to issue stock and it became a publicly held corporation. Two years later the firm moved to a 33-acre site complete with picnic areas, a softball field, and a tennis court in the Overlake Industrial Park in Red-

Sundstrand's main offices are located on thirty-three acres in Redmond. The first company to move into the area, Sundstrand has literally watched a vital economic sector of the greater Seattle area grow up around it.

mond. United Control was the first major corporation to make its headquarters on the east side.

In the early 1960s the company began developing and building cockpit voice and flight data recorders for commercial transport aircraft. These devices are the "black boxes" that are used in aircraft accident investigations.

In 1967 United Control was purchased by the Sundstrand Corporation of Rockford, Illinois, and its name was changed to Sundstrand Data Control. Just a few years after the acquisition, the company pioneered flight safety equipment with the invention of the Ground Proximity Warning Computer. This device orally notified flight crews of such problems as landing equipment that has not lowered or if the aircraft is dangerously close to the ground. Since its inception in the late 1960s this equipment has been credited with saving literally hundreds of aircraft. In 1975 the computer became a mandatory piece of equipment for all commer-

A Sundstrand employee tests the latest in electronic equipment in the early 1950s, a few years after the firm's founding.

cial aircraft.

Sundstrand Data Control is also responsible for the manufacture and development of various other types of avionic devices. The firm developed a visual display system to allow pilots to land in bad weather. Other products aid in the search for energy reserves and help monitor the effect of earthquakes on bridges, large buildings, and the Alaska Pipeline.

Today Sundstrand Data Control is an expert in nearly all phases of avionic equipment, and it has greatly expanded its customer base to include both national and international clients.

PEOPLES NATIONAL BANK OF WASHINGTON

Following Seattle's fire in 1889 the city was served by nine small commercial banks. City pioneers, including Bailey Gatzert, Jacob Furth, John Collins, John Leary, Arthur Denny, and the Schwabacher brothers pledged $100,000 for capital stock in a new bank. All of its founders had other "commercial" banking investments, so Peoples Bank was incorporated on December 19, 1889, as a "savings" bank.

Peoples Savings Bank opened for business on September 2, 1890, in the new brick Occidental Building at the corner of Yesler and James. J.R. Hayden was the bank's cashier, manager, and only salaried officer. Bailey Gatzert was the bank's first president as well as president of Puget Sound National Bank (later to become part of Seattle First National Bank).

Jacob Furth became Peoples' second president following Gatzert's death in 1893 and, like Gatzert, he simultaneously served as president of Puget Sound National. Furth's growing interests in the city's utility and transportation needs forced his resignation from Peoples. His office and interest became that of his successor, E.C. Neufelder, who like Gatzert and Furth had learned the banking business as a merchant. Neufelder noted Seattle's growth to the north, and he pur-

In 1934 Peoples National Bank of Washington moved its main office from Second Avenue and Pike Street to this building at 1414 Fourth Avenue.

chased a building at the corner of Second and Pike and moved Peoples from the Occidental Building.

Peoples grew modestly and prospered as a neighborhood savings bank. Neufelder kept the bank's capital at $100,000 and though its deposits grew to $5 million its lending limits were restrictively small. He died in 1923 and his interests were managed by E.S. McCord, the Neufelder family attorney.

Joshua Green was president of Puget Sound Navigation Company when he first took an interest in acquiring Peoples Savings Bank. The then-57-year-old Green had invested in banks since 1904 and was a director of the National Bank of Commerce at the time he began negotiations to purchase Peoples.

In 1926 Green purchased 88 percent of the bank's stock for $308,000. He gave Peoples an injection of new capital and spirit. He was a salesman, not a banker, and one of his first acts was to hire the successful banker and businessman, Albert Brygger, to operate his new enterprise. The bank's capital was raised to $250,000, and its deposits increased to $6.7 million during the first three months following Green's purchase.

Green and Brygger astutely observed that "savings" banks were not as popular as they once had been, and large deposits and new business would only come by cultivating substantial commercial accounts. The bank's real estate was sold and Peoples' capital was again raised, this time to $500,000, and its name was changed to Peoples Bank and Trust Company. Green applied his talents as a salesman and one by one, new accounts including Standard Oil of California; Carnation; Sinclair Oil; General Motors; Sears, Roebuck; and Mil-

Joshua Green, Sr., purchased controlling interest in Peoples Savings Bank in 1926.

waukee Railroad were established at the bank.

By 1933 Seattle's banking community had been weakened, but not devastated, by the Depression. Seattle's banks were mostly sound; however, the day following the closure of banks in Oregon and California, the city's banks were strained by depositors requesting their savings, in cash or gold. Though it remained sound, in just one day Peoples experienced a 30-percent reduction in its deposits. The day following the run a national banking holiday was proclaimed by President Franklin D. Roosevelt.

Peoples was immediately reopened following the banking holiday and, like other Seattle banks, its deposits began to build again.

Among other changes brought about by the Depression were new regulations that allowed branch banking. Peoples converted pre-Depression enterprises into branches. These included the First National Bank of Renton, Peoples First Avenue Bank, and later the West and North Seattle branches.

In 1934 Peoples moved from its small Second Avenue location into the building at 1414 Fourth Avenue, the empty but lavish and defunct home of Puget Sound Savings and Loan Association.

Peoples was perceptive of change, and "national" banks were meeting

Joshua Green, Jr. (seated), and Joshua "Jay" Green III represent the second and third generation of Peoples Bank builders.

with greater success than state-chartered banks. In October 1937 the bank received a national charter and its name was changed to Peoples National Bank of Washington in Seattle.

World War II brought about rapid social and economic change to the banking industry. Deposits grew faster than at any time in Peoples' history and women assumed the traditional male roles as clerks and tellers. Brygger retired in 1942 and Phillip Strack was elected president of the bank.

Following his return from military service in 1945, Green's only son, Joshua Green, Jr., renewed his interest in the bank. He had been with Peoples since 1929 and had witnessed the effects of the Depression on the bank. His banking policies were different than those of his father. He was a conservative banker, yet he was an aggressive expansion-minded businessman. He was elected Peoples' president in 1949.

By 1953 Green Jr. had directed Peoples' move into the agricultural banking regions of central Washington with the purchase of the three-branch Grant County Bank system, and the Othello State Bank. Again, Peoples was a growing bank following the postwar recession.

Green Jr. was elected chairman of the bank in 1962 and E.L. Blaine, Jr., was elected president, serving in that position until his retirement in 1967. Harold Rogers was elected president at that time. Green and Rogers expanded the bank's interest in mortgage banking with the acquisition of the $40-million Seattle mortgage firm of Burwell and Morford. In 1969 the bank purchased First Mortgage Company, and three years later it furthered its interests with the purchase of Olympic Mortgage Company. By the time Green opened the bank's new corporate headquarters in 1974, Peoples operated a sixty-branch system.

Joshua "Jay" Green III began his career at Peoples Bank in 1961 following a year of intensive training at New York's CitiBank. When he returned to Seattle he set about improving systems. He knew that being smaller was no excuse for not being competitive.

Prior to his election as Peoples' president in 1975, Green observed its competitors' use of computers. Green recognized that the bank must commit the money and man-

Peoples Bank moved into its twenty-story Fourth Avenue head office in 1974.

power to develop competitive electronic banking technology. He assigned the task to James Cairns, Jr., a creative manager with no prior computer experience.

To help offset the cost of developing new computer systems, Peoples sold its new electronic services. Traditionally, Peoples offered its financial strength and banking services to small correspondent banks. As banking computer technology advanced, the network of twenty-five Washington State commercial banks with combined assets in excess of one billion dollars has aided Peoples in its development of a sophisticated electronic banking network.

In 1979 Green was elected chairman of the board and Cairns was elected president of Peoples Bank.

The Peoples Bank of the 1980s is a strong, conservative, diversified, $2.2-billion, customer-oriented, regional commercial bank. Peoples employs nearly 2,400 men and women who staff its head office and over eighty branch locations in Washington State. Its business is concentrated in six major bank businesses, including consumer banking, corporate banking, trust, money management, electronic banking, and mortgage banking.

MOLBAK'S GREENHOUSE AND NURSERY

When Egon and Laina Molbak came to the United States from Denmark in 1950, the newlyweds promised their parents that they would stay no longer than five years. The Molbaks did not keep that promise. So far, their "visit" has stretched into a 36-year stay, and the Pacific Northwest is richer because of it.

In 1956, just a little over five years after the couple came to the United States, they purchased a 3.5-acre nursery in the then-rural community of Woodinville. There they began what was to become one of the most respected and well-known wholesale and retail nursery operations in the area— Molbak's Greenhouse and Nursery.

Egon, the son of an orchardist, was educated in Denmark in floriculture and trained in nursery management in the United States through the American-Scandinavian student exchange program. Because of his background, he was well aware of the difficulties that running a nursery can present, and

Molbak's main garden store was built in 1978.

the Molbaks' new venture was not immune from those difficulties.

Just one month after the Molbaks acquired the nursery, the greenhouse boilers went out on one of the coldest winter nights on record. The couple frantically built fires in buckets, covered much of the crop with newspapers, and walked back and forth through the five greenhouses carrying lighted newspaper torches. At 3 a.m. the previous owners, who still lived nearby, came over to help out. Through the efforts of the Molbaks and their neighbors, the crop was saved and financial disaster was averted.

Other crises followed, but dedication and many sixteen-hour days on the part of the Molbaks and their four children have kept the business going and have led to its expansion.

In 1966 the Molbaks added a small retail shop and began selling retail products year-round. Four years later they moved into retailing on a larger scale and purchased an additional 3.5 acres of adjacent land to accommodate the expansion. By 1979 Molbak's Greenhouse and Nursery needed even more space and another three

acres were purchased. A gift shop and Hallmark card shop were added in 1981. Two years later Molbak's moved to the city with the acquisition of the Seattle Garden Center branch in the historic Pike Place Market.

Molbak's currently employs the latest in nursery technology with the addition in 1984 of a computerized greenhouse. The new building automatically monitors the environment in each section of the greenhouse and adjusts to the needs of each plant group. The nursery's reputation has grown to the point that customers drive for miles to shop and browse at Molbak's. During the Christmas season Molbak's becomes a plant fantasyland that is a must-see for gardeners, as well as for those who just want to marvel at the endless wonders of nature.

Today Egon and Laina Molbak no longer spend sixteen hours a day building their nursery. In 1985 Egon assumed the position of Molbak's Greenhouse and Nursery chairman and turned the daily operations of the firm over to its new president, Jerry Wilmot. However, the couple still remain active in the management of their "growing" company.

FREDERICK & NELSON

In 1890 D.E. Frederick joined his friend Jim Meecham in his already prosperous plumbing and second-hand business. From a small store-front on First Avenue, the two men provided the kind of merchandise and service that was scarce in the frontier town of Seattle, and business was brisk.

Within a year after the formation of the partnership, Nels Nelson, a mutual friend, joined the business. Frederick and Nelson bought out Meecham shortly thereafter. The new company evolved from the plumbing and secondhand business, and soon the store was overflowing with new quality merchandise. From those beginnings came what is known today as Frederick & Nelson, a leading Northwest department store chain with fifteen branches in Washington and Oregon.

In its early years the growing business moved to several different facilities, each time greatly expanding the store. Finally, in 1916, Frederick & Nelson began construction of its current store location at Fifth and Pine in downtown Seattle. The new building, which was completed in 1918, was a giant five-story structure located in uncharted territory on the outskirts of Seattle's downtown. The two men were admired for their boldness in constructing a store of such magnitude so far out of town.

By 1929 D.E. Frederick was ready to retire from the retail business, and he sold the store to Marshall Field & Company of Chicago. The new owner further perpetuated the firm's philosophy that had served it so well in the past.

In 1946, in response to its customers' needs, Frederick & Nelson embarked on what was to become an aggressive expansion effort. That year the company opened its

Frederick & Nelson's downtown Seattle store at Fifth and Pine in 1936.

first branch store in the growing community of Bellevue. In 1947 the downtown Seattle store was expanded upward with the addition of five floors. This new addition doubled the size of the establishment and made it one of the largest department stores in the country. Continued vigorous growth in the state of Washington led to the expansion of the Bellevue store in 1956. Stores in Aurora Village, Southcenter, and a major distribution center followed in rapid succession through 1969.

In 1978 Frederick & Nelson opened two new stores in Tacoma and three in Oregon. A year later additional Oregon stores were completed, and a major establishment was opened in downtown Portland. The Olympia and Everett stores followed in 1980. The following year the downtown Seattle store introduced its "Arcade," which offers a complete marketplace of merchandise ranging from an epi-

In 1947 the downtown Seattle store was expanded with the addition of five stories, doubling the size of the establishment. Photo circa 1985

curean delicatessen to stationery and luggage departments.

In 1982 BATUS, a holding and management company for the U.S. business interests of its London-based parent, B.A.T. Industries, acquired Frederick & Nelson along with several other department stores nationwide. The new owners have continued to improve and renovate the Frederick & Nelson chain.

BERGMAN LUGGAGE COMPANY, INC.

In 1927 Fred Bergman and several partners began a small luggage-manufacturing business in Seattle's Pioneer Square. At first business was lively, and the new company's economic future looked bright. However, the financially troubled 1930s soon brought problems for the partnership, as they did for the rest of the nation.

During that time each partner sold out until Bergman was left with the entire operation. At that point he decided to give up the manufacturing aspect of the business in order to concentrate more fully on the sales aspect. That decision paved the way for what was eventually to become the largest retail luggage operation in the Northwest, with a worldwide reputation for quality at a fair price.

A great deal of the firm's phenomenal growth stems from the innovative ideas of Simon "Si"

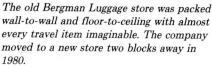
The old Bergman Luggage store was packed wall-to-wall and floor-to-ceiling with almost every travel item imaginable. The company moved to a new store two blocks away in 1980.

Hurwitz, who joined Bergman Luggage Company, Inc., in 1945. Soon after Hurwitz joined the business, it moved from its longtime Pioneer Square location to the Denny Regrade area, where it was to remain for many years.

During his early years at Bergman Luggage, Hurwitz served in every capacity from stockman to general manager. However, he made his first major impact on the store's direction while serving as promotion and advertising manag-

er. In that position Hurwitz introduced the company to its first direct-mail advertising campaign when he spent $800 on fliers, which he mailed to potential customers. In those days direct mail was a new concept and $800 was a large gamble. However, the gamble paid off, the store sold out of the advertised item, and Hurwitz initiated numerous other advertising campaigns in the years that followed.

From the beginning Bergman Luggage had a reputation for both quality and selection. Travel often consisted of a grueling train ride or a lengthy ocean voyage, and the luggage of the day was categorized by its function. Pullman cases held everything one would need for a five-day train ride. Train cases carried cosmetics and other personal items. Fortnighters could accommodate all the necessary belongings for a two-week trip, and steamer trunks provided space for lengthy trips at sea.

Whatever the need, Bergman

Si and Gerry Hurwitz, familiar faces to world travelers and Puget Sound shoppers alike, photographed just after the opening of the new downtown store.

Si Hurwitz, Puget Sound's "Mr. Luggage," was something of a one-man whirlwind in his Third Avenue store. He was still climbing ladders to retrieve stock needed to make a sale when he was in his seventies.

Even with six stores now in the chain, the main store, located in downtown Seattle at Third and Virginia, remains a landmark for travelers from all over the world.

Luggage carried the product. When interviewed in late 1985 Hurwitz recalled one piece the firm carried called the Oshkosh wardrobe trunk. The trunk cost $500 and was extremely heavy. In today's economy that same piece of luggage would be priced at $2,500, quite an expense for a single piece of luggage, but Bergman Luggage sold a surprising number of the Oshkosh trunks.

The luggage business has changed dramatically since the company was founded in 1927, with the trend toward lighter, smaller luggage that will fit under an airplane seat or in the overhead luggage compartment. However, the firm still maintains an extensive selection, with a price category to meet any budget.

For thirty years, from 1956 until his death on January 1, 1986, Si Hurwitz was sole owner and presi-

dent of Bergman Luggage. His wife, Geraldine, who had worked part time for a number of years while raising their family, joined her husband in the business on a full-time basis in 1967. In 1978 their son, Jay, left his career as a university professor and returned from the East Coast to assume the position of general manager of the company.

During the thirty years that Si Hurwitz owned and operated Bergman Luggage, the company underwent extensive expansion. Hurwitz first added to his selection and solidly established his reputation for "quality at a discount." The firm's physical expansion began in 1978, when Jay came aboard, with the opening of a new store in the Overlake area of Bellevue/Redmond.

In 1980 the company's head offices, warehouse, and store were moved from the Denny Regrade area, where the original store had been located for thirty-five years, to its present facility at Third and Virginia streets in downtown Seattle. In 1982 Bergman Luggage opened its Pavilion store in Tukwila, and the following year the company opened stores at both Northgate and Alderwood malls, as well as a clearance center at the Pavilion. In 1985, at the age of seventy-seven, Si Hurwitz was still

building, with the company opening a store in the Kitsap Mall in Silverdale, Washington, in November of that year.

Through all of the expansion, Bergman Luggage has maintained its reputation for quality merchandise and exceptional value by providing an overwhelming selection of nearly every major brand of luggage, ranging from the most to the least expensive, all at discount prices. This tremendous selection has enabled the firm to establish itself as *the* luggage store for Northwest customers as well as for many from far away, including overseas, who find their way to Seattle. In addition, a number of celebrities have made Bergman Luggage a "must" stop while on tour in the Seattle area.

Si Hurwitz, known as "Mr. Luggage" to many of his customers, continued to work at least six days a week at the store right through the 1985 holiday season. With his passing, his wife, Gerry, and son, Jay, face the challenge of building on the foundation he established as the company, now with seven stores, nears its sixtieth anniversary.

THE BOEING COMPANY

The Boeing Company has grown from a tiny, fledgling organization that entered the aerospace business on its founder's whim to an industry giant whose successes and failures profoundly affect the entire Seattle area.

In July 1916 William E. Boeing, the son of a wealthy Midwest timberman and an aviation enthusiast, decided that he could build a superior airplane. The young man teamed up with G. Conrad Westervelt, a Navy officer, and formed a business called Pacific Aero Products Company. Its first offices were located in a boat house on the shore of Lake Union near downtown Seattle.

The venture's work force consisted of just twenty-one employees, and its payroll for two weeks amounted to $703. The minimum wage was fourteen cents per hour, but test pilots could earn one dollar per hour. One year after its founding the firm's name was changed to Boeing Airplane Company, which was reduced to The Boeing Company in 1961.

The Boeing Airplane Company got off to a brisk start. Two of its first planes, called B&Ws after its founders, were sold to New Zealand, where they were used to pioneer airmail flights in that country and to train pilots. Other variations of the B&W were ordered by both the United States Army and Navy. This led to the firm's first large order for fifty Model C trainers soon after the United States entered World War I.

However, as soon as the armistice had been signed and the country was again at peace, Boeing was out of airplane orders. Bill Boeing and his associates seriously debated their future in the airplane manufacturing business. Meanwhile, Boeing employees marked time manufacturing sea-

The "Red Barn," original home of The Boeing Company. Built in 1910 to house a boat works, the Red Barn was converted to airplane production in 1915 and used in one way or another until 1970. It now houses exhibits for the Museum of Flight in Seattle.

sled boats and bedroom furniture.

However, the year 1921 brought encouragement to the tiny aerospace company. That year Boeing was awarded its first major postwar airplane order for 111 observation planes, and more orders followed quickly in its wake. By 1926 Boeing was ready for expansion.

That year President Calvin Coolidge decreed that airmail should be turned over to private enterprise, and the bidding war began. Boeing gambled the company and won the contract with a bid far below his competitors. Like the good businessman he was, he had risked the firm's future on a new plane called the Model 40. His gamble paid off, and The Boeing Company was profitably situated in the airmail business.

By 1929 Boeing had become one of the largest aircraft plants in the country. That year Bill Boeing decided to take the firm public and Boeing Company stock began selling briskly almost immediately. With the additional financial boost from stock sales, the corporation again began to expand. Soon the United Aircraft & Transport Corporation was founded, with Bill Boeing as its chairman. The new

From 1943 until the end of World War II, Boeing's Plant II facility was realistically camouflaged to deter aerial spying or attack.

concern was composed of several profitable aerospace-oriented firms, including Boeing Airplane Company.

However, just a few years after the consolidation, the federal government, in an antitrust action, forced the breakup of the firm, and served as the catalyst for William Boeing's resignation shortly thereafter. On September 26, 1934, the giant conglomerate was separated into three new companies—United Air Lines, United Aircraft Corporation, now United Technologies,

In late 1942 the new Boeing Plant II facility was filled with B-17s, including these nose sections of the "E" Model. More than 12,700 B-17s were built in all, nearly 7,000 by Boeing.

Seamstresses apply wing fabric for an MB-3A Army Air Corps pursuit plane in the early 1920s. The MB-3A could reach 19,500 feet altitude and top speeds of 140 r.p.m.

and Boeing Airplane Company.

The mid-1930s represented a time of uncertainty for Boeing. The competition was closing in; the Boeing 247 was barely making a profit; and the P-26 was losing money. The firm's new chairman, Claire Egtvedt, took action that resulted in the birth of the B-17. That plane became one of the company's brightest successes and played a major part in winning World War II.

When the war ended Boeing shifted into another down cycle. On September 1, 1945, the directors elected a new president, William Allen. The day after he accepted the position, all military contracts

for B-17s and B-29s were cancelled. More than 44,000 workers had to be laid off. In order to keep his core engineers and manufacturing team together, Allen ordered the development of a new commercial plane. The result was the 314 Stratocruiser. However, the luxury airliner was not a commercial success, and only fifty-six were built.

However, Boeing was not to be deterred, and it quickly undertook a new venture—the world's first jetliner. In 1954, when the prototype rolled out of the factory with the 72-year-old Bill Boeing as an honored guest, the company had officially launched the world into the jet age.

In 1958 Boeing won a contract from the Air Force to assemble and test a three-stage, solid-propellant missile called the *Minuteman*. Boeing factories were turning out both military and commercial aircraft at an astounding rate. In 1960 Boeing introduced the 727, which proved to be the world's most popular jetliner. In 1966 the company began producing the 747, still the world's largest commercial jetliner.

Also during the 1960s Boeing played a major role in the advancement of the space program. It built five lunar orbiters to photograph the moon, the first stage of the *Saturn V* moon rocket, a moon buggy, and other space-

oriented equipment. The firm also became involved with the technical integration and evaluation of the entire *Apollo* program.

However, by the late 1960s orders fell again, and Boeing faced another financial crisis. Under the leadership of a new chief executive, T. Wilson, the work force was reduced from 150,000 to 53,000 employees in an effort to save the company from financial disaster. The drastic measures worked, and by late 1971 the company was again on the rebound. By 1979 Boeing had added the 757 and the 767 to its repertoire, and its sales had increased to eight billion dollars.

Today Boeing is recognized as the world's leading manufacturer of airplanes. It employs 104,000 people, a major portion of whom are located in the Seattle area. It commands forty-seven million square feet of floor space including administrative buildings and factory space. In 1986 The Boeing Company manufactured its 5,000th commercial jet, making it the world's largest producer of commercial jets.

MAYER BROTHERS

The firm of Mayer Brothers, wholesale and manufacturing jewelers and silversmiths, was incorporated in Seattle on January 22, 1897. Its three founders, Joseph, Albert, and Markus Mayer, were brothers who had recently emigrated from the Rhineland in Germany, and who decided to stake their fortunes on the growing Puget Sound region.

The brothers established their first office in the Colman Building at First Avenue and Marion Street, and the company's first manufacturing division in the Colman Annex Building. There the business prospered, and the brothers saw their hard work pay off and their dreams become reality in their newly adopted country.

At one time the firm's manufacturing division employed over 100 fine craftsmen who produced jewelry items such as rings, lodge emblems, and charms, as well as silverware pieces including trophies, silver flatware, and silver hollowware.

As a result, Mayer Brothers was involved in the manufacture of some of the most exquisite and unique items produced in the

western United States. Nearly all of the many street clocks located in Seattle and throughout the western region of the state were made by the company. A number of those old clocks are still keeping time today, and Seattle has declared those left in the city to be historic landmarks.

Mayer Brothers was also selected to manufacture the sterling silver pieces that were commissioned by the State of Washington to be presented to the Navy for its newly built battle cruiser, the *Washington*. It took the company more than two years to design and manufacture the intricate pieces, all of which had the seal of the State of Washington incorporated into their design. These silver pieces are now aboard the U.S.S. *Constellation* and have been on display at the Museum of History and Industry in Seattle.

Mayer Brothers also was heavily involved in the design of gold nugget jewelry for Alaska, as a result of the early adventures of Albert and Markus Mayer. In 1897, shortly after the founding of the firm, the two succumbed to gold fever and journeyed to the Klondike in search of their fortune. After a grueling trip over both land and

water, the pair arrived safely in Dawson City, Yukon Territory, where they set up a jewelry store and staked their claim on Gold Bottom Creek. The brothers remained in Dawson City until 1904, when they returned to Seattle. However, their affinity for Alaska remained, and for thirty years Markus made semiannual sales trips to the state.

In 1951 Markus Mayer, Jr., assumed control of the company following the death of his father. Now seventy years old, Markus Jr. still runs the firm's day-to-day operations. For nearly eighty-eight years Mayer Brothers has served the jewelry industry as a wholesale distributor and manufacturer of jewelry. Today the family-owned business continues to serve the industry as a leading distributor of equipment, tools, parts, and supplies for jewelry manufacturers and watchmakers.

This photograph of the original location of Mayer Brothers was taken in 1906. The office for the wholesale distribution part of the business was in the Colman Building in the foreground, and the manufacturing department for the jewelry and silverware was in the small building in the background known as the Colman Annex Building.

Markus Sr. and Albert Mayer (in the bow of the boat), two of the three brothers that founded Mayer Brothers, at Lake Bennett in 1897. The boat was built with lumber whipsawed by hand from logs and was used to go down the Yukon River to Dawson City after the ice melted in the spring.

NORDSTROM, INC.

Nordstrom, now the nation's leading fashion specialty retailer, traces its roots to the Klondike gold fields and the hard work and good fortune of a young Swedish immigrant named John W. Nordstrom.

Nordstrom arrived in this country at the age of sixteen with just five dollars in his pocket. For some time he labored at numerous odd jobs before he headed north to the Klondike in 1897 along with thousands of other gold seekers. Alaska was good to Nordstrom, and he returned to Seattle two years later with $13,000 and a desire to settle down.

Once back in the area, he agreed to go into partnership with Carl F. Wallin, a Seattle shoemaker whom Nordstrom had met in Alaska. The pair opened their first shoe store in 1901, with a twenty-foot frontage on Fourth Avenue and Pike Street. The first day's receipts totaled $12.50, the sum of the store's only sale.

Hard work and diligence eventually paid off, and the business gradually grew. In 1929 Wallin sold his interest in the company to Nordstrom, and just one year later Nordstrom sold the business to his sons, Elmer, Everett, and Lloyd. Together the brothers built that single Seattle shoe store into the largest independent shoe chain west of the Mississippi.

In 1963 the brothers realized that the time for expansion was at hand. They decided to branch out into other areas of fashion and later purchased the Best's Apparel fashion specialty stores in Seattle and Portland.

That decision proved to be a wise one, and Nordstrom continued to expand at an astounding rate. Within six years the company, now known as Nordstrom Best, had seven apparel stores in Washington and Oregon in addition to

its twenty-seven shoe stores. By that time the firm's operations were in the hands of the third generation of Nordstrom descendants including sons Bruce, James, and John; son-in-law Jack McMillan; and friend Bob Bender.

The new generation had their own ideas about growth and implemented several new policies. The biggest change came in 1971 when, needing more financing for additional expansion, the family offered Nordstrom stock to the public for the first time.

The Wallin & Nordstrom shoe store at the Second and Pike Street location in downtown Seattle in 1915. The store remained at this site for twenty-two years.

launched a new division called Place Two, and more stores were added.

Two years later Nordstrom made a bold move into the highly competitive California market. Despite warnings that the state's retail

One of the newest Nordstrom stores located in West Los Angeles, California, at the Westside Pavilion. The 144,200-square-foot store opened on May 3, 1985.

In 1973 the Best name was dropped and the corporation formally became Nordstrom. Two years later Nordstrom moved into the Alaskan market and established its reputation for quality there as well. In 1976, with sales over $200 million, the company

market could not be penetrated, Nordstrom's California outlets prospered. Since that time the company has opened many additional California stores, with more slated for opening in the near future.

Today Nordstrom, the once-tiny Seattle shoe store, is the largest independent fashion specialty retailer in the nation, with sales of over one billion dollars recorded in 1985.

HOLADAY-PARKS, INC.

Today Holaday-Parks, Inc., is one of the largest mechanical contractors in the nation. It specializes in all types of commercial and industrial buildings and has a team of professional designers that is unequaled in the Northwest.

However, the firm's roots reach back to some of the Puget Sound's most arduous days. In 1889 Joe and Ben Hunt established a tiny sheet-metal firm in Tacoma called the J.&B. Hunt Company. From that humble beginning the two brothers and their nephew, Paul H. Holaday, succeeded in bringing warmth to the bone-chilled throngs of adventurers that roamed the Klondike in pursuit of the elusive golden dust. The company's much-appreciated contribution to the Alaskan gold rush was an air-tight, sheet-iron heater, with a jacket that allowed the heat to circulate.

By 1902 the Hunt brothers had decided to retire from the company, and the now-bustling business was purchased by Holaday and a partner. Under its new identity, Holaday & Bailey, the partnership progressed from making Klondike toe-savers to copper roofs, handmade copper hoods, and various sheet-metal products.

However, more tumultuous times were in the offing for the growing concern. About 1916 Bailey sold his interest in the business to B.A. Edworthy, Holaday's son-in-law, and the firm's name was

Holaday & Edworthy maintained its offices in Tacoma until 1952. That year the name was changed to Holaday-Parks, and the main office was relocated to Seattle. Photo circa late 1930s

changed to Holaday & Edworthy, Inc. Subsequently, Ruth Edworthy, Holaday's daughter, divorced her husband and assumed control of the Edworthy portion of the business. For the next twenty years Ruth, a woman of extraordinary fortitude, ran the daily operations of the company.

Under Ruth's leadership, the firm became involved in even more varied projects. During World War II the company was involved in ventilation projects for barracks, and after the war Holaday & Edworthy employees could be found on the DEW lines in Alaska as well as in the Puget Sound region.

In 1950 Ruth died suddenly, leaving her half of the company to Gerald T. Parks. Parks, who was

an orphan, was just seventeen years old when he began working for Holaday & Edworthy in 1929. Ruth had liked him so much that she eventually adopted him. Several years later Holaday, upon his death, also left his share of the business to Parks.

When air conditioning was introduced into commercial buildings in the 1950s, Parks guided the firm through an unprecedented period of growth. In 1952 he opened a new office in Seattle called Holaday-Parks, Inc. The company expanded to Fairbanks, Alaska, in 1972; it closed the Holaday & Edworthy division in Tacoma two years later.

In 1978 Gerald T. Parks, Jr., took over the management of the firm for his father, and in 1984, after his father's death, Gerald Jr. became its president. He continued the firm's expansion with the acquisition in 1985 of a subsidiary in San Francisco, California, called the James A. Nelson Company. Today Holaday-Parks, Inc., has full-service offices in all of its three locations, and its state-of-the-art mechanical contracting has been involved in some of the most prestigious and difficult projects in the area.

Bellevue Place, which is scheduled for completion in June 1988, will have a Holaday-Parks custom-designed heating, ventilation, and air-conditioning system.

THE SEATTLE POST-INTELLIGENCER

The Seattle Post-Intelligencer has played an integral role in Seattle's history since its founding on December 10, 1863, as the *Puget Sound Gazette.*

James R. Watson, the paper's first editor, had prepared a sample copy of the publication in Olympia and had distributed it free to Seattleites in 1862 as an early example of a market survey. The response was overwhelmingly positive, and Seattle's first newspaper was launched.

On August 5, 1867, the paper's name was changed to *The Weekly Intelligencer.* In 1878 two local papers merged with *The Intelligencer,* which had begun daily publication on June 1, 1876. Then, in October 1878, *The Seattle Post* began publication in direct competition with *The Intelligencer.* However, Seattle was not ready for two daily newspapers, and on October 1, 1881, the publications merged to become *The Seattle Post-Intelligencer.*

On June 6, 1889, *The Post-Intelligencer* became one of the many victims of the Great Seattle Fire. However, with some salvaged equipment, Leigh S.J. Hunt, the paper's owner, was able to publish a small, two-page edition from his home the next morning telling of the fire.

Before long Seattle was besieged by gold seekers on their way to the Alaskan gold fields, and the city's population exploded. Suddenly, the little *Post-Intelligencer* was turned into a metropolitan newspaper and became a powerful force in the Pacific Northwest.

For the next several years *The Post-Intelligencer's* circulation grew dramatically. In 1921 the publication became part of the Hearst Newspaper Group when it was purchased by that organization. In 1948 *The Post-Intelligencer* moved into a $5-million facility

at Sixth Avenue and Wall Street in Seattle. The new facility was one of the most modern newspaper plants in the United States at that time. By 1969 the paper had outgrown its headquarters, and an additional floor was built at a cost of five million dollars.

In May 1983 *The Post-Intelligencer* entered into a joint operating agreement with *The Seattle Times.* The purpose of the agreement was to preserve Seattle's two major editorial voices. Under the agreement, which is still in effect today, *The Post Intelligencer* and *The Times* operate with combined business departments. However, the editorial staffs of the papers remain separate.

Today *The Post Intelligencer* has a circulation of 200,000. In April 1986 the *Post-Intelligencer* moved its neon-lit globe of the world, one of Washington State's

People of the Pacific Northwest have been reading the headlines of history in The Seattle Post-Intelligencer *since before Washington became a state.*

most famous landmarks, to the top of a new five-story building at 101 Elliott Avenue West, on the shores of Elliott Bay.

Over the years, *The Seattle Post-Intelligencer* has strived to provide Seattle with a fair and accurate reporting of both local and world events. However, the newspaper's management has always considered that its responsibility to the betterment of the Seattle area goes far beyond its editorial policy. As a result, *The Post Intelligencer* has found additional ways to contribute to the community. One example is its Action Fund, which raises more than $225,000 from readers annually for distribution to various charities.

TRA

TRA Architecture Engineering Planning Interiors has been designing the Seattle skyline since 1911, when A.M. Young first established the firm under his own name.

Young, originally from England, came to Seattle in 1910 from the University of Michigan with a degree in structural engineering. He appreciated the opportunity offered by the Seattle area, as well as its natural beauty, and he decided to make the Emerald City his home.

Much of Young's early work involved association with local architects, and he came to believe that the best in architecture evolved from a close relationship with engineering. In 1920 Young formed a partnership with two Seattle architects he particularly admired, James Schack and David Meyers. This partnership designed many of Seattle's outstanding structures, including the Municipal Auditorium (now the Seattle Center Opera House) and the Arctic Building.

The Depression brought financial uncertainty to most of Seattle's architectural firms. Schack, Young and Meyers was no exception, and the partnership was dissolved. Young practiced on his own until 1936, when he began sharing office space with a young architect, Stephen Richardson. The pair worked together informally on several projects during the next five years, and in 1941 formed the firm of Young and Richardson. With World War II looming on the horizon, the partners began to be awarded government projects.

One of the firm's most challenging tasks during that period was the Boeing camouflage project. It involved engineering a three-dimensional cable and fabric structure that covered the entire Boeing

plant, camouflaging one of the nation's most important wartime assets from enemy detection. John S. Detlie, a young architect and U.S. Army officer, was assigned to monitor the project for the government. Detlie later joined the firm.

After the war Young and Richardson kept pace with the booming building industry by expanding and diversifying. Seattle landmarks constructed during that time included Children's Orthopedic Hospital, several buildings for the Port of Seattle and United Airlines at the Seattle-Tacoma Airport, and various University of Washington projects such as the Fisheries Center and Terry Men's Residence Hall.

In 1950 architects Detlie and William Carleton were advanced to partners, and the firm was then known as Young, Richardson, Carleton and Detlie. Four years later A.M. Young passed away, leaving a legacy of notable archi-

TRA partners (left to right): Arthur Sirjord, Jr., Allen Moses, George Oistad, Edward McCagg II, Phillip Jacobson, Jerome Ernst, Robert Nixon, and Gerald Williams.

tectural structures dotting the Puget Sound area.

In 1956, with Detlie's departure, the firm's name was changed to Young, Richardson and Carleton. Growth continued with the firm strengthening its reputation and expanding through the addition

Sheraton Tacoma Hotel. Completed in 1984, the hotel has won seven design awards, including the Honor Award, Seattle Chapter, American Institute of Architects.

of mechanical engineering and graphic services. Among representative projects of the 1960s were the Aerospace Laboratory and a women's residence hall for the University of Washington, the State of Washington's Highway Administration Building, a second major addition to Group Health Hospital, and numerous elementary, junior, and senior high schools. The firm also began considerable activity in the specialty of airport planning and design.

In 1967 Allen Moses, Phillip Jacobson, James Hussey, and John Rogers were made partners, and the firm became The Richardson Associates. That year also saw a commitment to offer a program of full engineering services. Two years later interior design services were added. A major downtown landmark, the Peoples National Bank Building, was designed during this time as was the Northwest Trek Wilderness Park and a major expansion of Seattle-Tacoma International Airport.

In 1970, fifty-nine years after its founding, the firm moved from the Central Building to the remodeled and restored Seattle Chamber of Commerce Building for which A.M. Young had been the original structural engineer. That same year Richardson retired. He had been the firm's guiding force for almost thirty years and had led it to a high level of professional stature. Under his guidance, the firm had grown from two professional individuals to a full-service organization employing more than eighty-five people.

The year 1970 also saw the addition of planning services. Since that time the firm's efforts in that field have won numerous awards for excellence, including recent recognition for the Manson Bay Park design from the Seattle Chap-

ter, American Institute of Architects and the Washington Chapter, American Society of Landscape Architects. Overall, the firm's various disciplines have earned more than 120 design awards.

In 1973 Arthur Sirjord, Jr., and Gerald Williams became partners, and The Richardson Associates diversified further by starting electrical engineering services in 1975. Engineering services also were offered as a separate organization in 1975 with the creation of Engineering Consultants Inc. Foreign work was reorganized as TRA International Inc. in 1977.

During the past decade the firm gradually branched out from the Puget Sound area. Projects and studies have been performed throughout the United States, Guam, Samoa, the Philippines, Mexico, Peru, and several Middle Eastern countries. In 1977 the firm changed its name to TRA and also established a branch in Anchorage, Alaska, known as TRA/Farr. The Nevada Corporation of TRA Consultants, Inc., was opened in Las Vegas in 1979 to act as prime architect and engineer on the $315-million expansion of McCarran International Airport. A project office was opened in Boston in 1986. The past ten years also brought the retirements of Rogers and Hussey and the addition of four partners: Edward McCagg II in 1978; Robert Nixon, 1983; George Oistad, 1984; and Jerome Ernst, 1986.

Today TRA and its subsidiary

TRA Columbia Building. Built in 1926, TRA's Seattle headquarters has a carefully preserved and restored facade. The firm has offices in Las Vegas, Nevada; Anchorage, Alaska; and Boston, Massachusetts.

companies perform professional services, both domestic and foreign, through a staff of nearly 200. Because of its diversification, the firm is able to thrive despite the recurring economic cycles that often affect the environmental design profession. If A.M. Young were alive today, he would hardly recognize TRA with its advanced technology, vast resources, and numerous disciplines—now including the recently added program management services. However, upon closer inspection, Young would surely recognize the firm's continuing attainment of quality and dedication to service, which he initiated seventy-five years ago.

Seattle-Tacoma International Airport. Among the country's most admired airports, Sea Tac continually updates and improves its facilities to accommodate growing numbers of travelers. The airport's terminal area development has been a TRA project for the past three decades.

NORTHGATE CENTER, INC.

Today regional shopping centers are commonplace. However, in the late 1940s, when Allied Stores employee Rex Allison and architect John Graham, Sr., first conceived of such a plan, it was an entirely new concept. The result of the forward thinking of those two men was Northgate Center, now recognized in the shopping center industry as the first planned regional shopping mall.

In order to build the sort of complex the two men envisioned, they needed an extensive amount of land, and a parcel of adequate dimensions did not exist within the then-established areas of Seattle. However, the partners were not to be deterred. They climbed into Allison's plane to search for an appropriate parcel of land. Eventually, they spotted fifty-two acres of land to the far north of Seattle, and they settled on that spot for their new shopping complex.

Allison persuaded a group of local investors to back the project, but they soon lost interest, and the future of the development was in jeopardy. Allison then convinced Allied Stores of the viability of the project, and that firm agreed to back the complex.

With the John Graham Company as the architect and the Howard S. Wright Company handling the construction, ground was broken for Northgate Center in 1949. One year later, on April 21, 1950, the shopping center's only anchor store, the Bon Marche, opened for business. In May of that year the complex held a grand opening with forty stores participating.

In addition to the innovative concept of the regional shopping center, Northgate Center was the first mall to employ an underground tunnel for delivery service to its stores. As the shopping mall

Recognized in the shopping center industry as the first regional shopping center, Northgate opened with one major department store (The Bon) and forty specialty stores.

began to take shape and more stores started to lease space, the shopping center industry looked on with interest and more than a little skepticism. However, Northgate did not falter. More stores were gradually added and the center continued to attract customers from miles around, often jamming the roads near the facility.

In the early 1960s Northgate Center was modernized with the addition of a sky shield to protect customers from the rain. By 1965 Northgate had doubled its size, adding both JCPenney and Nordstrom as additional anchor stores. That same year the Bon Marche increased its size considerably, and a new wing was added to the hospital medical building. In addition, Interstate 5 from downtown Seat-

tle was opened, with an exit to Northgate.

Despite the construction, the mall remained open and business continued to increase. In 1975, after the completion of the work, Northgate hosted a "Re-Grand Opening Celebration." At the time Northgate added Lamont's, its fourth department store, and several boutiques for a total of 115 stores.

Today Northgate Center is a Seattle fixture. It has over 125 stores and services and is serviced by a major health facility. The shopping center that began with just one department store and only 600,000 square feet of space has grown into a major retail center with a total of 1.1 million square feet of active retail and service space.

Today over 120 specialty stores and services are located in Northgate Center, including four major department stores (The Bon, Lamons, Nordstrom, and JCPenney), a major health facility/hospital, a movie theater, and parking for over 7,000 vehicles.

PATRONS

The following individuals, companies, and organizations have made a valuable commitment to the quality of this publication. Windsor Publications and the Museum of History and Industry gratefully acknowledge their participation in *Where Mountains Meet the Sea: An Illustrated History of Puget Sound.*

Adams News Co., Inc.*
Advanced Technology Laboratories
Robert M. Arnold
Avtech Corporation*
Bergman Luggage Company, Inc.*
The Boeing Company*
Bogle & Gates*
Ben Bridge*
The Bryant Corporation
The Callison Partnership, Ltd.*
Capital Industries, Inc.*
CAREAGE*
Case Construction Company, Inc.
CH2M HILL*
Coldwell Banker Real Estate Finance Services
Continental Incorporated*
Peggy Corley
Dain Bosworth, Inc.
Darigold, Inc.*
Charles L. Divelbiss, M.D.
Diggs & Jack Docter
Edgewater Inn*
First Interstate Bank of Washington*
Four Seasons Olympic Hotel
Doug Fox Travel*
Frederick & Nelson*
Lyle & Marnette Hall
Holaday-Parks, Inc.*
Hurlen Construction Company
J.L. Johnson & Company
Jones Washington Stevedoring Company*
Karr, Tuttle, Koch, Campbell, Mawer, Morrow & Sax A Professional Service Corporation*
King Broadcasting Company
King County Medical Blue Shield*
Abie Label & Associates Inc.

Lease Crutcher and Lease Kissee Construction Companies*
F.R. McAbee, Incorporated
J.M. McConkey & Co., Inc.*
Manson Construction and Engineering Company*
Mayer Brothers*
Metal Goods' Div. Alcan Aluminum Corp.
Molbak's Greenhouse and Nursery*
Nordstrom, Inc.*
North Star Casteel Products, Inc.*
Northgate Center, Inc.*
Nyman Piledriving, Inc.
Overall Laundry Services, Inc.*
Pacific International Underwriters
Pacific Lutheran University*
PEMCO Financial Center*
Peoples National Bank of Washington*
Puget Power*
Prudential Bank*
Quarante Club of West Seattle
Rainier Bancorporation*
Earl F. Reilly, Jr.
Roffe, Inc.*
Rothschild and Company*
Sam's Tire Service, Inc.*
Seacon Terminals Inc.
Seattle Daily Journal of Commerce
Seattle Mortgage
The Seattle Post-Intelligencer*
The Seattle Times*
Seattle Trust
Seattle University*
Sellen Construction Company, Inc.*
Source Northwest, Inc.*
F.G. Steele
Strobe Data, Inc.
Sundstrand Data Control*
Touche Ross & Co.*
TRA*
Harry Truitt's Lighthouse Diving Center, Inc.
Van Waters & Rogers
Veca Electric Co., Inc.
Washington Dental Service*
Washington Mutual Savings Bank*
Washington Natural Gas Company*

Wright Runstad & Company*
Wright Schuchart*
WYCO, Inc.
Ziff-Davis Technical Information Services

*Partners in Progress of *Where Mountains Meet the Sea: An Illustrated History of Puget Sound.* The histories of these companies and organizations appear in Chapter 9, beginning on page 209.

SELECTED BIBLIOGRAPHY

Avery, Mary W. *History and Government of the State of Washington.* Seattle: University of Washington Press, 1961.

Bagley, Clarence B. *History of King County, Washington.* Chicago: The S.J. Clarke Publishing Co., 1929.

Bancroft, Hubert Howe. *History of Washington, Idaho, and Montana.* (Volume XXXI of Bancroft's Works). San Francisco: The History Company, 1890.

Binns, Archie. *Northwest Gateway.* Garden City, NY.: Doubleday, Doran and Co., 1943.

Blankenship, Mrs. George E. *Early History of Thurston County, Washington.* Olympia: 1914.

Chasan, Daniel Jack. *The Water Link, A History of Puget Sound as a Resource.* Seattle: University of Washington Press, 1981.

Clark, Norman H. *Mill Town, A Social History of Everett.* Seattle: University of Washington Press, 1970.

Coman, Edwin T., Jr. and Helen M. Gibbs. *Time, Tide and Timber.* Stanford, California: Stanford University Press, 1949.

Denny, Arthur A. *Pioneer Days on Puget Sound.* Seattle: Alice Harriman Co., 1908.

Denny, Emily Inez. *Blazing the Way.* Seattle: Rainier Publishing Company, 1909.

Evans, Elwood and Edmond S. Meany (eds.). *The State of Washington.* Tacoma: Washington State World's Fair Commission, 1893.

Fuller, George W. *A History of the Pacific Northwest.* New York: Alfred A. Knopf, 1941.

Hawthorne, Julian (ed.). *History of Washington.* New York: American Historical Publishing Company, 1893.

Humphrey, Robert M. *Everett and Snohomish County, A Pictorial History.* Norfolk, Va.: The Donning Company, 1984.

Johansen, Dorothy O. and Charles M. Gates. *Empire of the Columbia.* New York: Harper and Brothers, 1957.

Kirk, Ruth, with Richard D. Dougherty. *Exploring Washington Archaeology.* Seattle: University of Washington Press, 1978.

McCallum, John D. *Dave Beck.* Vancouver, B.C.: Gordon Soules Book Publishers, 1978.

McCurdy, James G. *By Juan de Fuca's Strait.* Portland: Binfords and Mort, 1937.

McCurdy, James G. with Gordon Newell. *Indian Days at Neah Bay.* Seattle: Historical Society of Seattle and King County, 1981.

McDonald, Lucile. *The Lake Washington Story.* Seattle: Superior Publishing Company, 1979.

Meany, Edmond S. *Mount Rainier, a Record of Exploration.* New York: The MacMillan Company, 1916.

_____. *Vancouver's Discovery of Puget Sound.* New York: The MacMillan Company, 1935.

_____. *Origin of Washington Geographic Names.* Seattle: University of Washington Press, 1923.

Meeker, Ezra. *Pioneer Reminiscences of Puget Sound.* Seattle: Lowman and Hanford, 1905.

_____. *Seventy Years of Progress in Washington.* Tacoma: Allstrum Printing, 1921.

Miles, Charles and O.B. Sperlin (eds.). *Building a State.* Tacoma: Washington State Historical Society, 1940.

Morgan, Murray. *Puget's Sound.* Seattle: University of Washington Press, 1979.

Morgan, Murray and Rosa. *South on the Sound.* Woodland Hills, California: Windsor Publications, Inc., 1984.

Nesbit, Robert C. *He Built Seattle, A Biography of Judge Thomas Burke.* Seattle: University of Washington Press, 1961.

Newell, Gordon (ed.). *The H.W. McCurdy Marine History of the Pacific Northwest.* Seattle: Superior Publishing Company, 1966.

Newell, Gordon. *Rogues, Buffoons and Statesmen.* Seattle: Superior Publishing Company, 1975.

Phillips, James W. *Washington State Place Names.* Seattle: University of Washington Press, 1971.

Prosser, William Farrand. *A History of the Puget Sound Country.* New York: The Lewis Publishing Company, 1903.

Richardson, David. *Pig War Islands.* Eastsound, Washington: Orcas Publishing Company, 1971.

_____. *Puget Sounds, A Nostalgic Review of Radio and TV in the Great Northwest.* Seattle: Superior Publishing Company, 1981.

Richie, Art and William J. Davis (eds.). *Pacific Northwest Goes to War.* Seattle: Associated Editors, 1944.

Ruffner, W.H. *A Report on Washington Territory.* New York: Seattle, Lake Shore and Eastern Railway, 1889.

Snowden, Clinton A. *History of Washington.* (4 vols.): New York: The Century History Company, 1909.

Speidel, William C. *Sons of the Profits.* Seattle: Nettle Creek Publishing Co., 1967.

Spencer, Lloyd, and Lancaster Pollard. *A History of the State of Washington.* (2 vols.) New York: The American Historical Society, Inc., 1937.

Stevenson, Shanna B. *Lacey, Olympia, and Tumwater, A Pictorial History.* Norfolk, Va: The Donning Company, 1985.

Washington State Data Book, 1983. Olympia: Office of Fiscal Management, 1984.

Warren, James R. *King County and Its Queen City Seattle.* Woodland Hills, California: Windsor Publications, Inc., 1981.

Warren, James R. and William R. McCoy. *Highlights of Seattle's History.* Seattle: Historical Society of Seattle and King County, 1982.

Washington, A Guide to the Evergreen State. Tacoma: Washington State Historical Society, 1941.

Watt, Roberta Frye. *The Story of Seattle, Four Wagons West.* Seattle: Lowman and Hanford Company, 1932.

Wing, Robert C., with Gordon Newell. *Peter Puget.* Seattle: Gray Beard Publishing, 1979.

PERIODICALS

Washington Historical Quarterly, Pacific Northwest Historical Quarterly, Oregon Historical Quarterly, The Sea Chest (Journal of the Puget Sound Martine Historical Quarterly), *Portage* (Journal of the Historical Society of Seattle and King County), *Puget Soundings,* and others.

NEWSPAPERS

The Seattle Times, The Seattle Post-Intelligencer, The Puget Sound Business Journal, The Weekly, and *The Eastside Journal-American.*

INDEX